WHAT'S MINE IS YOURS

WHAT'S MINE IS YOURS

HOW COLLABORATIVE CONSUMPTION IS CHANGING THE WAY WE LIVE

Rachel Botsman and Roo Rogers

Collins

Collins
An imprint of HarperCollins*Publishers*
77–85 Fulham Palace Road
London W6 8JB

www.harpercollins.co.uk

First published in the USA in 2010 by HarperBusiness,
an imprint of HarperCollins*Publishers*

This revised and updated edition 2011

1 3 5 7 9 10 8 6 4 2

A catalogue record for this book is
available from the British Library

ISBN: 978-0-00-739591-0

Designed by Janet M. Evans
Images in chapters 4, 5 and 6 by Nicholas Blechman
Collaborative Consumption logo and website designed by UnderConsideration

Printed and bound in Great Britain by
Clays Ltd, St Ives plc

Mixed Sources
Product group from well-managed
forests and other controlled sources
www.fsc.org Cert no. SW-COC-001806
© 1996 Forest Stewardship Council
FSC

FSC is a non-profit international organisation established to promote the
responsible management of the world's forests. Products carrying the FSC
label are independently certified to assure consumers that they come
from forests that are managed to meet the social, economic and
ecological needs of present or future generations.

Find out more about HarperCollins and the environment at
www.harpercollins.co.uk/green

For my nana, Evelyn Amdur

– Rachel

For Bernie, Ruby & Mei

– Roo

CONTENTS

In October 2007, designers from all over the world travelled to San Francisco to attend the annual industrial design conference. The city's hotel rooms had been sold out for months. Joe Gebbia and Brian Chesky, old friends and graduates from the Rhode Island School of Design, were among the ten thousand people planning to attend. The classmates had recently moved into a big loft in South of Market, San Francisco, or SoMa, as it is known, to start a business. During a conversation Gebbia and Chesky had about making some quick money to help pay their rent, they asked themselves, 'Why not rent our extra room and advertise it on the conference website?' They did, and made close to $1,000 in just one week.

Chesky and Gebbia thought that people in their twenties would respond to their offer. Three people ended up staying: a male designer from India who read about the idea on a local design blog and who saw it as a great way to meet new people; a thirty-five-year-old woman from Boston who thought it was better value than a hotel; and a forty-five-year-old father of five from Utah. 'It completely blew away our assumptions,' Gebbia recalls. The friends were also surprised that they didn't feel like they had strangers in their own home. 'They are strangers until you have a conversation with them,' Chesky explained.

Convinced they could start a business matching visitors who wanted rooms with locals who wanted to rent out extra space, Chesky and Gebbia, joined by Nathan Blecharczyk, a close friend and Web developer, built a simple website in early 2008. They initially thought of the idea 'air beds for conferences' solely for large events such as the Republican and Democratic conventions – where hotels were unavailable because they were sold out or unaffordable. 'When Obama announced he was speaking in a 75,000-seat arena, and there were only 40,000 hotel rooms in Denver, the maths just really worked in our favour,' Chesky recalls. Their website's traffic grew. They appeared on CNN and in the pages of *The New York Times* and *The Wall Street Journal*. During the first few months of the launch, the trio were surprised by both the number and the mix of people wanting to rent out space as well as by the diversity of travellers – families, newlyweds, students, and even businessmen – willing to pay for a rented room.

Chesky, Blecharczyk and Gebbia realized that conferences were just a narrow slice of the larger market. On the whiteboard in their apartment, they drew a spectrum. On one side they wrote 'hotels' and on the other they scribbled rental listings such as craigslist, youth hostels, and nonmonetary travel exchanges such as Couch-Surfing that help people travel by creating a network of couches available to sleep on for free. In the middle was a big white space, an untapped market: people looking for reasonably priced accommodations with the added benefit of a local experience. They were, however, wary that this opportunity appeared so large and untapped for a logical reason – trust.

Was the act of attending the same event, whether a political rally, a music festival or a design conference the critical factor in building trust between strangers? Would people stay with one another if they just shared an interest such as photography? What about if they were alumni who had graduated from the same university? Was it possible to create an entirely open peer-to-peer marketplace for people to stay anywhere around the world? These were questions the three men chatted about for several months before agreeing that the answer could be 'yes' to all of the above. The success of other matchmaking services such as eBay indicated that trust could be built. By August 2008, Airbnb.com, their company's website, was born. 'The name came from the idea that with the Internet and a spare room, anyone can become an innkeeper,' explains Blecharczyk.

In October 2010, Airbnb.com had over 210,000 registered users, with more than 28,000 properties across 8,122 cities in more than 157 countries. In the UK alone, there are 13,295 Airbnb members, with over 1,100 of them playing host in 1,362 properties. Just as eBay is for goods, the site is a diverse marketplace for spaces. Listings include everything from a 'Charming studio in Bastille, Marais' for $90 a night, to a 'Harlem Haven Private Apartment, New York' for $120, to an entire villa in the 'Bophut Hills in Koh Samui, Thailand' for $275 per night. Chesky marvels, 'When we started I never thought people would be renting out tree houses, igloos, boats, villas and designer apartments.'

For the most part, the people and places are not vetted, inspected or interviewed by Airbnb. It's up to users to determine if they want to host a guest or if they want to stay with someone based on kaleidoscopic photos of the property, detailed profiles and other users' reviews. As the site has grown, in fact, the founders have removed rules they initially thought would be required. They took away the initial cap on charges of $300 because they realized that people were using the Airbnb community for far more than budget accommodation. Today you can find castles for rent in England for $3,000 a night. The only fixed rules on Airbnb are that the travellers must be able to ask the host questions before they book, and rooms can't be a commodity, which excludes most hotels. 'A Marriott in New York City and a Marriott in Ireland will look exactly the same,' Chesky says. 'And you don't know what room you are getting or even what floor you are on. We are providing the opposite.'

Blecharczyk has since moved with his wife to a bigger apartment in Palo Alto. In January he made $1,200 from renting out their extra

bedroom via Airbnb to three different individuals for a total of fifteen days in January 2010. When the founders launched, they didn't
consider that the service would enable people to use their spare
space as an investment rather than it being a liability. Some users
have an extra bedroom in an expensive neighbourhood, so why not
rent it out every now and again? Angela Rutherford moved into a
large two-bedroom loft in New York's financial district. After having
previously lived alone, she was hesitant about sharing her room
with a full-time roommate. Instead, she decided to furnish the spare
room and rent it out on Airbnb for about fifteen nights per month. 'I
can control when I'm sharing the space and when I'm not,' she explained. 'I use the extra cash to help pay off my credit card debt, and
it covers about half the rent.'

The motivation for hosts using Airbnb is typically a blend of making extra money and meeting new people. The children of Jill Banou-
nou from Denver went to college: 'I have an empty room now and it's
interesting to have people every once in a while.' Stephanie Sullivan
from Pittsburgh needed extra money to help pay for the maintenance
on her 110-year-old home and loves having people stay. Matthias
Siebler from Boston used the money to pay for an entire trip to England so he could attend an old friend's wedding. Sandra Bruce from
Washington is 'hosting to save for my retirement. I also like having
the company.' Some people have started their own business with the
extra money; for others it has helped them keep their home.

In January 2010, the team received this email from a woman
named Kendra Mae Tai, a host in New York City: 'Hi Airbnb, I am
not exaggerating when I tell that you literally saved us. My husband
and I just married this past May after losing both of our jobs and our
investments in the stock market crash last year. We slowly watched
our savings dwindle to the point where we did not have enough
money to pay our rent. At that point, I listed our apartment on your

website and received so many requests. . . . You have given us the ability to keep our home and travel together and the peace of mind of knowing we can make it through this challenging time in our life. Thank you so much.'

Remarkably, out of the ten thousand completed trips to date there have been no reports of theft. Sometimes an apartment is not clean or someone does not show up, but these cases are rare. Chesky believes that a 'trusted intermediary' and secure payment system have a lot to do with this record. When making a booking, guests put the reservation on hold using a credit card or PayPal account. Hosts are not paid in full until twenty-four hours after a guest has checked in. Airbnb charges hosts a standard 3 per cent service fee and travellers an additional 6 to 12 per cent depending on the reservation price. Aside from turning Airbnb into a real business with a profitable revenue model that has been growing at more than 10 per cent every month since they launched, the founders believe that some form of payment 'puts both parties on the best behaviour and makes the whole process more reliable.'

When Chesky told his grandfather about the idea behind Airbnb, 'It seemed totally normal to him. My parents had a different reaction. I could not figure out why at first.' Chesky later realized that his parents grew up in the hotel generation, whereas his grandfather and his friends would stay on farms and in little houses during their travels. Airbnb is not very different from that experience. 'We are not the modern invention, hotels are.' Indeed, prior to the 1950s, staying with friends or friends of friends was a common way to travel. Airbnb is an old idea, being replicated and made relevant again through peer-to-peer networks and new technologies.

There is now an unbounded marketplace for efficient peer-to-peer exchanges between producer and consumer, seller and buyer, lender and borrower, and neighbour and neighbour. Online exchanges mimic the close ties once formed through face-to-face exchanges in villages, but on a much larger and unconfined scale. In other words, technology is reinventing old forms of trust. Chesky predicts, 'The status quo is being replaced by a movement. Peer-to-peer is going to become the default way people exchange things, whether it is space, stuff, skills or services.'

The Rise of Collaboration

Over the past couple of years, we started to notice that stories and business examples like Airbnb weren't unusual. At dinner parties, instead of bragging about their new Prius, friends boasted how they had given up their cars altogether by becoming 'Zipsters' (members of the car-sharing service Zipcar). More and more friends were selling stuff on craigslist and eBay; swapping books, DVDs and games on sites such as Swap and OurSwaps; and giving unwanted items away on Freecycle and ReUseIt. On a trip to Paris, we saw cyclists pedalling around on sleek-looking bikes with the word 'Vélib' (Paris's bike-sharing scheme) on their crossbars. A friend in London told us about her new favourite Channel 4 programme called *Landshare*. And we kept hearing about the number of people joining Community Supported Agriculture (CSA) programmes or local co-ops. We saw stats and stories about online cooperation and the growth in virtual communities. Every day there are more than 3 million Flickr images uploaded; 700,000 new members joining Facebook; 50 million 'Tweets'; and 900,000 blogs posted. There are twenty-three hours of YouTube videos uploaded every minute, the equivalent of Hollywood releasing more than 90,000 new full-length films into theatres each week.[1]

'Collaboration' had become the buzzword of the day with economists, philosophers, business analysts, trend spotters, marketers and entrepreneurs – and appropriately so.

We stumbled on articles about sharing, bartering, lending or swapping, often with some kind of 'co' in the headlines, such as 'Co-Housing for Gen X & Y', 'Co-working: Solo but Not Alone', 'Couch Surfing: This Isn't Just About a Place to Crash', 'Can Community Co-Ops Revive Our Towns?' 'Social Networking for Communes', 'Global Collectivist Society Is Coming Online,' 'Living Together: Modern Answer to the Commune', and 'Governing the Commons'. Even science, social psychology and economic journals brimmed with popular articles about the self-organizing behaviours of ants, the 'intelligence' of swarming honeybees, and the cooperation of schools of fish and flocks of birds.

The more we examined these trends, the more convinced we were that all of these behaviours, personal stories, social theories and business examples pointed to an emerging socioeconomic groundswell; the old stigmatized C's associated with coming together and 'sharing' — cooperatives, collectives, and communes — are being refreshed and reinvented into appealing and valuable forms of collaboration and community. We call this groundswell Collaborative Consumption.

The collaboration at the heart of Collaborative Consumption may be local and face-to-face, or it may use the Internet to connect, combine, form groups, and find something or someone to create 'many to many' peer-to-peer interactions. Simply put, people are sharing again with their community — be it an office, a neighbourhood, an apartment building, a school or a Facebook network. But the sharing and collaboration are happening in ways and at a scale never before possible, creating a culture and economy of *what's mine is yours*.

Every day people are using Collaborative Consumption — traditional sharing, bartering, lending, trading, renting, gifting and swapping, redefined through technology and peer communities. Collaborative Consumption is enabling people to realize the enormous benefits of access to products and services over ownership, and at the same time save money, space and time; make new friends; and become active citizens once again. Social networks, smart grids and real-time technologies are also making it possible to leapfrog over outdated modes of hyper-consumption and create innovative systems based on shared usage such as bike or car sharing. These systems provide significant environmental benefits by increasing use efficiency, reducing waste, encouraging the development of better products, and mopping up the surplus created by over-production and -consumption.

In this book, we have organized the thousands of examples of Collaborative Consumption from around the world into three systems – **product service systems, redistribution markets** and **collaborative lifestyles**. Together these systems are reinventing not just *what* we consume but *how* we consume.

Although the examples of Collaborative Consumption range enormously in scale, maturity and purpose, they share similar underlying principles essential to making them work that we explore throughout this book – **critical mass, idling capacity, belief in the commons** and **trust between strangers**.

Collaborative Consumption is not a niche trend, and it's not a reactionary blip to the 2008 global financial crisis. It's a growing movement with millions of people participating from all corners of the world. Many of these participants may not even realize that they are part of this groundswell. To illustrate the explosive rise of Collaborative Consumption, let's first look at the growth stats behind a few mainstream examples: Bike sharing is the fastest-growing form of transportation in the world,[2] with over 500,000 trips being made in the first six weeks of operation for London's Barclays Cycle Hire. Zilok, a leader in the peer-to-peer rental market, has grown at a rate of around 25 per cent since it was founded in October 2007.[3] Two billion dollars worth of goods and services were exchanged through Bartercard, the world's largest business-to-business bartering network in 2009, up by 20 per cent from 2008.[4] UK-founded Zopa, the first online peer-to-peer lending marketplace in the world, did more business in its fifth year, at £35.5 million (March 2009 to March 2010), than in the previous four years combined at £34.5 million. By October 2010, Zopa members had lent over £100 million between each other. Freecycle, a worldwide online registry that circulates free items for reuse or recycling, has more than 5.7 million members across more than eighty-five countries. More than twelve thousand items are 'gifted' every day through the network.[5] U-Exchange, one of the most successful of all swap sites, saw a 70 per cent increase in new members in 2008, and the membership of the trading site Swap grew tenfold in 2009 over the previous year. On thredUP, a clothing exchange for children's clothes, approximately twelve thousand were exchanged within the first eight days of launching in April 2010. Landshare, a site that connects gardenless would-be growers with unused spare land, has more than 55,000 members across the UK today. CouchSurfing, a global website that connects travellers with locals in more than 235 countries and territories, is currently the most visited 'hospitality service' on the Internet.[6] In the United States, there are more than 2,500 CSA schemes – where people pay a sum of money at the beginning of the year to a local farmer who will deliver a weekly box of fresh produce throughout the growing season – compared with only 1 in 1985. In the UK, there are more than 100,000 people on the waiting list for an allotment (a plot of land that can be rented by an individual for growing fruits and vegetables) and in some parts of London the wait is up to forty years.[7] In the midst of the global financial crisis, when the federal government was bailing out the 'Big Three' car companies, car-sharing membership increased by 51.5 per cent in the United States.[8] By 2015, it is estimated that 4.4 million people in North America and 5.5 million in Europe will belong to services like the one from Zipcar, whose membership alone more than tripled in 2009.[9] UK-based WhipCar, the first neighbour-to-neighbour car-sharing service had over 1,000 owners accepting bookings within the first six months of launch. We could go on. Collaborative Consumption is a snowball idea, one with enough heft to keep gathering momentum and enough adhesion to keep growing bigger.

Many of the companies we explore in this book are already profitable or have growing revenue models. The more established companies are making hundreds of millions in revenue (Netflix made $359.6 million and Zipcar $130 million in 2009), while others like SolarCity and Swap are just starting to turn a profit. Specific sectors of Collaborative Consumption are predicted to experience phenomenal growth over the next five years. The peer-to-peer social lending market led by the likes of Zopa and Lending Club is estimated to soar by 66 per cent to reach $5 billion by the end of 2013.[10] The consumer peer-to-peer rental market for everything from drills to cameras is estimated to be a $26 billion market sector. The swap market just for used children's clothing (0 to 13 years) is estimated to be between $1 billion and $3 billion in the United States alone.[11] Car sharing or per hour car rental is predicted to become a $12.5 billion industry. Even organizations such as CouchSurfing and Freecycle that were set up for a purpose not explicitly about profitability are helping create consumer acceptance and paving the way for similar businesses with a revenue model. CouchSurfing, a nonprofit organization, created the space for the likes of Airbnb and CrashPadder. And it's not just the companies making money. As *The Economist* noted, individuals involved in Collaborative Consumption are becoming 'microentrepreneurs.'[12] Some people are making a little money on the side and others are making significant income from peer rental of products and spaces that would otherwise be sitting unused and idle. The average New Yorker participating in Airbnb is making $1,600 per month. And that is just the average. Renters on Zilok are making over $1,000 a year from renting out just one item such as a camera or bike. It is estimated that an owner of a saloon car such as a Camry can make over $6,250 per year through peer-to-peer car rental sites such as RelayRides, Gettaround and Whipcar by renting the car for twenty hours a week. Some owners, such as 'Dave,' a twenty-six-year-old designer, are using Whipcar to help pay for general living costs. Others, such as sixty-six-year-old 'Maureen', hardly use their car and use the extra rental money to pay for holidays.

People may throw an 'out of necessity' brick at Collaborative Consumption, claiming that it will slow down or crumble when the economy fully recovers and prosperity returns. But not only is Collaborative Consumption driven by consumer motivations that extend far deeper than cost savings, the habits started to stick and spread before the financial collapse of 2008. Economic necessity has just made people more open to new ways of accessing what they need and how to go about getting it.

When the great recession hit in 2008, some pundits and economists heralded the end of consumerism, while some suggested that consumers needed to be prodded to shop again. Either way, they assumed that the traditional model of consumerism, the one in which we buy products, use them, throw them away and then buy more, would continue, even if at a hobbled rate. While the 'spend more, consume more' way out may be a short-term fix, it is neither sustainable nor healthy.

While the rampant and unregulated financial system led to investors losing millions in Ponzi schemes, hedge funds, insurance companies and even savings banks, everyday people pursuing the supposed American dream felt the worst impact. In all corners of the world, millions lost their homes, their jobs, their buying power and their confidence. But within weeks of the crash, there were signs of a new and increasing consumer awareness, tinged with anger. We have been living in a society that for more than fifty years has encouraged us to live beyond our means, both financial and ecological. As Thomas Friedman wrote in a *New York Times* op-ed, '2008 was when we hit the wall – when Mother Nature and the market both said: "No more."' While the world awaits a new big idea to reinvigorate and rebalance our economy, we believe the transformation will start to come from consumers themselves.

The convergence of social networks, a renewed belief in the importance of community, pressing environmental concerns and cost consciousness are moving us away from top-heavy, centralized and controlled forms of consumerism towards one of sharing, aggregation, openness and cooperation.

To build on an idea Charles Leadbeater discussed in his book *We-Think*, in the twentieth century of hyper-consumption we were defined by credit, advertising and what we owned; in the twenty-first century of Collaborative Consumption we will be defined by reputation, by community, and by what we can access and how we share and what we give away.[13]

The phenomenon of sharing via increasingly ubiquitous cyber peer-to-peer communities such as Linux, Wikipedia, Flickr, Digg and YouTube is by now a familiar story. Collaborative Consumption is rooted in the technologies and behaviours of online social networks. These digital interactions have helped us experience the concept that cooperation does not need to come at the expense of our individualism, opening us up to innate behaviours that make it fun and second nature to share. Indeed, we believe people will look back and recognize that Collaborative Consumption started *online* – by posting comments and sharing files, code, photos, videos and knowledge. And now we have reached a powerful inflection point, where we are starting to apply the same collaborative principles and sharing behaviours to other physical areas of our everyday lives. From morning commutes to co-working spaces to the way we borrow and lend money to the way fashion is designed, different areas of our lives are being created and consumed in collaborative ways.

This book does not posit that we need to pick between owning or sharing. In the future, most of us will have our feet in both camps, just as successful business models such as Airbnb may become a hybrid of both traditional commerce and collaboration. Collaborative Consumption will sit side-by-side and eventually may go head-to-head with the old consumerist model, much as blogs such as the *Huffington Post* now compete with hundred-plus-year-old newspapers such as *The New York Times*. But in the same way that the one-way flow of information from the media is over, we are reaching the close of a pure one-way consumerist culture based on just owning more and more stuff. 'Sharing is to ownership what the iPod is to the eight track, what the solar panel is to the coal mine. Sharing is clean, crisp, urbane, postmodern; owning is dull, selfish, timid, backward,' *New York Times* journalist Mark Levine commented recently.[14]

Concepts and connotations of 'sharing', 'collectivism' and 'communalism' need to be updated. In his classic novel *Through the Looking-Glass*, Lewis Carroll writes, '"When I use a word," Humpty Dumpty said, in rather a scornful tone, "it means just what I choose it to mean – neither more nor less." "The question is," said Alice, "whether you can make words mean so many different things." "The question is," said Humpty Dumpty, "which is to be master – that's all".'[15] Meanings of words can change as our cultural acceptance of ideas is reframed.[16] Hotels don't call their business 'bed sharing' for good reasons, and as Jonathan Zittrain, a professor of law at Harvard University, says, craigslist does not call its ride-sharing board 'hitchhiking.'

Collaborative Consumption is not asking people to share nicely in the sandbox. On the contrary, it puts a system in place where people can share resources without forfeiting cherished personal freedoms or sacrificing their lifestyle. A distinguished political scientist who shares this view is seventy-six-year-old Indiana University professor Elinor Ostrom. In October 2009, while we were writing this book, she won the Nobel Memorial Prize in Economic Sciences, along with Oliver E. Williamson. Ostrom is the first person ever to win the award with a proven theory on the efficiency of commons-based societies and how they work. Michael Spence, a senior fellow at the Hoover Institution, commented shortly after Ostrom won the prize that her work demonstrates that 'economics is not really fundamentally about markets, but about resource allocation and distribution problems.'[17] From alpine grazing meadows in Switzerland to irrigation canals in Spain to forests in Japan, Professor Ostrom has spent her life studying commonly managed resources and probing how they succeed or fail. Her research has demonstrated that even in capitalist societies, if simple rules are applied, a self-organized commons can work. Individuals will cooperate to act in the common good.

Perhaps what is most exciting about Collaborative Consumption is that it fulfils the hardened expectations on both sides of the socialist and capitalist ideological spectrum without being an ideology in itself. It demands no rigid dogma. There are, of course, limits to the system, specifically situations where people simply won't and can't give up on individual ownership or doing things by themselves. But this rigidity, too, could shift.

Although this book is a good-news book about promising solutions and long-term positive change, we start out by showing how the system of consumerism that we live with today – the system that is now our collective habit – was manufactured. Entire books have been written on this subject, and it is not our goal to provide another detailed history or critique of the rise of consumerism in the twentieth century. Ultimately, we are much more interested in the future. But if we can look back and deconstruct what got us on what cultural critic Juliet Schor calls the consumer escalator, 'ever moving upward', we can then look forward to figuring out how to get off it.[18]

WHAT'S MINE IS YOURS

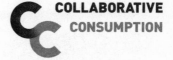

COLLABORATIVE
CONSUMPTION

PART

1

CONTEXT

ONE | **Enough Is Enough**

Way out in the Pacific Ocean, just east of Japan and west of Hawaii, a gigantic accidental monument to the waste of modern consumerism has formed. The Great Pacific Garbage Patch is the largest landfill in the world, except that it is not on land; it's in the ocean. This swirling mass of rubbish is estimated to be roughly twice the size of Texas and in some parts one hundred feet deep, if not deeper. It's a floating stew of 3.5 million tonnes of garbage, 90 per cent of which is plastic, containing everything from bottle caps and toys to shoes, cigarette lighters, toothbrushes, nets, babies' dummies, wrappers, takeaway containers and shopping bags from all corners of the world.

For years the patch was out-of-sight, out-of-mind, lying just beneath the surface of the water, invisible to satellites. The patch is located in a remote part of the ocean that is usually dodged by sailors because of its gentle breezes and extreme high pressure systems and shunned by fishermen, who call it the 'desert' due to its lack of fish. Charles Moore, a sailor, environmentalist, organic farmer and onetime furniture repairman, discovered the patch by accident on

3 August 1997. He was on his way home with his crew after finishing in third place in the Los Angeles–to-Hawaii sail race known
as the TransPac, when he decided to take a shortcut. He steered the
Alguita, an aluminium-hulled catamaran, into the North Pacific Sub-
tropical Gyre – a part of the ocean known for its vortex of swirling
undercurrents that trap debris. Moore, an old sea dog who had been
voyaging in the Pacific since childhood, knew that the region lacked
the wind to propel the boat but was not worried, as the *Alguita* was
equipped with engines and an extra supply of fuel.

In the week it took them to cross the Gyre, the crew were aston-
ished to find themselves surrounded by so much floating rubbish in
such a desolate place, thousands of miles from land. As Moore later
wrote in his story about the discovery, 'I often struggle to find words
that will communicate the vastness of the Pacific Ocean to people
who have never been to sea. Day after day, the *Alguita* was the only
vehicle on a highway without landmarks, stretching from horizon to
horizon. Yet as I gazed from the deck at the surface of what ought to
have been a pristine ocean, I was confronted, as far as the eye could
see, with the sight of plastic.'

Moore resolved to return to the area as soon as he could on a
proper trawling and research mission with marine scientists to start
to learn what was going on. And so he did, just over a year later,
with a team of volunteers and a net apparatus resembling a manta
ray that skimmed the ocean surface. The crew found 'a rich broth of
minute sea creatures mixed with hundreds of thousands of plastic
fragments – a plastic-plankton soup'.[1] Venturing out on inflatable
dinghies, they picked up everything from a cathode-ray tube for
televisions to a traffic cone to a gallon bleach bottle so brittle it
crumbled in their hands. Birds and fish mistake the plastic for food,
especially the bottle caps, which Moore calls 'poison pills'. One bird,
when dissected, contained 1,603 pieces of plastic.[2]

The Great Pacific Garbage Patch, sadly, isn't a lone phenomenon, though it is perhaps the biggest of them all. Together, these areas could cover 40 per cent of the sea. 'That corresponds to a quarter of the earth's surface,' Moore says. 'So 25 per cent of our planet is a toilet that never flushes.'[3] To convey the scope of the problem, Moore likes to give the example of Pagan Island (between Hawaii and the Philippines), where there is a 'shopping beach'. 'If the islanders need a cigarette lighter, or some flip-flops, or a toy, or a ball for their kids, they go down to the shopping beach and pick it out of the plastic trash that's washed up there from thousands of miles away.'[4]

Rubbish has been tossed into the seas for centuries. In preindustrial culture, it was broken down over time by microorganisms, as the materials, for the most part, were safely biodegradable. Today we have a spectacular abundance of products heavily dependent on plastic, a material that in any shape or form is 100 per cent nonbiodegradable. The 100 million tonnes of plastic produced each year will always exist; it just 'photo degrades' by the sun into smaller pieces and then smaller pieces resembling confetti.[5] Even the 5.5 quadrillion lentil-size plastic polymers, known as 'nurdles', made each year for our plastic-wrapped and packaged world are too tough for even the most voracious bacteria to break down. Plastic now outweighs surface plankton six to one in the middle of the Pacific Ocean.[6]

The Great Pacific Garbage Patch is a hideous illustration of the way we've ignored the negative consequences of modern consumerism. In the past fifty years, we have consumed more goods and services than in all previous generations put together.[7] Unfortunately, the consume-and-dispose engine is only going faster. Since 1980, we have consumed one-third of the planet's resources – forests, fish, natural minerals, metals and other raw materials.[8] Deforestation in the tropics destroys an area the size of Greece every year – more than 250 million acres. Americans are some of the world's worst environmental offenders. A child born today into a middle-class American family will live to about eighty years old and consume on average 2.5 million litres of water, the wood of 1,000 trees, 21,000 tonnes of petrol, 220,000 kilos of steel and 800,000 watts of electrical energy. At these rates, the average American child will produce in his or her lifetime twice the environmental impact of a Swedish child, 3 times that of an Italian, 13 times that of a Brazilian, 35 times that of an Indian and 280 times that of a Haitian.[9] If everyone on the planet lived like the average American child, we would need five planets to sustain them during their lifetime.[10]

Sadly, it would seem that the vision of unlimited consumption that Victor Lebow, a retail analyst, put forward in 1955 has come to fruition. 'Our enormously productive economy,' he said, 'demands that we make consumption our way of life, that we convert the buying and use of goods into rituals, that we seek spiritual satisfaction, our ego satisfaction, in consumption. The economy needs things consumed, burned up, worn out, replaced, and discarded at an ever increasing rate.'[11]

A big part of the problem is that many of our consumer behaviours have become so habitual that we are unaware of our impact. Psychologists call this consumer 'lock-in', as it can be difficult to make deliberate choices about what to buy and what not to buy because habits, routines, social norms and cultural values lock us into unsustainable behaviours. One example would be buying bottled water.[12] These behaviours stick because individuals acting in their own self-interest feel immediate gain, but they will not feel the losses from the impact of their actions for many years to come. We are always tempted by immediate self-gratification. At the same time, our brains cannot comprehend the cumulative impact at a collective level. If all the world's 1 billion personal computers were switched off for just one night, it would save enough energy to light up New York City's Empire State Building – inside and out – for more than thirty years.[13] Artist Chris Jordan, who creates arresting images about unimaginable statistics of western culture, puts it this way: 'As individuals we do these things all the time every day. But when millions of people go about these unconscious behaviours it can add up to a catastrophic consequence that nobody wants, and that nobody intended.'[14]

The Emergence of Throwaway Living

In 1907, Hugh Moore and his college roommate, Lawrence Luellen, dropped out of Harvard to pursue a business idea. At the time, people drank at public water fountains from the same 'tin-dipper' cups, which were rarely washed and never replaced. The friends, aware of recent findings that diseases were spread through sharing cups like these, spotted a moneymaking opportunity. Luellen had come up with the idea of a water vending machine with paper cups, and together he and Moore bought a factory, located next door to Alfred Schindler's Dixie Doll Company. Shortly after, they introduced the first paper cup, known as the 'Health Kup'. Moore, who never liked the original name for the cup, noticed the word 'Dixie' every day, as it was printed on the doll company's front door. 'Dixie Cups' were born.[15]

The idea was not a runaway success. But eight years later, Moore and Luellen repitched Dixie Cups for 'clinical use'. The friends and business partners became known as 'The Cup Campaigners' with a widespread education blitz telling the public that single repeat-use metal cups at water fountains were the main source for germ contamination. Only disposable cups were sanitary. They distributed a pamphlet with a graphic illustration of a cup in the shape of a skeleton perched on a fountain. This campaign was not all propaganda. The common drinking cup did spread serious diseases, in particular tuberculosis and smallpox, and in this sense the disposable paper cup did have a positive impact on society. Fast-forward to today, and a staggering 220 billion paper and plastic cups are used worldwide per year, with 146 billion cups consumed in North America alone. A day's worth of cups is as high as a forty-two-storey building.[16]

For manufacturers, a product that is thrown away after being used, forcing the customer to keep coming back for more, creates endless profit potential; a potential first discovered in the years after World War I, when there was a great need to find new uses for the abundance of materials produced for the war piled high in warehouses. For example, an absorbent material made from celluloid that had been used for military bandages and gas mask filters later gained a new use as the disposable Kotex sanitary towel. Manufacturers also had to figure out how to transform the wartime ethic of thrift and reuse – darning socks, keeping odd pieces of string, using tea leaves to clean carpets, and sewing rags into rugs – into a culture that embraced 'throwaway habits' and the willingness to spend money on new 'stuff'. During the war, the US government produced posters declaring 'Waste Not, Want Not.' By late 1917, the government was giving shops across the country signs to display in their windows reading 'Beware of Thrift and Unwise Economy', to help encourage repetitive consumption.[17]

Advertisers touted mass-disposable goods as more convenient, time-saving and hygienic than reusable products. They became increasingly attractive in the early fifties as more women entered the workforce, were pressed for time and had greater disposable income. It is not surprising that it was against this backdrop that entire lines of disposable products flooded the market, including Kleenex tissues, Q-tips, Band-Aids, paper towels, paper straws, disposable shopping bags and so on. And along with these products came the boxes and cartons they were packaged in and the ads, catalogues and window displays to promote them; more stuff used and then thrown away. Thirty years later, in 1955, *Life* magazine ran a front cover with the headline 'Throwaway Living' and a photo of a three-child family tossing various disposables high in the air, including paper plates and trays, aluminium pie pans, and nappies. The overall message was liberation for housewives, as disposability became synonymous with convenience and a metaphor for freedom.[18]

Looking back on these relatively simple and useful inventions, you may wonder: What was the harm? People embraced new products in the name of progress, and these products have their benefits. The crucial shift was when the cultural acceptance of disposability broadened past health concerns. How did disposable cups become ubiquitous in our homes and offices, where people have easy access to sinks to clean their own mugs or glasses? How did disposability change from a symbol of health to one of waste and environmental mess? And therein lies the constant tug-of-war between what is seen as progress at the time and future damage.

When Leo Baekeland invented Bakelite, the first man-made plastic, in 1907 − the same year Moore and Luellen started to pursue their cup idea − he intended to make a material that could be bent, moulded, twisted and plied in a number of different ways. It's impossible that he could have foreseen that Americans alone would one day dispose of about 100 billion plastic bags each year. Most are used just once and discarded.[19] The stories of the paper cup and plastic waste both follow the 'law of unintended consequences', where the actions of people have unanticipated and unintended effects, in some cases more significant than the intended effects. Sociologist Robert K. Merton identified five sources of unintended consequences: ignorance, error, immediate interest, basic values and self-defeating prophecy. Two of these sources are particularly relevant to hyper-consumption: first, ignorance (it's impossible to anticipate everything); and second, the imperious immediacy of interest. By the latter Merton was referring to instances in which an individual wants the intended consequence of an action (or product) so much that he purposefully chooses to ignore any long-term unintended effects. Both shoppers and manufacturers engage in a combination of these as they participate in the modern-day consumer system.

Just like the Great Pacific Garbage Patch, the environmental effects of consumerism sit just below the surface, a hidden history of materials, resources and impacts. The amount of waste matter generated in the manufacture of a single laptop computer, for instance, is close to four thousand times its weight.[20] The tiny micron chip inside that same computer requires 1.7 kilograms of materials to produce and its production generates 100,000 times its weight in waste.[21] Until recently, much of the hazardous e-waste from products including old computers, mobile phones and televisions from wealthier nations was shipped to countries in the developing world, including China, Pakistan and Bangladesh. Even though restrictions imposed in the Basel Convention by the United Nations have slowed the export of e-waste exportation, it continues on a gargantuan and destructive scale.[22] For the most part, marketers don't put this kind of information on the label. That's the 'ignorance' part of Merton's analysis. But we keep our laptops for only two years on average (it was six years in 1997).[23] That is a conscious choice we make in the immediacy of self-interest. As John Thackara says in Inside the Bubble, 'It's the accumulation of such tiny, unnecessary acts that weigh so heavily on the planet.'[24]

We are now a society addicted to 'throwaway habits', and many of us are anaesthetized to the consequences. In Britain, every man, woman and child in the country combined produces enough waste to refill London's Royal Albert Hall every two hours.[25] According to the EPA, only 30 per cent of this rubbish is recycled or composted, 13 per cent is incinerated, and the other 57 per cent ends up in landfills. What exactly do we throw out – and why is there is so much of it?

David Chameides, an Emmy award-winning cameraman in Los Angeles, wanted to find out. He decided to conduct an experiment: he

would not throw anything away for one whole year. Chameides kept
every single item of rubbish that he created at home and on the road in
the cellar of his house. A large tin box was used to hold bags of waste
paper, and rubbish bins to hold the rest. Most of the family's leftover
food was given to the dog and the rest was put into a worm composter.
Dave created some rules. Any waste that was not safe – medical waste
from doctor's visits, for instance – would be disposed of. The experiment did not apply to his wife and two children. Beyond that, he didn't
create a masterplan for his year of no trash.[26] Dave even admits, 'If I had
totally thought it through, I might not have done it.' But he did take the
experiment seriously, so much so that he even brought the rubbish
back in a suitcase from a romantic getaway with his wife in Mexico.
Airport screeners baffled by the extra holdall of Mexican rubbish that
went through the X-ray machine interrogated the couple.

Soon after he began his experiment, Dave realized the obvious
solution. The best way to reduce the amount of trash he produced
was to cut back on the amount he consumed in the first place. By
taking his own containers to the fishmonger to avoid the wrapping
and paying a company to stop his junk mail, he limited his waste for
a whole year to thirty pounds (after subtracting recyclable waste),
roughly the amount the average American produces in six days.[27]

All the 'good stuff' we throw away represents just a small
amount, given that for every rubbish bin of waste we put out on the
pavement, seventy additional bins of waste were produced upstream
in production and distribution to make the waste in your bin.[28]
Annie Leonard explains in her book The Story of Stuff, 'Guess what percentage of total material flow through this system is still in product
or use 6 months after their sale in North America. Fifty per cent?
Twenty? NO. One per cent. One! In other words . . . 99 per cent of
the stuff we run through this system is trashed within 6 months.'[29]
And the stuff we throw away is just one half of the waste. The other
half is all the stuff we buy and never or rarely use.

Self-Storage Self

Think, for a moment, about something you bought that you never ended up using. An item of clothing you never ended up wearing? A book you never read? Some piece of electronic equipment that never even made it out of the box? It is estimated that Australians alone spend on average $10.8 billion AUD (approximately $9.99 billion USD) every year on goods they do not use – more than the total government spending on universities and roads. That is an average of $1,250 AUD (approximately $1,156 USD) for each household.[30] All the things we buy that then just sit there gathering dust are waste – a waste of money, a waste of time, and waste in the sense of pure rubbish. As the author Clive Hamilton observes, 'The difference be-tween the stuff we buy and what we use is waste.'[31] Rubbish and storage are just two different endgames of the same problem.

We live in a world where our drawers, closets, walk-in ward-robes, attics, garages, sheds and cellars are bloated with mountains of objects we rarely use and forget we even have. By the early 1990s, American families had, on average, twice as many possessions as they did twenty-five years earlier.[32] So much stuff has been bought that it doesn't fit into our homes anymore, and so we rent storage to extend the capacity to own more things. Just as Cyril Northcote Parkinson, a British civil servant, mused in The Economist in 1955 that 'Work expands so as to fill the time available for completion,' many of us fall victim to Parkinson's Law when it comes to storage: more space increases our tendency to acquire more stuff. Just as plastic migrates to the Great Pacific Garbage Patch, these things get stored away, out-of-sight, out-of-mind.

If you've ever travelled from an airport into a city, say London or New York, and noticed the abundance of self-storage warehouses along the route, you begin to see the extent of the problem. These buildings sit on the sides of orbital motorways, sprout from the landscape of suburbia or are wedged into commercial strips in a city's central core. Regardless of their location, they look the same: grey, massive cinder blocks with halogen lamps glaring 24/7.

In 1964, Russ Williams, a Texas oil industry businessman and avid fisherman, got the idea to open 'mini-warehouses' called the A–1 U-Store-It U-Lock-It U-Carry the Key from his own need to store boats and oil field equipment securely but accessibly. He designed the first facility based on the pattern of side-by-side garages often found in apartment complexes with block partitions and panel garage doors. It was just one hundred feet by thirty feet in size and was painted yellow and black to draw attention to it. Williams realized that his residential customers wanted to store not just boats but items they did not have room for in their homes. The idea caught on so fast that it was hard to keep up with the demand. Williams built more and more facilities until he eventually owned (with various partners) 2,500 across the United States.

Today there are more than 53,000 personal storage facilities – more than seven times the number of Starbucks – in the United States. This amounts to a staggering 2.35 billion square feet or more than 38,000 football fields put together in America alone.[33] If you put out your arms, you create about seven square feet around you. That is roughly how much self-storage space there is for every man, woman and child in America. It means every single person in the country could comfortably stand together inside self-storage units.[34] And self-storage is now a $22 billion-per-year industry in the United States – surpassing domestic Hollywood box-office sales. On average we spend more on self-storage than milk, coffee and even beer. Rentable storage has increased by 740 per cent in the past two decades.[35] As Chris Sonne, a storage expert at Cushman & Wakefield, comments, 'That's two or more self-storage facilities opening every day for fifty years. That beats McDonald's.' About 30 per cent of the storage boom comes from use by businesses storing things such as

payment records, office equipment, and inventory, but the rest of
the expansion has come from people storing possessions that no
longer fit in their homes.[36]

So what are we cramming into these storage units? Camping
gear, lawn mowers, roller skates, pet cages, bread makers and other
electronic gadgets, back issues of *National Geographic* magazine, old
souvenirs, children's bicycles, a computer monitor that just might
work one day, a clarinet we played in primary school, years of bank
receipts, an old sofa – the list goes on. But for the most part, it is 'just
stuff' we no longer want cluttering our homes but pay to store anyway.

Rich Ellmer is a self-storage veteran who has owned and operated more than two hundred Cypress Storage Units in Austin, Texas,
since 1976. Over the past quarter of a century, Ellmer has seen the
same storyline unfold many times. People rent a space and start off
thinking they will rent it for a month or two. They end up keeping
it a lot longer, for years, sometimes more than a decade, with some
renters never clearing out their stuff. Every month, a fee is automatically debited from their bank account, on average ranging from
$99 to $195 depending on the amount of storage. 'Generally, after
six to eight months, the money people pay for the storage exceeds
the value of the items,' Ellmer says. 'It's easier just to write a cheque
for another month and pay. People just don't want to be bothered.'
Gradually, however, some of his tenants realize that the stuff they
are keeping is worth less than what they are paying to store it and
one day just ask for it all to be thrown away.[37]

The phenomenal growth of the self-storage industry becomes
even more disturbing when you think that the size of the average
American home has more than doubled over the past half century,
growing from 983 square feet in 1950 to 1,140 square feet in the
1970s to 2,434 square feet in 2005. In 1950, only 1 per cent of homes
built had four bedrooms or more, but 39 per cent of new homes had

at least four bedrooms in 2003. Garages have become almost obliga-tory, with only 8 per cent of new homes built without a garage, as opposed to 53 per cent built without one in 1950.[38] And when you consider that the average number of people per household has de-clined from about 4.5 in 1916 to 3.3 in 1970 to 2.6 today, this growth seems to be driven by our need to have more room to keep more stuff. As Tom Vanderbilt puts it in his article on self-storage in *Slate*, 'So, let's get this straight – houses got bigger, *average family sizes got smaller*, and yet we still need to tack on a billion-plus square feet to store our stuff?'

The Things You Own End Up Owning You

There is something sad about all this stuff we work so hard to buy, can't live with, but inevitably can't bear to part with. In the same way that we focus on where to bury our waste, not where the waste came from, we also spend inordinate amounts of energy and money storing excess stuff rather than asking the hard truths of why we have so much in the first place. The comedian George Carlin riffed on this in his classic stand-up routine about stuff: 'The whole mean-ing of life has become trying to find a place to put your stuff. . . . Have you ever noticed how other people's shit is shit and your stuff is stuff?'[39] The controversial David Fincher film *Fight Club* struck a painful chord with viewers who have ever experienced that addic-tive feeling of always wanting more, regardless of how much they have. Most people remember two lines from the movie: 'The first rule of Fight Club – you do not talk about Fight Club' and 'The things you own end up owning you.'

Tyler and Jack, the two main characters in the film, seem to represent the stark choice that modern consumerism offers, best summarized by esteemed German social psychologist Erich Fromm as 'To Have or to Be?'[40] Jack (Ed Norton) is a stereotypical thirty-year-old insomniac yuppie who keeps trying to fill his emotional void and feel 'complete' with the things he acquires. 'I flip through catalogues and wonder what kind of dining set defines me as a person.' But no matter what Jack buys, he's never satisfied. That's before he meets Tyler (Brad Pitt), who throughout the film takes anticonsumerist jabs such as, 'You are not the clothes you wear. You are not the contents of your wallet. . . . You are not your grande latte. You are not the car you drive. You are not your fucking khakis. You're the all-singing, all-dancing crap of the world.' Tyler shows Jack that acquiring more and more stuff is a meaningless pursuit devoid of purpose and fulfilment. 'God damn it . . . Advertising has us chasing cars and clothes, working jobs we hate so we can buy shit we don't need.' The main theme of *Fight Club* runs counter to much of what consumer advertising preys on; we won't find happiness or the meaning of our lives in the shopping centre or in the click of a mouse.

Research has proved that people who can afford to buy and hold on to more material goods are not necessarily more satisfied with their lives. Indeed, the reverse is often true. Economist Richard Layard has researched the relationship between growth, hyper-consumerism and happiness. His findings are illustrated by a graph on which one line represents per capita income and personal consumption since 1950 and shows a soaring increase (it has more than doubled) while the other line, marking Americans and Britons who describe themselves as 'very happy' in an annual Gallup survey, remains flat.[41] In fact, the number of people describing themselves as 'very happy' peaked in 1957 just as the conspicuous cycle of 'work and spend', and a revolution of rising materialistic expectations, began. Happiness became an elusive moving target. Nothing was ever enough.

Telling societal indicators paint a vivid picture of this decrease in well-being. Since 1960 teenage suicide rates have tripled in the

United States; the prison population has quintupled; and the percentage of babies born to unmarried parents has sextupled. Not exactly indicators of a satisfied consumer society. And it is only getting worse, as indicated by the massive increase in depression, anxiety, insomnia, heart disease and obesity since the eighties.[42] As political scientist Robert Lane comments in *The Loss of Happiness in Market Democracies*, 'The appetite of our present materialism depends upon stirring up our wants – but not satisfying them.'[43] Economists describe this emotional phenomenon as the 'hedonic treadmill'. We work hard to acquire more stuff but feel unfulfilled because there is always something better, bigger and faster than in the present. The distance between what we have and what we want, the 'margin of discontent',[44] widens as the number of things we own increases. In other words, the more we have, the more we want.[45]

We are taught to dream and desire new things from an early age, as we are frequently asked, 'What do you want for Christmas?' or 'What do you want for your birthday?' Susan Fournier and Michael Guiry, former associate marketing professors at Harvard Business School, conducted a study called Consumption Dreaming Activity. They asked participants, 'What things would you like to own or do someday?' Contrary to the researchers' expectations, the lists varied little regardless of sex, income, education or standard of living. Generally speaking, lists were full of desires for material possessions; almost half the sample (44 per cent) mentioned new cars; more than one in four (29 per cent) listed luxury items such as yachts, antiques, jewellery and designer clothes; and 16 per cent just asked for the money – enough to buy anything they could possibly want. Where the study gets most interesting is not just the type of items respondents wrote down but the level of detail and elaboration they included; 42 per cent of all things listed were described vividly. One participant wrote down wanting not just a car but 'an emerald green

Jaguar'. As the professors noted, 'This level of detail and elaboration could reflect that consumers have "perfect things" in mind when they formulate wish lists.'[46] Here we see the amount of time and headspace most of us give to future purchases. Not only do the things we own fill up our closets and our lives, but they also fill our minds.

TWO | All-Consuming

On Friday 28 November 2008, Jdimytai Damour, a thirty-four-year-old Wal-Mart temporary security guard, was trampled to death at 5:00 a.m. by a stampede of frenzied shoppers. The two-thousand-plus crowd had been gathering at the Valley Stream, New York, shop since 9:00 the night before by a sign that read 'Blitz line starts here.' By dawn they were chanting, 'Push the doors in.' According to witnesses, the doors shattered under the weight of the crowd rushing forward, mowing down Damour, a big man at 270 pounds, who was doing his best to keep the crowd under control. What was the crowd in such a craze for? The bargains promised inside included the latest fifty-inch plasma HDTV, on sale for a price of $798.

The paramedics who came to help were also jostled and stepped on by the shoppers. Damour was pronounced dead of asphyxiation just after 6:00 a.m. Unbelievably, after the police declared that the shop was closed because it was now a crime scene, people kept shopping. Some even refused to leave, yelling, 'I've been queuing since yesterday morning.' The next day, when this same Wal-Mart reopened, crowds lined up again.

The courts have not yet concluded the Damour manslaughter case, but reports indicate that there were 'so many contributing causes to this tragedy' that it will be difficult to assign individual blame. No matter who is to blame for the incident, Damour's terrible end is a sad and chilling metaphor for our culture at large – a crowd of exhausted consumers knocking down the doors and ploughing down people simply to buy more stuff.

Hyper-Consumption

Thorstein Veblen, a Norwegian economist and sociologist, first coined the term 'conspicuous consumption' in 1899.[1] He used the term to describe the nouveau riche, a class emerging during the nineteenth century made up of people eager to display their wealth and social power. They spent lavishly on visible goods such as jewellery and clothing to show they were prosperous and to differentiate themselves from the masses. In this sense, the nouveau riche, just like their counterparts in earlier Roman, Greek and Egyptian civilizations, bought and consumed goods for self-advertisement as much as, if not more than, utility.

What interests us the most is not the luxury status or elitist side of conspicuous consumption that Veblen referred to, but the excessive mass consumption binge kick-started in the 1920s that exploded in the mid-1950s. We refer to the endless acquisition of more stuff in ever greater amounts as 'hyper-consumerism', a force so strong that there are now more shopping centres than high schools in America.[2] There is now more than sixteen square feet of shopping centre for every man, woman and child in the United States.[3] Our challenge is not the fundamental consumer principle in itself but the blurred line between necessity and convenience; the intoxicating addiction of defining so much of our lives through ownership; and the never-ending list of things we 'have to have'. And hyper-consumption has brought us to a place where the real cost of a bargain is that some consumers will trample over a man in the quest for a 'good deal'.

There are four big forces that have played a critical role in manipulating and feeding hyper-consumption: the power of persuasion; the buy now, pay later culture; the law of life cycles; and the 'just one more' factor. These forces offer some way of making sense of why we consume at the rate and in the way we do and help answer the question: How did we end up with so much stuff?

Power of Persuasion

In 1917, twenty-six-year-old Edward Bernays went to work for President Woodrow Wilson. His first job was to help form the Committee on Public Information alongside renowned political journalists Walter Lippmann and George Creel. By this time, the word 'propaganda' was gaining a sinister connotation in the West due to its association with communism, so Bernays coined the term 'public relations' as a positive alternative. The committee crafted the irresistibly patriotic slogan 'Making the World Safe for Democracy' to influence gun-shy America into an anti-German frenzy to go 'over there' and fight in World War I. They used newsprint, posters, radio, telegraph, cable and films to broadcast this message.

After the war, Bernays, like many PR political gurus of that time, went to Madison Avenue, where he applied his talent for influencing the masses to the nascent advertising industry. He received a letter from his uncle Sigmund Freud asking for money. 'I disdain to ask you for this favour, but times are hard in Austria and my research thus far has not been well received. Is there a way I might borrow from you a sum to help cover some recent expenses?' Freud wrote.

Bernays, knowing his uncle was fond of cigars, enclosed a box of Cubans along with the cheque. Grateful for the loan and the gift, Freud sent Bernays a copy of his unpublished book, *A General Introduction to Psychoanalysis*. Within his uncle's writing, Bernays found the scientific backing for his ideas about the power of emotions to persuade. The book reinforced his profound belief that you could manipulate consumers' behaviour by connecting with them on a deep subconscious level, particularly their drives towards aggressiveness and sexuality. To get people to want stuff, desire should be linked to rudimentary human patterns – what we admire, what we despise, what we love, and what we hate and fear.[4] He was so impressed, in fact, that he arranged for his uncle's book to be published in America. Freud became famous, and to a lesser degree, so did Bernays as the father of spin.

Bernays understood the power of psychology to design effective public marketing campaigns. 'If we understand the mechanism and motives of the group mind, is it not possible to control and regiment the masses according to our will without their knowing about it?' Bernays wrote.[5] He reasoned that if he could tap into people's desire to feel good, powerful and sexy, he could sell just about anything, and he proudly referred to this concept as the 'engineering of consent'. We call it the power of persuasion. From soap to silk to bacon to even Wall Street stocks, Bernays got consumers to buy not what they needed but what they desired, connecting not just to who the consumer is but who he or she wanted to be. He realized that the power in this principle was that unmet desires have no fixed point. One of his favourite techniques for influencing consumer wants was to use indirect third-party endorsements. 'If you can influence the leaders,' he posited, 'either with or without their conscious cooperation, you automatically influence the group which they sway.' Through techniques such as these, he didn't just change what people bought; he transformed time-honoured social habits.

In the mid-1920s, despite the widespread popularity of cigarettes, it was not considered acceptable for ladies to smoke in public. The American Tobacco Company hired Bernays to change this social norm. He realized that the real desire for women was not the cigarettes themselves but the liberty to pursue the same things as men. During the 1929 New York Easter Parade, he arranged for a group of attractive young debutantes, including his own secretary, Bertha Hunt, to march in their Sunday best. On Bernays's signal, the women all lit up a Lucky Strike cigarette. Hunt's press release described the march as 'Lighting the Torches of Freedom' in the interests of gender equality. And being the master of PR, Bernays saw to it that the media throughout the world covered the event. The idea was that anyone against the idea of women smoking would appear to be against their liberty and freedom. Although this did not completely do away with the taboo against women's smoking, the number of women taking up smoking skyrocketed (American Tobacco's revenues jumped by $32 million in 1928 alone).[6] In his memoirs, Bernays wrote, 'It was on this day I learned that age-old customs could be broken down by a dramatic appeal, disseminated by the network of media.'[7]

When you consider that the average person sees more than three thousand advertising messages per day, it is not surprising that we have become so seduced by the pull of the new and the desire for more.[8] Influencers such as Bernays were part of a wider force, which engineered and reinforced a system that converted consumers' wants into needs into everyday habits.

The Diderot Effect

In 1919, an advertisement from the department store Sears exhorted, 'Use your electricity for more than light.' Before World War I, the average household did not have an electric toaster, blender or dishwasher, or electronic waste disposal. Families used other means, even if it took a bit longer to toast a piece of bread or wash the dishes. The consumer revolution had barely begun, yet we learned to need and depend on these gadgets. Few people today will deny that these products make our lives easier, and most of us use them every day. But around the same time, superfluous gadgets also entered the kitchen, such as the spiral slicer and other garnishing tools as specific as melon ball scoopers. If you have ever created dramatic spiral strands, ribbons or thin slices from vegetables such as a cucumber, you have probably used a spiral slicer. Advertisers not only touted the slicer as the 'clever, easy and sophisticated way' to add colour to meat platters and to make bland one-colour vegetables such as carrots 'more attractive', but also pulled out the health card, attempting to convince mothers that fancy slicing was the way to get their children to eat more vegetables. Products such as these, which could never be considered a necessity, mark the crossing of a critical line, the line of needing a new invention for rational reasons including hygiene and safety to you-never-know-when-you-might-need-it reasons devised by advertisers.

When you think that garnishing tools were introduced about ninety years ago, it starts to make more sense how kitchens today became stuffed with items such as ice cream machines, bread makers, mushroom brushes, chocolate fondue fountains, popcorn makers, iced tea brewers and strawberry slicers. Most of us buy these contraptions on impulse, possibly learn how they work, use them once, and spend time trying to find a good place to store them, until we admit that we are never going to make homemade ice cream and spend more time working out how to get rid them. In 2009, an average home in the UK contained twenty-five electrical appliances – an increase of 60 per cent in just the last five years alone.[9] How did we lose sight of our real needs?

In his essay 'Regrets on Parting with My Old Dressing Gown', eighteenth-century French writer Denis Diderot tells the story of how the gift from a friend of a beautiful scarlet dressing gown changed his home. Initially delighted by his gift, Diderot discarded his old gown that he had worn for as long as he could remember. But in a short time, his pleasure turned sour as he began to feel as though the rest of his possessions and surroundings were shabby in comparison with the new gown. One by one he replaced the familiar but well-worn furnishings of his study. He replaced his old chair, for example, with an armchair covered in Moroccan leather. And the rickety old desk? That was out, too. In came an expensive new writing table. Even the beloved prints that had hung on his walls for years were taken down to make way for newer, more costly prints that matched the elegance of the new robe. 'I was absolute master of my old dressing gown,' Diderot wrote, 'but I have become a slave to my new one.'[10]

Today, consumer researchers call this kind of trading up the Diderot Effect. In the way that Diderot's new smart gown had the unexpected effect of 'forcing everything else to conform to its elegant tone', we have been persuaded ever since the 1920s that we need complementary groups of possessions (colour, style or the up-to-dateness of an item). Ralph Lauren will take over an entire floor of Bloomingdale's to market a self-contained universe to convince us of the need for a 'total home environment'. Shoppers can purchase matching Ralph Lauren wallpaper, glasses, sheets, rugs, slippers and, yes, even a dressing gown.[11] Similarly, when women were exposed to an advertisement in *Good Housekeeping* or *Ladies' Home Journal* for, say, a Swan electric kettle, in the background was the 'ideal' kitchen with the perfect housewife surrounded by her Swan electric toaster, fridge, dishwasher and so on. It was not about buying the kettle per se, but about aspiring to the complete lifestyle conveyed in the picture.

There is a line in the 1999 Oscar-winning film *American Beauty* when the main character Lester (played by Kevin Spacey) starts to rebel against his cookie-cutter life. In a voice-over, he mocks his wife Carolyn's materialism. Carolyn works in her manicured rose garden. She is put together in a matching outfit. Lester remarks, 'That's my wife, Carolyn. See the way the handle on the pruning sheers matches her gardening clogs? That's not an accident.'

This materialistic image of what life should be started to be embodied everywhere – films, radio, magazines, political speeches, advertising – and all was wrapped up in the famous idea of the American dream. The concept of the American dream, and the image of the perfect suburban home that went with it, became such an inherent part of the fabric of American culture and even a global advertisement to the rest of the world on the way to live that it became un-American to challenge it. Douglas Rushkoff comments in *Life Inc.*, 'It was less important for this life to provide actual satisfaction as for it to produce a class of people who behaved as if they were satisfied.'[12] This desire created a relentless pressure to buy more stuff. Now the barrier that companies needed to overcome was giving people an easy way to pay for it.

Buy Now, Pay Later

Richard Feinberg, a consumer psychology professor at Purdue University and a pioneer in consumer behavioural economics, has long studied the influence of credit cards on our spending decisions. One of the first experiments he conducted, with the help of a local restaurant, involved recording the size of the bill, the size of the tip, and the method of payment – cash or credit card – for 135 customers. He found that people who paid by credit card left tips 2 per cent higher than those who paid by cash.

To make sure this was not simply a case of credit card customers being wealthier than cash customers (or company expense-account diners), Feinberg followed up with a controlled experiment in a laboratory. He randomly assigned one group of undergraduate students to a lab with MasterCard signs and logos intentionally placed in the corner. He told the subjects this paraphernalia was for another experiment and to pay no attention to it. A second control group had no credit card-related materials. He showed both sets of participants identical pictures of various products, such as a dress, a tent and a typewriter. For each item he asked, 'How much would you be willing to pay for it?' Remarkably, Feinberg's participants exposed to the red and yellow logo (even though they were told to ignore it) were willing to pay up to three times more for products relative to the control group. The study showed that mere image exposure to a credit card logo is sufficient to affect what people will pay. Feinberg also discovered that students answered the questions faster in the 'MasterCard' group room, an indicator that people think less or at least for shorter moments when they spend with plastic.[13]

Feinberg's experiments, as revealing as they were, didn't involve people making decisions about actual purchases. To follow up, MIT economists Drazen Prelec and Duncan Simester conducted a study in 2001 based on real bids for real commodities (the study was later appropriately named Always Leave Home Without It).[14] MBA students from MIT participated in two real auctions, one for a pair of tickets to a Boston Celtics game, and the other for tickets to a Boston Red Sox game. The Celtics tickets were not just any tickets, mind you; they were for the last regular-season game with the Miami Heat, a game the Celtics had to win to clinch the division title. Tickets had been sold out well in advance and could be bought only from touts. The Red Sox tickets were for a regular-season baseball game with the Toronto Blue Jays.[15]

The students who volunteered for the experiment reported to a classroom at lunchtime and were handed a sheet of paper that described the prizes and gave instructions on how to record their bids.

No information on market values for any of the prizes was given, but descriptions read like this: 'One pair of 3rd row balcony tickets for Celtics-Miami game, Sunday April 19'. The students were told not to discuss their answers or anything else about the bid sheet. Unbeknownst to the participants, two different versions were handed out at random. Half the sheets stated that payment was required by winners in cash, the 'cash condition' sheet. It included a note that they had to indicate whether they had 'ready access to a local cash machine'. The other sheet stipulated that payment must be with a credit card.

The results were clear. Students who agreed to pay with cash bid an average of $28.51 for the Celtics ticket, but the students who agreed to pay with plastic bid an average of $60.24 – an incredible 113 per cent premium over the cash bids. The outcome for the Red Sox tickets showed the same pattern, but the price premium for credit card bids over cash was lower, at 76 per cent, perhaps because these seats were not as desired or rare. Were the students who bid with credit cards less able to constrain their desire and more reckless with their bidding? And given that the bids were for items of an uncertain value, how much does this experiment apply to the world of goods with a price tag?

Dilip Soman, a marketing professor at the Hong Kong University of Science and Technology, designed a study to look at this very point. Soman intercepted forty-one students after they had made purchases at the campus bookstore and asked them to recall the exact amount they had spent. Of the respondents who had paid by credit card, only 35 per cent could recall the amount; the remainder either named a figure far lower than the true amount or confessed that they had no idea.[16]

These experiments appear to demonstrate how credit cards – or even just credit card symbols – alter our perception of the value of a product. But they illustrate deeper clues into what is going on in our brains when we buy. When cash tangibly leaves our hands, we are more conscious that we are spending money than when we use a card.[17] What economists such as Feinberg, Prelec and Simester have shown is that credit cards, in contrast, make the transaction less 'real', detaching the act of purchase from payment. The behavioural experts call this phenomenon 'decoupling'. Perhaps it is this decoupling that explains why credit cards have become the ultimate enablers or, more accurately, tranquillizers of shopping.[18] Indeed brain imaging experiments indicate that the insular cortex, the region of the brain often associated with addictions and negative feelings, experiences less activity when people pay with credit cards over cash. George Loewenstein, a neuroeconomist at Carnegie Mellon, points out that 'the nature of credit cards ensures that your brain is anaesthetized against the pain of payment.'[19]

It's hard to imagine life before credit cards. In stark contrast to the shopping behaviour this plastic device has come to facilitate, the basic idea for the credit card was invented by an individual, not a corporation, and for a practical reason. In 1949, in Major's Cabin Grill, New York City, Frank McNamara, head of Hamilton Credit Corporation, took his partners to dinner. Their conversation centred on the problems of a customer who had borrowed some money from Hamilton Credit, but was now unable to pay it back. When the bill arrived, it was Frank's turn to pay, but he realized to his embarrassment that he'd left his wallet in another suit pocket at home. He called his wife and asked her to drive over and bring him money, vowing to himself that he would never let this mistake happen again. At this moment he thought about the troubled Hamilton customer who could not pay his debts and his own personal embarrassment. 'What if there was some way to pay the bill without cash in hand?' Frank mused. Thus inspired, Frank developed the first dual-party credit card, Diners Club, and the credit card was born. In the credit card industry, this dinner is often referred to as the 'First Supper'.

In just one year, twenty thousand people became card holders. Five years later, that number had increased tenfold. Other banks took note of the popularity of this new payment device, but the idea didn't gain mass appeal until 1957. That was the year when the nation became obsessed with the story of Mr Harold Bortzfield and his wife from Lancaster, Pennsylvania, who set off on an around-the-world thirty-day trip with nothing more than an airplane ticket and a Diners Club card. Shortly thereafter American Express introduced the first 'general-purpose' 'Don't Leave Home Without It' credit card made of plastic, and then along came 'Master the Moment' from MasterCard, 'It's Everywhere You Want to Be' from Visa, and so on. The critical turning point in the history of credit cards was when American Express introduced the option of maintaining a revolving balance in 1959. Cardholders no longer had to pay their bills in full but could carry a balance from one month to the next. Joe Nocera writes in his book *A Piece of the Action: How the Middle Class Joined the Money Class*, 'Thus did Americans begin to spend money they didn't yet have; thus did the unaffordable become affordable.'[20]

Between 1989 and 2001, credit card debt nearly tripled, soaring from $238 billion to $692 billion. In 2007, it was up to $937 billion. The equation is simple: the more credit we have, the more stuff we can afford to buy, the more resources are consumed and the more waste is created. The credit card (or more specifically, credit card debt) has become as much a symbol of American life as apple pie, with US citizens holding more than 1.3 billion cards. There are more than four credit cards for each American. In contrast, the Chinese have only a total of 5 million credit cards, for all 1.2 billion of the population.[21] In Western Europe, there is only 0.23 credit card per person.

Think about your own credit card statement for a second (that is if you are not the one in four who has never looked at his or her statement).[22] What are the four logical pieces of information missing from it? You probably guessed the first two: your statement of interest and fees paid. But what about the interest rate itself and the length of time it will take you to pay off your debt at your current minimum monthly payment? This missing information begins to explain why the average family carries, often ignorantly, $8,000 of debt (over eight cards) and pays $1,000 a year in interest and fees alone.[23] The nation's credit card charges amount to more than $1.8 trillion a year.[24] So what have we spent all this credit on?[25]

Of course most of us benefit from credit cards at some point in time. As the credit card industry says, 'We provide the credit, in many cases, for people to start businesses . . . to buy more, to live a better life, to do things that they could never do any other way.'[26] So what's the problem? Looking at the buying habits of a spectrum of consumers, we can see that credit cards have fuelled different types of unhealthy spending habits: accelerated spending, mindless spending, and latest and greatest spending. By no means are these three types mutually exclusive. It is common for one consumer to get caught in the trap of all three. The result, though, is the same and obvious: consumers spend more than they can afford and buy new stuff faster, more easily and more often.

Accelerated spending is the 'I've got to have it right now' shopping mentality that leads us to make purchases we can't afford. David Laibson, an economist at Harvard, notes, 'Our emotional brain wants to max out the credit card, order dessert, and smoke a cigarette. When it sees something it wants, it has difficulty waiting to get it.'[27] Most people's brains are not wired to do the 'buy now, pay later' calculation, as we struggle to understand the principles of exponential growth (which is precisely what credit card interest is). Jonathan Zinman, an economics professor at Dartmouth College, uses an old puzzle to illustrate this point. Imagine a chessboard with $1 on the first square, $2 on the second, then $4, $8, $16 and so on.

How many dollars on the final sixty-fourth square? Okay, so if you are like us, your brain does not even try to figure it out, but instinct would suggest it is somewhere around $100,000. Actually, the sixty-fourth square contains $9,000 quadrillion.[28] When we borrow money to buy something now, we do not contemplate the interest hangover. Our brain can't compute the cost of our actions, at least in the moment.

Mindless spending is the 'I don't know what I spent my money on' type of spending that can take the form of aimlessly wandering around the shopping centre or popping into shops during your lunch break and coming home with things you never intended to buy. The moment when a person shifts from being a conscious consumer shopping for a specific item to an impulse buyer has been named the Gruen Transfer, after architect Victor Gruen, who constructed the first shopping centre in 1956.[29] Gruen's original vision for the centre was to create an 'idyllic shopping environment' and a 'kernel of the community' – a grand plan far removed from the disorienting and sprawling maze we experience today.

Latest and greatest spending translates into 'I've got to get it because it is bigger (or smaller), better, faster or even just newer.' In most instances the existing product still functions; nevertheless it cannot fulfil our desire to have the latest version available. We tend to value whatever is new and original over what is old, durable or used.[30] This tendency is not so far removed from the 'utopia' described in Aldous Huxley's classic fantasy Brave New World, where children are indoctrinated from birth to consume. Newness as a trait is something to be cherished.[31] In Huxley's imagined world, these children undergo conditioning from teachers who whisper in their ears as they sleep, 'I do love having new clothes. Ending is better than mending . . . old clothes are beastly. We always throw away old clothes. . . . The more stitches, the less riches; the more stitches . . .'[32] The philosophy of Mustapha Mond, the dictator of

Brave New World, is 'We don't want people to be attracted by old things. We want them to like the new ones.'

Law of Life Cycles

Mobile phones have now achieved the dubious status of having the shortest life cycle of any electronic consumer product.[33] The average person in America and Britain discards his or her mobile phone within eighteen months of purchase, even though mobile phones will last for ten years on average. (In Japan, the time span from purchase to discard is merely a year.) Every year more than 130 million still-working mobile phones in the United States and 15 million in the UK are retired. Only a small fraction are reassembled for reuse.[34] The iPod is not far behind the mobile phone in claiming the 'shortest life cycle' crown. For a product introduced in 2001, it is remarkable that by 2009 it had already gone through six 'generations' of the first 'Classic' model (and that does not even include the extensions of the family such as the Shuffle, Nano, Mini and Touch). If you were one of those consumers who 'upgraded' to every new iPod that had come onto the market from 2001 to 2009, you would now own eighteen iPods.[35]

We are addicted to new products. According to Colin Campbell, a professor of sociology at the University of York, we suffer from 'neophilia'. Campbell argues that novelty seeking is a new phenomenon. 'Pre-modern societies tend to be suspicious of the novel. It is a feature of modernity that we are addicted to novelty.'[36] Medieval period fashions changed slowly and slightly over the course of a thousand years. Clothing was primarily a matter of necessity rather than of ever-changing fashion.

The stories of the founding fathers of the automobile industry, Henry Ford and Alfred P. Sloan, illustrate a dividing line between comfort with the tried and true and the endless chase of the new. One believed in a hyperthyroid economy that could be sustained only through a constant consumer demand for new goods, while the other, the master of mass production, initially rejected force-fed repetitive consumption.

Henry Ford learned the honest values of quiet country living on a small farm in Dearborn, a rural town just west of Detroit. He spent most of his childhood tending the fields and milking cows. But it was clear from a young age that Henry would not be a farmhand forever. Indeed, he had a gift for mathematics and loved tinkering with machines of all kinds, especially watches. When he founded the Ford Motor Company in 1901, Ford knew that he wanted to make owning a car possible for everyone. Ford, committed to social change, believed a 'one size fits all' approach to cars could be a great class leveller. He realized this dream with the introduction of the first Model T in 1908, a car that was simple to drive, cheap, easy to repair, and durable.

Alfred Sloan, in contrast, had a wealthy and privileged upbringing in New Haven, Connecticut. He studied electrical engineering at MIT, where students were taught to focus on inventing the 'next big thing'. After graduating at the top of his class, he joined Hyatt Rolling, a small ball bearings manufacturer, acquired by General Motors in 1916. At the age of twenty-six, he became president when his father, a prosperous businessman, bought the company. When Sloan became president of GM in the early 1920s, he faced the threat of an ever-expanding used-car market and an ever-lowering price tag of the Model T. It was around the same time that he brought the new Chevrolet to market. Observing how the fashion and textile industries were growing at a rapid rate by updating designs, he proposed that consumers would trade up for style as much as for technological improvements long before their old cars wore out. He convinced his team to restyle the body covering of what was essentially a nine-

year-old piece of technology under the banner of 'product innovation'. The Chevrolet was a remarkable success and the idea of
'perceived obsolescence' and 'change for change's sake' was born.
Obsolescence was now built not just into the product itself, but into
our minds. GM went so far as to define its strategy as choreographed
cosmetic 'upgrades' to 'Keep the Consumer Dissatisfied'. In 1929,
Charles Kettering, director of research for Sloan, wrote an article
declaring, 'The key to economic prosperity is the organized creation
of dissatisfaction. . . . If everyone were satisfied no one would want
to buy the new thing.'[37] This cry became an increasingly popular
concept as companies realized they no longer had a production
problem but rather had a demand problem. They needed to shift
their attention to finding new ways to sell existing products.

For fifteen years Ford showed a fanatical dedication to sticking
with the Model T's original design (with the exception of a few
minor changes). In 1922, he proclaimed, 'We have been told . . .
that the object of business ought to be to get people to buy frequently and that [it] is bad business to try to make anything that will
last forever. . . . Our principle of business is precisely to the contrary.
. . . We never make an improvement that renders any previous
model obsolete.' Ford maintained consumer demand by competing
on costs, bringing the price of the Model T down from $950 in 1909
to $290 by 1924 through the efficiencies and scale made possible by
the assembly line.[38] But by 1927, with most families who could afford one owning a car, the increasing competition of GM's lavish
and continual design 'improvements' and the rumblings of the Great
Depression, this strategy faltered. After the 15 millionth Model T
rolled off the assembly line, production halted, and cars such as the
Model A and V-8 with multiple different styles of models were born.
Henry Ford lost the battle to obsolescence.

The efficiencies of mass production only grew during World
War II. Goods rolled off assembly lines faster than they could be

consumed, jamming warehouses. As Vance Packard writes in the The *Waste Makers*, 'The challenge was to develop a public that would always have an appetite as voracious as its machines.'[39] Advertisers called the time between when a product was made and when that product was purchased by the consumer 'time lag'. To reduce that gap, manufacturers induced people to buy more and more products, faster, and to create desire even when customer needs were already met. Perceived obsolescence, making products feel out-of-date, less desirable, and in need of replacement, was a strategy mastered by the car makers, but it was not enough. Consumers still controlled their desires to update or upgrade. Manufacturers needed to take this decision out of their hands.

Designing for the Dump

In Arthur Miller's *Death of a Salesman*, Willy Loman, the aging salesman with an unwavering devotion to the American dream, laments, 'Once in my life I would like to own something outright before it is broken! I am always in a race with the junkyard!' His outburst continues, 'The refrigerator consumes belts like a goddamn maniac. They time those things. They time them so when you've finally paid for them, they're used up.' Willy was experiencing the pains of 'death dating', the idea of deliberately building into the product different ways to shorten its life, carefully controlled by the manufacturer.

Planned obsolescence was a concept first suggested not by an economist, a manufacturer or even an advertiser, but by a Manhattan real estate broker. In 1932, Bernard London wrote a twenty-page pamphlet called 'Ending the Depression Through Planned Obsolescence'. London proposed starting a government agency that would determine the 'lease of life' of every manufactured product, be it a car, a hair comb, a ship or even a building. After the allotted time expired, 'these things would be legally dead.' Consumers would have a choice: they could give up the item, and be paid part of the price of a new one, or use the product past its 'expiration date' and pay a penalty tax. While the regulatory details of London's concept were not enforced, the principle of the proposal was adopted by product designers in the fifties who started to 'design for the dump'.

During the twentieth century, the average human life span in the United States increased by more than thirty years, twenty-five years of which are attributed to advances in medicine and public health.[40] In contrast, over the last fifty years, the life span of everyday 'durable' goods including refrigerators, toasters and washing machines has decreased anywhere between three and seven years. In 1901, Shelby Electric Company produced an incandescent 'Centennial' lightbulb. The original, more than one hundred years later, still lights up the fire station in Livermore, California, where it was first installed. In contrast, in 1932, a memo circulated at GE stating, 'We should change the life of the 200-watt 110–120 volt PS 30 bulb lamp from 1,000 hours . . . to 750 hours.'[41] GE, like many other companies, shortened the life span of its products to increase sales.

Just One More Factor

For many families today, the idea of owning one television is as odd as having, say, just one pair of shoes. In 2004, both America and the UK crossed a telling threshold: the average home had more televisions in it than people (there are on average three sets in the typical home and 2.55 people).[42] As a person is unlikely to watch two televisions at once, how did we end up being convinced that we need more than one television per person in our homes?

In the late 1950s, industrialists were worried. The Smiths had caught up with the Joneses. A degree of mass affluence meant that the average American family (and much of Europe) was satisfied with what it had, owning a home, new appliances and a car. Markets for goods were getting saturated while consumer demand was slowing. Social commentator Vance Packard summed up this phenomenon when he noted, 'The way to end glut was to produce gluttons.'[43] Manufacturers needed people not simply to want to keep up with the Joneses, but as Gregg Easterbrook wrote in The Progress Paradox, to have a desire to 'call and raise the Joneses'.[44] Given that most people had one of everything, consumers needed a plausible excuse to buy 'just one more' of a product they already owned, and so the surplus doctrine of choice was born.

Psychologist Jonathan Haidt conducted a simple experiment that we can re-create here. Pick a word from the following list most appealing to you: constraint, limit, barrier, choice. Odds are that, like the participants in the research, you picked 'choice', as the first three have negative associations.[45] We often believe as consumers that the more choice the better, even if it is more of the same. And this feeling relates not just to the hundreds of thousands of brands we have to choose from every day, but also to which car to drive, television to watch and phone to call on, and even which bathroom to use. As psychologists such as Barry Schwartz have shown in books such as the The Paradox of Choice, choice confuses us not only about how to satisfy our wants, but about what those wants are. This uncertain disorienting effect is what manufacturers wanted to create. If we don't feel satisfied, satisfaction may be just one more purchase away. By 2005, according to Juliet B. Schor, a professor of sociology at Boston College, the average consumer purchased one new piece of clothing every five and half days.[46]

The more our houses and lives bloat with stuff, the heavier and more trapped we feel. As Neal Lawson wrote in All Consuming, 'The more we consume the less space we have to be anything other than consumers.'[47] Similarly, the more space and time we spend dedicated to accumulating stuff in our lives, the less room we have for other people. Our drive for material wealth entailed the exclusion of our most basic social needs, such as family and community bonds, personal passions and social responsibility. We thought we could fill these needs through shopping and buying and accumulating more and more stuff. Some critics describe our era of hyper-consumerism as 'autistic capitalism'. Regardless of nomenclature, we know two things about this disorder of hyper-consumption. First, it was driven by a belief that money – and the almost instinctual accumulation of what money can buy – equalled happiness. The second thing we know is that this disorder is fixable. The system of consumerism may seem like an immovable fact of modern life. But it is not. That the system was manufactured suggests that we can reshape those forces to create a healthier, more sustainable system with a more fulfilling goal than 'more stuff'.

<table>
<tr><td>THREE</td><td>From Generation Me
to Generation We</td></tr>
</table>

Anyone who has travelled in rural Africa knows that one adjective describes its economy: 'more.' The people there need more. They need more water, food, infrastructure, education, health and governance. This lack of the most basic resources and the consequent poverty also confronted Adam Smith more than two hundred years ago. Smith, the great Scottish economist, sought a way out of the agrarian squalor of the eighteenth century. He believed a more productive society would lead to a wealthier society. In *The Wealth of Nations*, Smith argued that humans are motivated by self-interest and 'self-love', and that the exploitation of this trait leads to greater wealth for all and a more effective distribution of labour.[1]

Looking back, one can understand why Adam Smith wanted to work out how to get the economy to produce more. Britain in the 1700s was not a nice place to live. The average life expectancy was just thirty-five years. Dead dogs, cats, rats and even horses decayed on the cobblestone streets, and raw waste spilled everywhere, creating a breeding ground for diseases such as bubonic plague, tuberculosis and smallpox. Medicine was still so primitive that in 1775 more than eight hundred deaths recorded in the Bills of Mortality were attributed simply to 'Teeth'.[2] Most people lived in just one room in buildings made of crumbling bricks. It was not unusual for such buildings to collapse.

But today, in a rampant consumer economy, 'more' has lost its meaning. Smith would probably be mystified by how his simple goals of increasing productivity and achieving market efficiency have become an ideological threat to our economy, society and planet. In *When Corporations Rule the World*, David C. Korten writes, 'Smith did not advocate a market system based on unrestrained greed. He was talking about small farmers and artisans trying to get the best price for their products to provide for themselves and their families. That is self-interest – but it is not greed.'[3]

Adam Smith and later Milton Friedman both believed that an individual pursuing his own self-interest promotes the good of society as a whole. In Chapter Two, we saw how in just a few generations, this concept was transformed from a relatively healthy narrative of technological ingenuity to a frenetic quest for personal identity through brands, products and services, before finally becoming an extreme system of insatiable consumerism. So much so that by the 1950s, the dawn of hyper-consumerism, we started to perceive ourselves first and foremost as a society of individual consumers, and as a group of citizens second. We ended up believing that we were better off relying on corporations rather than cooperating with each other. Collective- and community-based values were shunned in favour of consumer independence and a mind-set of 'me, me, me'.

The promises of individuality and independence were wrapped up in the falsehood that 'what's mine is mine' and that complete self-reliance was the ultimate goal. Douglas Rushkoff writes in his book *Life Inc.*, 'Each home was to be its own fiefdom. Self-sufficiency was part of the myth of the self-made man with his private estate, so community property, carpools, or sharing of almost any kind became anathema to the suburban aesthetic.[4] And that neighbour on the other side of the fence, do we even know him well enough to borrow his ladder? Sadly, neighbours being 'total strangers' is more the norm these days than the exception. A recent survey shows that three-quarters of Americans confess that they don't know their next-door neighbours.[5] In the UK, six out of ten people don't know their neighbours' names.[6] It would seem that the consumer culture of 'more' helped businesses get bigger while prizing us further and further apart.

Through the fifties and sixties, manufacturers and marketers encouraged American workers to give up their hobbies and free time for the choice of bigger cars, better homes and more technology. The result was a dramatic decline in 'social capital'. Robert Putnam, a political science professor at Harvard University, was responsible for popularizing the concept of social capital, defining it as 'the trust, norms, and networks that can improve the efficiency of society by facilitating coordinated actions'.[7] In his book *Bowling Alone*, he traced the decline in social capital through a study of American membership in bowling leagues. Putnam found that between 1980 and 1993, while the total number of people who bowled in America increased by 10 per cent, the number of bowling leagues decreased by 40 per cent. And as Putnam notes, 'Lest this be thought a wholly trivial example, nearly 80 million Americans went bowling at least once during 1993, nearly a third more than voted in the 1994 congressional elections.'[8] In short, the more people who bowl alone, the fewer conversations over beer and pizza, and the greater the overall decline in human interaction. The less time people spent socializing, the more time they spent in the office or shopping. The irony is that while Americans tripled their capacity to consume between 1980 and 2000, they found themselves with far less time to enjoy the fruits of their labour.[9] As former president Bill Clinton said in a 1993 speech, 'Most Americans are working harder for less.'[10]

Edmund Burke, the great Irish statesman, philosopher, and – as one might now call him – futurist, was ahead of his time when he wrote in 1757, 'The great error of our nature is not to know where to stop; not to be satisfied with any reasonable requirement . . . but to lose all we have gained by an insatiable pursuit of more.' It is this 'insatiable pursuit of more' that we must now address. Adam Smith remarked that Burke was 'The only man I ever knew who thinks on economic subjects exactly as I do.'[11] They both wanted to create a better society through competition but with a healthy balance between pursuit of self-interest and pursuit of the greater good. Over two centuries later, their vision might be taking shape.

We may be coming out of the consumer trance we have been living in for the past fifty or so years. At the heart of this transformation are two interlocking phenomena. The first is a values shift. There is a growing consumer consciousness that infinite growth and consumption based on finite resources are not a viable combination. Consequently, we are finding ways to get more out of what we buy, and more importantly, out of what we don't buy. At the same time, we are starting to recognize that the constant quest for material things has come at the expense of impoverishing relationships with friends, family, neighbours and the planet. This realization is causing a desire to re-create stronger communities. We are experiencing a tipping point from the pursuit of 'what's in it for me?' towards the mind-set of 'what's in it for us?' But more than that, we are beginning to see that self-interest and collective good depend on each other. It is in my self-interest to stop global warming; it is in my self-interest to participate in elections; it is in my interest to correct an online entry on Wikipedia.

Reclaiming Old Virtues

Our awareness of the false promises of our consumer economy is not new. Just as mass consumerism was taking hold, a visionary tried to halt the emerging culture of materialism. Cereal giant Kellogg Company founder W. K. Kellogg decided in 1930, right around the start of the Great Depression, that most of his fifteen hundred employees would go from a traditional eight-hour to a six-hour workday. Company president Lewis Brown championed the initiative, announcing at the time, 'Four six-hour shifts . . . instead of three eight-hour shifts, will give work and paychecks to the heads of three hundred more families in Battle Creek.'[12] The existing workforce took a slight pay cut, but Kellogg raised the hourly rate to offset the loss and promised production bonuses to encourage people to work hard.

But Kellogg wanted to do more than provide and save jobs. He recognized that rather than passing time, like previous generations, people were spending it, getting lost in the ever-accelerating cycle of work and consumption. This mania was leaving them disconnected from their communities. Benjamin Hunnicutt explains in his book *Kellogg's Six-Hour Day* that Brown and Kellogg hoped to show that the 'Free exchange of goods, services, and labor in the free market would not have to mean mindless consumerism or eternal exploitation of people and natural resources.'[13] It was a bold vision, and it worked – for a while.

The workers in Battle Creek embraced the extra two hours. Beyond the time spent at home with their family and friends, the time also created a sense of freedom to pursue leisure interests. Women sewed, gardened, visited neighbours and cooked together. Men exercised, hunted, visited libraries and explored other hobbies. As Hunnicutt writes, 'Those extra two hours were precious and offered an opportunity to

craft the employee's sense of family, community, and citizenship. . . .
The modern discipline of alienated work was left behind for an
older . . . more convivial kind of working together.'[14]

Kellogg's six-hour workday produced not just a qualitative social
benefit by creating 'happier' employees with more leisure time.
There were quantitative results for the company, too. The shorter
workday influenced employees to work harder. On average, ninety-
six boxes of shredded wholewheat biscuits were packed per hour
instead of eighty-three.[15] Overhead costs, labour costs and the number of work-related accidents also decreased. The company polled
workers in 1946 (after the programme had been temporarily suspended) and found that 77 per cent of men and 87 per cent of women
would choose a thirty-hour week even if it meant lower wages.[16]

Despite its success and popularity, Kellogg stopped its experiment in 1943. The labour shortage and product demand from World
War II pushed the company back to an eight-hour workday. President Roosevelt launched a series of policy initiatives that led to the
standard forty-hour working week that for the large part we still
adhere to today. These political forces were impossible for even Kellogg to resist. As one employee later commented, 'Everybody
thought they were going to get rich when they got that eight-hour
deal and it really didn't make a big difference. . . . Some went out
and bought automobiles right quick and they didn't gain much on
that because the car took the extra money they had.'[17]

Today there is a conscious movement to return to the same intentions that motivated the six-hour Kellogg working week. Across
America, and much of Europe and Australasia, we are seeing a drive
to reclaim leisure time to self-educate, self-relate and revive neglected
forms of social capital. The urge to regain meaning and community
in our lives is popping up everywhere – and perhaps nowhere more
obviously than in our kitchens. Roo used to visit his Grandma Dada
in her middle-class home in Wimbledon every Saturday. When Roo

walked in the door, he would run to the fridge. Everything you needed to know about Dada could be understood in the way she cooked. She had a routine. The first Saturday would be a roast chicken, the leftover bones would be turned into stock for the following Saturday's risotto, the leftover risotto would be used for the following Saturday's stuffed tomatoes, and the leftover stuffed tomatoes would be turned into pasta sauce. Roo and his brothers would joke that when there was something that she couldn't reuse she'd turn it into the soap she made them wash their hands with. There is more to this process than resourcefulness. For Dada, making lunch was about finding balance through a value system that integrated her history, as well as her sense of responsibility to her family and community. Roo thought of his grandmother in June 2009 when he, his wife and their fourteen-month-old daughter took a trip to China to visit distant relatives. They stayed on the fifty-seventh floor of the JW Marriott in Shanghai. As they walked around the breakfast buffet, he was struck with an intense feeling that what lay before him wasn't rational. Smoked salmon from Scotland, lobster from Maine, French croissants, Italian spring water and Costa Rican coffee. The sense of globalized freedom that the buffet offered felt overwhelming and oppressive. But most of all, the choices were without meaning. He was in Shanghai, and he wanted a Chinese breakfast and something that made him feel his fourteen-hour flight had transported him somewhere new. And here is where his grandmother's old world and his own new world values meet, in the desire to find purpose and an authentic story behind what we buy, make, do and create.

Return of the Local Marketplace

In high school, Rob Kalin would skip classes to shoot and develop his photographs. He graduated with a D-minus average but won admission to a studio programme at Boston's Museum of Fine Arts.

Over the next six years, Kalin attended half a dozen colleges before finally finishing his degree, with a major in classics, from New York University in 2004. He was twenty-five years old at the time and pessimistic about how his degree would help him in the job market. The son of a carpenter, he grew up with a 'hands-on' approach to life. He started to make furniture in his Brooklyn apartment, turning IKEA kitchen work surfaces into stereo speakers and reclaimed wood into desks. But Kalin discovered it was hard to sell his stuff, even online. There was a lot of 'advice and hand-holding' for artisans but no viable marketplace to exhibit and sell their creations. At the same time, he was not a fan of brick-and-mortar chain stores. He would just walk around and see shelves upon shelves of 'anonymous mass-produced products' – and think that he wanted to create the opposite experience.

In early April the following year, Kalin was sitting in a big orange chair facing his apartment window. He started to sketch the initial ideas for his vision – a vibrant community of people across the globe connecting with and helping one another, and ultimately buying and selling unique handmade goods direct, with no big middleman. Working with three friends and fellow NYU graduates – Chris Maguire, Haim Schoppik and Jared Tarbell – Kalin transformed his initial scribbles into a live website in just two months. Etsy was born. In just three years, Etsy has attracted 200,000 sellers, a million registered users and more than $27 million in funding.[18]

Etsy connects buyers with independent creators of all things handmade, the result being that you pay less and the seller makes more. In 150 countries, from Australia to England to South America, more than 3 million people are buying and selling everything from 'myrtle wood electric guitars' to 'crocheted bath puffs' to 'bookcases handcrafted from canoes'. At the same time, through forums and live chats, as well as via offline crafts events and workshops known as Etsy labs, the Etsy community provides these artists not just with the platform but with the information and support they need to earn a living. 'This human-to-human relationship of the person who's making it with the person who's buying it is at the core of what Etsy is,' Kalin explained.[19]

Kalin posits that handmade 'isn't a fad, it's a resurgence', and indeed the growth and sales of Etsy have been phenomenal. In November 2008, when much of the consumer world was in a panic, Etsy had twelve record sales volume days in the month; $10.8 million of goods were sold – a 27 per cent increase over October; and 135,165 new members joined the community. In the first six months of 2009, more than $70 million worth of goods were sold and more than 1 million new sellers and buyers joined.

Etsy is a throwback to the way consumerism used to be, individuals buying from individuals, and re-creating old forms of virtual market bazaars. It is a part – or you could say a pioneer – of the resurgence in the popularity of older craft industries – knitting, printmaking, crochet, ceramics, quilting, woodworking and so on. More and more people are looking to reconnect with the ties and variety of local and custom-made goods that got lost in mass production. Chain-store culture and shopping centre-fuelled conformity have created extraordinarily impersonal experiences with products that have no history, story or person behind them. In his book *What Would Google Do?* Jeff Jarvis observed, 'Everything's the same; nothing's unique; and that takes the fun out of making, buying and owning. But the small-is-the-new-big world could bring variety back. The craftsman lives again on Etsy.'[20]

In 2009, Kalin travelled to the World Economic Forum in Davos, Switzerland, to talk to world leaders about Etsy's vision to 'create millions of local living economies that will create a sense of community in the economy again'. In a prepared video message made for the Forum, sitting on an old sofa covered in a pink and red quilt, and surrounded by patchwork cushions, a brightly coloured oversize toy octopus and two teddy bears (obviously all made by Etsy sellers), Kalin explained that 'these millions of local living economies around the world are more sustainable for the planet than a small number of huge conglomerate companies.' Kalin is a realist as well as an idealist. He admits that 'there can't be no mass production altogether' but is equally 'flabbergasted that anyone would shop at Wal-Mart to save twelve cents on a peach instead of supporting a local farmer'.[21] These days it seems more and more people agree with him.

There are currently more than 5,750 local farmers' markets in the United States, compared with 1,700 in 1994, making them the fastest-growing part of our food economy.[22] To put that in perspective, there are more than a thousand more farmers' markets in the United States than there are Wal-Marts – one out of every three of them started since 2000. There are now 550 farmers' markets in the UK, compared to one in Bath in 1997. Significantly, 9 out of 10 people in the UK would shop at a farmers' market if they had the choice. There is a newfound interest in being self-reliant and eating reasonably priced fresh produce that is not being carted all around the country and back again. Something deeper and more poignant is happening here. We are seeking to restore the missing link between producer and consumer. The experience of going into a supermarket to walk through aisle upon aisle stacked high with boxed, bagged or canned food is, for many consumers, starting to feel empty and even wrong. Sociologists studying shopping behaviour report that shoppers have ten times more conversations at farmers' markets than at supermarkets.[23] As it turns out, many of us would rather stroll around a farmers' market and chat with the people who have grown our food and find out what's tasty and in season.

The recent resurgence in the desire to 'eat local' was symbolically celebrated when a 1,100-square-foot patch of the manicured South Lawn of the Obama White House was dug up and turned into a vegetable garden for the first time since World War II. It would seem that the Obamas have inspired thousands to follow suit. In 2009, seed sales were up by 19 per cent and the number of homes growing their own vegetables increased by a staggering 40 per cent.[24,25]

Etsy and the local food movement are part of a mass re-evaluation of what and how we consume. They are also a part of a deep shift around three core values that lay the groundwork for a new consumer mind-set. The first is simplicity; consumers are yearning to go back to a time when markets meant community-based, traditional relationships with strong ties. When you purchase an item from Etsy or pick up a piece of homemade cheese from a farm stand, there is a history or story behind it. There's a person behind it. The second is traceability and transparency – the notion that 'local is good again' and that consumers want to know whom they are buying from and learn more about the product than just its immediate purpose. As Michael Pollan wrote in The Omnivore's Dilemma, 'Instead of looking at labels, the local food customer will look at the farm for himself, or look the farmer in the eye and ask him about how he grows his crops or treats his animals.'[26] And the last is participation; people are increasingly seeking to be active participants more in control of their world – rather than passive 'victims' of hyper-consumption.

Today there is an unprecedented degree of interconnectivity as well as an infrastructure for participation. Our immersion in innovative information, communication and technology (ICT) platforms, specifically online social networks and handheld mobile devices, is the second phenomenon driving us towards a 'we' mind-set.

The 'We' Generation

Chris Hughes co-created one of the defining businesses of the past decade, Facebook. Unlike his partners and Harvard roommates, Mark

Zuckerberg and Dustin Moskovitz, Hughes was not interested in the
software itself. Instead, he wanted to work out the ways that people
would want to connect and share stuff with one another and how an
online community could enrich the lives of its users – a passion that
led to his nickname 'the Empath' among Facebook insiders. Hughes
left Facebook in February 2007 just when it was taking off, with
more than 10 million active users. His new calling was not another
business start-up but to head the online organizing campaign for
Barack Obama, who at the time was the underdog junior senator
from Illinois. It was Obama's belief in the collective power of citizens
that drew Hughes away from Facebook. He admits, 'I wouldn't have
left Facebook for any other person or at any other time.'[27]

The Obama campaign recruited Hughes because he knew perhaps better than anyone else how to use the Internet to coordinate
and inspire supporters. Within a couple of months, Hughes led the
launch of My.BarackObama.com (which became known as MyBO)
and the Vote for Change sites. Hughes created a multitude of tools,
such as the 'MyBO Activity Tracker'. It gave people control of their
campaign experience, but, also important, it turned the process of
political canvassing into an interactive game, one with a serious
prize – the presidential election. In this game, the users got 15
points for every event hosted, 15 points for every donation made to
their personal fund-raising page, 3 points for every event attended
and 3 points for a blog post. The site's scoring system was weighted
to give more points for offline activity than online activity. A single
score was aggregated and posted on the user's profile, and then
scores were ranked to reward only the recent activities so that users
would be encouraged to keep up participation. As Hughes puts it,
'The more work you've done recently, the higher the number will
be.'[28] A system of work and reward creates a market-like mechanism
and appeals to our self-interest. MyBO hit the sweet spot of collaboration and healthy competition. By the time of the presidential elec-

tion in November 2008, $30 million had been generated on more than 70,000 personal fund-raising pages and at more than 200,000 grassroots community events. And more young people between the ages of eighteen and thirty-five participated and voted in an election than ever before. Hughes's role was so critical that *Fast Company* dubbed him 'The Kid Who Made Obama President'[29] – a designation he achieved before he even celebrated his twenty-fifth birthday.

In the same year that Hughes was driving My.BarackObama, Rainer Nõlvak, an Internet entrepreneur; twenty-six-year-old Tiina Urm; and Ahti Heinla, one of the founders of Skype, masterminded a national grassroots cleanup day in Estonia called Let's Do It. Ahead of the day, they got 720 volunteers to scour the country and photograph sites using mobile phones to pinpoint more than 10,500 locations where rubbish had been illegally dumped. These sites were plotted using custom-made rubbish-mapping software to create what they called the 'the ugliest map ever'. Then, on 3 May 2008, they rallied 50,000 Estonians (many of them Millennials) – 4 per cent of the population – to arrive at the sites with spades and bags to clean up the mess. An operation that otherwise would have taken the Estonian government three years and cost an estimated 22.5 million euros took just five hours (give or take a few months of planning) and cost only half a million euros.[30] Let's Do It is just one example of thousands that show the power of the 'we mind-set' combined with technology to produce collective action. The participants as well as the entrepreneurs are often Millennials, just like Chris Hughes, who admits that he can work only on projects that will have 'far-reaching social and life-changing impact but that are also fun, modern, and smart'. 'Smart' is a word Hughes uses a lot. When we had the chance to ask Hughes if he thinks his generation is more responsible, he answered in his calm yet astute way, 'It's not that we're more responsible, it's that we make smarter choices. We know, and I mean really know, that money doesn't equal happiness.

We know what's important and not important. We still buy a lot, but we don't buy needlessly.'

In March 2010, Hughes launched his third social venture, called 'Jumo' – a word in the African language that Yoruba translates as 'together in concert'. It's a site designed to connect individuals and organizations working to change the world. For Hughes and other Millennial entrepreneurs, the idea behind Jumo is philanthropy, social networking and volunteerism all rolled into one.

The Millennials are not a generation of Mother Teresas. They are not all do-gooders shunning well-paid jobs and luxuries for a utopian dream. Statistics show that they are as competitive, commercial and ambitious as any other generation in history. But they are abandoning the prevailing ethos of their parents' generation of baby boomers and adhering more to the values of their grandparents, the war generation. In a 2006 *USA Today* poll, 61 per cent of thirteen- to twenty-five-year-olds felt personally responsible for making a difference in the world; 81 per cent have volunteered in the past year; 69 per cent consider a company's social and environmental commitment when deciding where to shop; and 83 per cent trusted a company more if it was socially/environmentally responsible.[31] While the Millennials grew up with an abundance of wealth and opportunity unimaginable to their grandparents, it was an abundance that came with a real cost. As Bill McKibben writes in his book *Deep Economy*, 'For most of human history, the two birds More and Better roosted on the same branch. You could toss one stone and hope to hit them both. Now you've got the stone of your own life, or your own society, gripped in your hand, you have to choose between. It's More or Better.'[32]

In the 1990s a movement arose that warned us we were turning our backs on the bedrock of 'traditional' societal values. Pastor Jerry Falwell railed against video games, the Internet and 'godless' films, and former vice president Dan Quayle's and the media's rant against

Murphy Brown turned into a political circus. But today it is this generation of 'valueless' children that is changing the world with sophisticated inventions such as Meraki (a low-cost Internet service for poor
communities), new funding models such as Kickstarter, Profounder
and Prosume (a 'crowdfunding' model for creative projects), powerful online networks such as Meetup (an online platform that
makes it easy for people with shared interests to organize local face-
to-face groups), and community tools such as WordPress (an open-
source blogging software). All these ventures were founded by
entrepreneurs under thirty. Regardless of what term you use to describe them (Generation Y, Generation We, or Millennials), one
consistent trait connects them: they are coming of age in an increasingly collaborative world. Sharing and collaboration have become as
second nature as the bi-directional telephone call, as people meet up
in chat rooms and social forums; upload music, books and videos;
and share thoughts and daily actions with the rest of the world.

Value shifts have happened before, such as the activist movements of the sixties and seventies. For new habits, ideas and visions
to stick, they need a network and platform that transform principles
into behaviours on a global scale. The shifts we have been discussing
in this chapter are occurring at a time when an extraordinary con-
fluence of technological and cultural development makes the realization of these values not just possible but long lasting. Sharing has
always depended on a network – but now we have one that is redefining its scope, meaning and possibility. That network is, of course,
the Internet.

'Sharing Nicely'

On 26 June 2008, The New York Times declared that Osama bin Laden
faced his first significant threat. Was this threat from the CIA? Or the
National Security Agency? Or the unmanned drones flying across

Afghanistan? No. In an article titled 'Fight Terror with YouTube', journalist Daniel Kimmage wrote that Osama bin Laden's first credible challenges came from popular online network applications such as YouTube, Facebook, Twitter and MySpace that make his political media power, based on both anonymity and accessibility, vulnerable to disruption. 'The Qaeda media nexus, as advanced as it is, is old hat. If Web 1.0 was about creating the snazziest official Web resources and Web 2.0 is about letting users run wild with self-created content and interactivity, Al Qaeda and its affiliates are stuck in 1.0.' Social networks and 'self-created content' provide people with a platform to be heard and can unite 'a fragmented silent majority and help it to find its voice in the face of thuggish opponents . . . the ensuing chaos will not be to everyone's liking, but it may shake the online edifice of Al Qaeda's totalitarian ideology.'[33]

The disruptive power of Web 2.0 that Kimmage highlighted in his article extends way beyond Al Qaeda's radical demagoguery. He refers instead to the new rules of social networks that break down the barriers of elitism and hierarchy and promote a world of openness, participation and empowerment. In their book *Wikinomics*, Don Tapscott and Anthony D. Williams describe these rules as 'weapons of mass collaboration' and argue that they may give birth to a golden era equal to the Italian Renaissance or Athenian democracy.[34] Social networking is probably the most inclusive and culturally disruptive development of our time. Even those on the isolated peripheries of our society, such as someone in Siberia or on the equator, or someone with a unique hobby such as collecting miniature Polish pipe organs, can find a group to share and connect with based on common interests.

Every investigative journalist knows that the key to breaking a news story is that money always leads to the top. Whether it's Al Capone or Bernard Madoff, taxes or Ponzi schemes, money is linked to power and control. If we apply these principles to Web 2.0, we find a surprising new relationship between money and power. The Internet is inherently democratic and decentralized. One of the first celebrated examples of this autonomous force was in 1991 when a twenty-one-year-old Finnish student posted a simple request on Usenet (a global discussion forum) for help from his mother's Helsinki apartment. 'I'm doing a (free) operating system (just a hobby, won't be big and professional like gnu) for 386(486) AT clones. This has been brewing since April, and is starting to get ready. I'd like any feedback on things people like/dislike . . .'[35] This hobby of Linus Torvalds's would turn into Linux, the most prominent example of open-source software and the self-organizing power of the Internet.

The roots of Linux can be traced back to Richard Stallman's GNU Project at MIT to develop a comprehensive code that would be free and available around the world, but in 1981 a fundamental technological advancement was missing that made the difference between Stallman's rebellious idea and Torvalds's revolution: networked collaboration. When Torvalds announced his idea, he received thousands of responses from all over the world, even though the population of the Internet was then less than 10 per cent of its present size.[36] Today, Linux is used by more than 18 million people around the globe[37] and there continue to be more than 128,500 geographically dispersed volunteer programmers building and improving the software.[38] These people are working together with a unified goal: to create the world's best operating system.

Linux was by no means a fluke. The Web has amassed millions of volunteers to create coordinated projects that produce cooperative value. Take Clickworkers.com, a NASA experiment set up to map the surface of Mars. When you click on the site, the first question it asks is, 'What task would you like to help with?' The pull-down menu gives the following options: 'Mark Mars Craters', 'Classify Mars Craters', 'Catalog Mars Landforms', and 'Mark Asteroid Craters'. Given that the professional field of study for astronomy requires a bachelor's degree in physics, mathematics or engineering followed by several years of master's, doctorate and fellowship work, one would expect that Clickworkers would offer these choices to a closed group of handpicked elite scientists. Instead, the site is made up entirely of amateur volunteers. By the end of the study in 2001, there were more than 85,000 users and 1.9 million entries recorded.[39] Perhaps even more astounding was the accuracy of the work. According to NASA, the quality of Clickworkers entries was virtually indistinguishable from that of a professional geologist with years of experience identifying Mars craters.[40]

On 17 November 2009, NASA launched a similar experiment called Be a Martian to encourage volunteers to help map the planet Mars. The number of images and amount of data on the Red Planet returned by spacecraft since the 1960s are now so large that scientists cannot hope to study all the material by themselves. NASA has turned the project into a game where you earn points for 'being a mapmaker' or 'counting impact craters'. As these projects are voluntary, they attract only participants passionate about the subject and motivated to engage with a group of people to help solve real challenges. The same principle applies to SETI@home, which stands for 'Search for Extraterrestrial Intelligence', set up in 1999 by Space Sciences Laboratory at the University of California, Berkeley. In the essay 'Sharing Nicely', Yale Law School Professor Yochai Benkler pointed to the world's largest distributed computer network to highlight the trend towards sharing and to prove the potential of a distributed network. The goal of SETI was to apply collective power to look for intelligent life outside Earth. To date 5.2 million global volunteers have downloaded a small screensaver that identifies when their home computer is idle. At that time the computer is networked, and groups collaboratively download problems to calculate. When the problem is solved, the computer sends the results back to the main terminal. As a result, according to Guinness World Records,

SETI@home has calculated some of the largest computations in history.

Power in Numbers

The power of mass collaboration is by no means restricted to the open software movement. But the start of projects such as Linux in the late nineties and early 'noughties' was a pivotal milestone in the timeline of co-creation. Programmers were foot soldiers in pioneering new attitudes and innovative behaviours around sharing. The likes of Linus Torvalds showed how the Internet created a boundless automated open infrastructure for sharing, but also an ethos of wanting to be a part of something bigger than our individual consumer selves. Open, collaborative projects appealed to a participant's need for individuality and autonomy and at the same time provided a sense of belonging to a community.

The collective power of physically dispersed yet virtually connected individuals only became stronger and more apparent through the 2000s. Crowdsourcing, a concept coined by Jeff Howe as the 'act of taking a job traditionally performed by a designated agent (usually an employee) and outsourcing it to an undefined, generally large group of people in the form of an open call', became an important business idea. It is now a well-documented phenomenon applied to the creation of collective repositories of content (Wikipedia), products (the T-shirt company Threadless, where all the designs are created by the user community), new business ideas (Procter & Gamble's Connect & Develop), and even problems such as climate change (MIT's Climate Collaboratorium). What the success of crowdsourcing has shown is that as people move from hyper-individualistic consumer behaviours, a 'me mind-set', to a 'we mind-set', an empowering dynamic emerges. Specifically, online networks bring people together again, making them more willing to leverage the old rule of thumb: there is power in numbers. And impacts of online sharing and collaboration are not confined to the virtual world. They are spilling off-line, creating change within our cultural, economic, political and consumer worlds.

Using the Internet to Get Off the Internet

Cindy Gallop is a magnetic character. Half English and half Chinese, she represents a unique and fruitful collision between two worlds. A talk with Cindy may include an in-depth conversation about altruism, advertising, martinis or running. For more than twenty years, Gallop had an illustrious career in branding and advertising. In 2003, Advertising Women of New York voted Gallop Woman of the Year. The following year, at the pinnacle of her success, she voluntarily resigned as chairman of the ad agency BBH. She wasn't having any midlife career crisis, but she wanted to do something different – to help change the world, her way.

Gallop just turned fifty when we were writing this book. She is a living example of how the values of the Millennial generation are in no way confined to a certain age group – older and younger people share the same open, interactive and collaborative traits and habits often ascribed to Millennials. She is fascinated by how much passion and energy is invested in the virtual worlds – Mafia Wars, Facebook, Second Life and so on. Indeed, the last time Rachel spoke with Gallop, the conversation turned to FarmVille, a 'social game' application on Facebook that had more than 90 million active users and 62 million daily users in October 2010.[41] They both were curious about why millions of people, more than 1.2 per cent of the world's population, wanted to manage a virtual farm and devote on average twenty to twenty-five minutes a day to laborious tasks such as managing a pumpkin patch or ploughing the land. This adds up to a staggering 78 years every month collectively spent growing virtual crops that nobody can eat. Gallop is not judgmental of the explosive online gaming phenomenon; instead she is determined to figure out how to take the passion and effort people invest online and harness it, in her words, to 'get shit done to make the world a better place'.

Gallop agrees with Scott Heiferman, one of the three founders of Meetup, that a blurry line is emerging between online and off-line communities. There are over 277,000 Meetup members based in the UK involved in over 3,000 dedicated Meetup groups. More than 2.5 million people around the world respond to some kind of Meetup invitation every month and more than 2,000 local groups, from stay-at-home mums to small business owners to walking clubs, get together face-to-face each day.[42] 'We are using the Internet to get off the Internet and form a twenty-first-century civil society,' Heiferman commented.[43]

In 2006, a couple of years after leaving BBH, Gallop found herself thinking, 'How could I take all the good intentions most of us have on a daily basis, our single biggest pool of untapped natural resource, and transform them into shared actions?' Like Chris Hughes on Obama's campaign, Gallop also knew she had to make her initiative fun and avoid the 'yawn factor' by adding a healthy dose of what she refers to as 'competitive collaboration'. She launched IfWeRanTheWorld.com early in 2010. It's essentially a crowdsourcing project based on the similar principles of microfunding sites such as Kiva or Kickstarter. People are motivated to do big things by taking easy steps or microactions that in Gallop's words 'can bring about great leaps'. When you arrive at the site, you are asked to complete the statement, 'If I ran the world, I would____.' Gallop illustrates how it works with a simple example. 'The blank would be filled with something like "plant a garden to feed the local homeless".' On the IfWeRanTheWorld platform, the user and the community all help break down the goal into microactions that friends, family, neighbours, businesses, celebrities or total strangers can all help complete. As Gallop explained in a recent interview with *Wired*, 'One person might secure the site, another might convince a local nursery to donate seeds, someone else might know a graphic designer with the time and inclination to create promotional leaflets, another participant could print those, while volunteers plant, harvest, and distribute crops – and so on.'[44] Her vision is for IfWeRanTheWorld to become the 'Google of Action'.

From her years spent in advertising, Gallop was well aware that people are looking for new outlets to express their individualism, but that they also possess an equally strong sense of the extraordinary power of doing things together to improve society.[45] The problem Gallop is determined to crack is the large gap created by good individual intentions that never translate into collection action. 'I am all about making things happen, and quite frankly, I have a low tolerance for people who whine and moan about stuff and never do anything to change it.' But even Gallop admits, 'I can be just as guilty as anybody else. After reading *The New York Times*, I'll go, "Oh my God. That's terrible. I must do something about that. I'll turn the page, and the moment's gone".'[46]

IfWeRanTheWorld is in its early days, but Gallop has already received an outpouring of support from all around the world. Like Meetup, Linux, MyBO, Clickworkers and Kickstarter, IfWeRanTheWorld is part of a re-establishment of community relationships not just through local activities but through the vast global infrastructure of the Internet. In this sense, the very concepts of 'neighbour' and 'community' are being redefined and expanded as the 'Me' generation is being replaced by the 'We' generation.'

Reconnection Beyond Consumerism

On 29 June 2009, Bernard Madoff stood in front of Judge Denny Chin of the US District Court in New York, pleaded guilty to an eleven-count criminal complaint, and was sentenced to 150 years in prison, the maximum sentence allowed. Madoff's notorious crime was the creation of a $65 billion Ponzi scheme, the largest investor fraud ever committed by a single person. But while Madoff's actions were abhorrent and the punishment was fitting, we have all in some way been a part of and fallen victim to a far greater Ponzi scheme.

The last two hundred years of industrialized growth have been a Ponzi scheme. We have depleted our natural resources, spewed poisonous gases into our atmosphere and created wasteful products that will far outlive our own existence. In essence we have taken without the intent of giving or ever repaying. The results can no longer be swept under the proverbial carpets of 'liberal conspiracy' or 'consumer denial'. Whether we consider the Great Pacific Garbage Patch or the economic collapse in 2008, we have run out of ways to shelter ourselves from our own destructive habits. As Joe Romm, a physicist and climate expert, puts it, 'We created a way of raising standards of living that we can't possibly pass on to our children. You can get this burst of wealth that we have created from this rapacious behaviour. But it has to collapse. . . . Real wealth is something you can pass on in a way that others can enjoy.' [47]

Our concurrent economic and environmental crises can be seen as two separate problems, or as overwhelming collateral damage, or as an opportunity. As Picasso said, 'Every act of creation is first an act of destruction.' We have witnessed the power of economic markets to create efficiencies that have produced extraordinary leaps of innovation and standards of living. At the heart of this lies the human impulse for self-interest and survival. If we can channel this energy away from consumer excess into community bonds and planetary survival, we may reverse the errors of our past. We are seeing compelling examples of individuals and communities rediscovering a sense of meaning and reconnection beyond consumerism. The old consumer doctrine that has been carefully scripted and controlled by corporate evangelicals such as Edward Bernays is within a generation being fundamentally disrupted. The next chapters will introduce a new promising economic and social mechanism that starts to balance individual needs with those of our communities and planet – what we call Collaborative Consumption.

2

GROUNDSWELL

FOUR	The Rise of Collaborative Consumption

Why is it that we spend so much time teaching children how to share their toys nicely but for adults sharing becomes a loaded concept? We share our roads, parks, schools and other public spaces, but we draw the line in other areas of our life, such as our personal belongings. As a society, we are wary of the old C's associated with sharing: cooperatives, collectives and communal structures. The words themselves are loaded with stigmas and unfortunate associations. Perhaps we fear they will jeopardize our cherished personal freedoms of individuality, privacy and autonomy.

But we only need to look to one of the smartest creatures on the planet, the bottlenose dolphin, to see that we can have it both ways. Like other mammals, dolphins have innate cooperative and coordinated behaviours they use when hunting fish and looking after each other. Dolphins live in close-knit family pods of about six to ten dolphins. But in the open waters of the Pacific and Atlantic oceans, several pods may join temporarily (for several minutes or hours) to form larger groups of more than one hundred or even occasionally more than one thousand dolphins for the purpose of easy 'cooperative feeding'. They will encircle a large shoal of fish from all sides, much like cowboys herding cattle, using their bodies as a wall, with large males often roaming the periphery of a pod to protect it against predators. This group herding slows down the fish and forces them into a tight ball. The dolphins then take turns diving under or into the ball to catch fish easily. Dolphins have other techniques, as when the older dolphins dive below a shoal, sending the school swimming upward to the rest of the pod who are waiting to feed. But the cooperative principle is always the same: the more dolphins in the herd, the easier it is to catch more fish, and the greater individual and collective benefit.

If we're looking for a role model for group cooperation, we could do worse than to imitate bottlenose dolphins. They take advantage of strong, closed networks (their family) and open networks of weak ties (other dolphin pods).[1] In the aggregation, the pod completes tasks and solves problems in ways that would be unimaginable for a single dolphin. And if you have ever seen dolphins riding on ocean swells or jumping high in the stern wakes of boats, you know that their group behaviour does not undermine their autonomy. They fulfil our two basic needs: individual freedom and collective security.

For centuries we behaved like dolphins, coming together to get what we needed and sharing access to food, land and other resources. Going back millions of years to our Palaeolithic ancestors in the Stone Age, humans grouped into tribes or bands of approximately twenty-five to one hundred people who survived by gathering plants and hunting wild animals in packs. As with dolphins, the chances of getting food were greater if the tribe hunted and foraged cooperatively. Following a kill, the meat was cut into pieces and shared with everyone in the camp. Cooperative efforts continued throughout recorded history. Babylonian farmers relied on each other to share equipment, build barns, harvest crops and even defend the land. Anthropologists believe that this mutualism (people helping each other) and reciprocity ('I'll give you meat today, you give me meat in the future') are hardwired human behaviours that serve as the basis for human cooperation and are the core of our existence.

Michael Tomasello, an American development psychologist, has researched cooperation in young children. When infants as young as fourteen months see an adult (even one they have just met) who needs a door opened because his or her hands are full, they will immediately try to help. From around the time of their first birthday, infants will point at objects that an adult pretends to have lost. And if you drop something in front of a two-year-old, he or she is likely to pick it up for you.[2] In his recent book *Why We Cooperate*, Tomasello argues that empathy and cooperative behaviours are not learned from adults or done out of expectation of a reward. Children are sociable and cooperative by nature. But by the age of three, children start to adhere to 'social norms' shaped by culture. At this stage, concerns of how others in a group will judge them can encourage or discourage collaboration. The likelihood of reciprocation informs their choices of whom they share with and they will share more generously with a child who has already been nice to them. Tomasello also believes that human beings have a selfish streak and that 'cooperativeness and helpfulness are, as it were, laid onto this self-interested foundation'.[3]

For the past fifty years, children have grown up in a hyper-individualistic society, so it is not surprising that their inherently selfish side has overshadowed their equally natural social inclination to share. But today this tendency may be changing. Over the past couple of years a quiet yet powerful revolution of collaboration has risen up and is gaining momentum throughout our cultural, political and economic system. We are relearning how to create value out of shared and open resources in ways that balance personal self-

interest with the good of the larger community. People can participate without losing their autonomy or individual identity. As Neal
Gorenflo, founder of the online community Shareable, puts it, 'Communities can help people become more than they are as individuals.
In other words, we benefit from a "collaborative individualism".'

An increasing number of Millennials have grown up with Collaborative Consumption. But these habits are not confined to one
generation. While you need to be a bit Web savvy to participate in
many forms of Collaborative Consumption, you do not need to be a
technology geek or computer sophisticate, nor do you need to live in
a major city. Indeed, from the masses of baby boomers addicted to
eBay (21 per cent of all users are over fifty years old)[4] to the Gen
Xers increasingly using bartering services, people are participating
in different types of Collaborative Consumption from a diverse array
of subcultures and socioeconomic and demographic groups.

There are also two distinct ways to participate in Collaborative
Consumption, each with a different appeal to different people. You
can play the role of 'peer provider' by providing assets to rent, share
or borrow. Or you can play the role of 'peer user' consuming the
available products and services. Some participants may choose to do
both, but others may feel comfortable on one end of the spectrum.
The participant who wants to make money renting his or her car
through WhipCar or other unused items through sites such as Ecomodo is likely to have different motivations from the 'user' who
rents these items. Similarly, the person looking for a high rate of return through a loan on social lending sites such as Zopa is there for
different reasons than the peer borrower who needs the money.

Some collaborative consumers are forward thinking and socially
minded optimists, but others are individuals motivated by a practical urgency to find a new and better way of doing things. That practical urgency may be to save money or time, access a better service,
be more sustainable, or allow closer relationships with people rather

than brands. For the most part, the people participating in Collaborative Consumption are not Pollyannaish do-gooders and still very much believe in the principles of capitalist markets and self-interest. In his book *From Counterculture to Cyberculture* Fred Turner envisioned that these citizens desire a world in which 'Each individual could act in his or her own self-interest and at the same time produce a unified social sphere, in which we're "all one".'[5]

Collaborative Consumption Systems

Swap trading, time banks, local exchange trading systems (LETS), bartering, social lending, peer-to-peer currencies, tool exchanges, land share, clothing swaps, toy sharing, shared workspaces, co-housing, co-working, CouchSurfing, car sharing, crowdfunding, bike sharing, ride sharing, food co-ops, walking school buses, shared microcrèches, peer-to-peer rental – the list goes on – are all examples of Collaborative Consumption. Some of these may be familiar already, some not, but all are experiencing a significant growth surge. Although these examples vary in scale, maturity and purpose, they can be organized into three systems – product service systems, redistribution markets and collaborative lifestyles – which are the subject of the next three chapters.

Product Service Systems (PSS)

An increasing number of people from different backgrounds and across all ages are shifting to a 'usage mind-set' whereby they pay for the benefit of a product – what it does for them – without needing to own the product outright. This is the basis of product service systems (PSS), which are disrupting traditional industries based on models of individual private ownership. In a PSS, a service enables multiple products owned by a company to be shared (car sharing, solar power, launderettes), or products that are privately owned to be shared or rented peer-to-peer (Zilok, TheHireHub, Erento). PSSs can also extend the life of a product (repair services offered by Steelcase, or Interface Carpets, for example). The obvious environmental advantage of this system is that an individually owned product with often limited usage is replaced with a shared service that maximizes its utility. For users the key benefits are twofold. First, they don't have to pay for the product outright. It removes the burdens of ownership such as maintenance, repair and insurance, and enables us to make the most of the assets we do own. And second, when our relationship with things moves from ownership to use, options to satisfy our needs, whether for travel, leisure, work, food or children, change and increase.

Redistribution Markets

Social networks enable used or pre-owned goods to be redistributed from where they are not needed to somewhere or someone where they are, fuelling the second type of collaboration consumption, redistribution markets. In some instances, the marketplace is based on entirely free exchanges (Freecycle, Kashless, Around Again); in others the goods are sold for points (Barterquest, UISwap) or for cash (eBay, Flippid), or the markets are a mixture (Gumtree and craigs-list). Goods such as makeup, accessories, clothes, books, toys, games, baby clothes and DVDs can be swapped for similiar goods (thred-Up, BigWardrobe, SwapStyle), or goods of a similar value (Swap, SwapSimple, SwapCycle, ReadItSwapIt). Often exchanges are conducted between anonymous strangers, but sometimes the marketplaces connect people who know each other (Share Some Sugar, NeighborGoods). Regardless of the specifics of the exchange, a redistribution market encourages reusing and reselling old items rather than throwing them out, and also significantly reduces waste and resources that go along with new production. Redistribution is the fifth 'R' – reduce, recycle, reuse, repair and redistribute – and is increasingly considered a sustainable form of commerce. It challenges the traditional relationship between producer, retailer and consumer, and disrupts the doctrines of 'buy more' and 'buy new'.

Collaborative Lifestyles

It is not just physical goods such as cars, bikes and used goods that can be shared, swapped and bartered. People with similar interests are banding together to share and exchange less tangible assets such as time, space, skills and money, in what we call collaborative lifestyles. These exchanges are happening on a local level and include shared systems for working spaces (The Cube London, The Trampery, Lemon Studios, Hub Culture), goods (Ecomodo, ThingLoop), tasks, time and errands (Camden Shares, Southwark Circle, SPICE Timebank Wales), gardens (Landshare, Edinburgh Garden Share), skills (Brooklyn Skillshare), food (Neighborhood Fruit, Lourish) and parking spaces (ParkatMyHouse, Park-UK). But collaborative lifestyles are also happening worldwide as the Internet enables people to coordinate, scale and transcend physical boundaries in activities such as peer-to-peer social lending (Zopa, YES-Secure, Quakle) and travel (CouchSurfing, Airbnb, Roomorama, CrashPadder). A high degree of trust is often required with collaborative lifestyles because human-to-human interaction, not a physical product, is often the focus of the exchange. As a result, they generate a myriad of relationships and social connectivity.

Across product service systems, redistribution markets and collaborative lifestyles, motivation can range from saving money to making money, from convenience to meeting friends, from saving space to saving time, from feeling a part of a community to 'doing the right thing'. Sustainability is often an unintended consequence of Collaborative Consumption. It is unintended in the sense that the initial or driving motivation for a company or the consumer may not be about 'being green'. As eBay announced on Earth Day in 2008, 'We never set out to be a green business, we realized it's intrinsic.' These positive unintended or unexpected consequences happen because sustainability and community are an inherent, inseparable part of Collaborative Consumption and not an afterthought or add-on.

Real and meaningful progress in sustainability can be achieved only when both the consumer and the company are motivated to change their behaviour. Collaborative Consumption has the benefit of being in the user's self-interest, without emphasizing guilt or personal sacrifice. In addition, habit changes have to be easy and desirable for the average person, while creating value for business and society. And when a new behaviour yields strong rewards, it is more likely to stick.

The power of Collaborative Consumption to change behaviour and for that behaviour to stick is illustrated by the 'Low-Car Diet Challenge' experiment, a marketing campaign conducted by Zipcar, the world's largest car-sharing service. Zipcar members can reserve a car twenty-four hours a day, seven days a week on the Internet, by using an iPhone app, or by phone for periods as short as one hour in any of the forty-nine US cities it operates in, as well as Vancouver, Toronto and London. On 15 July 2009, 250 participants from thirteen cities around the world – many of them self-confessed 'car addicts' and so-called car-sharing 'rookies' – committed their keys and their consciences to not using their own vehicle for a month. Instead, they utilized public transportation, walked and biked, and resorted to a car (they were given a Zipcar membership) only when necessary.[6] The survey conducted after the challenge showed that living without a car had a positive impact on participants' wallets, bodies and communities. They increased their usage of public transportation by 98 per cent, reduced their vehicle miles travelled by 66 per cent, and on average saved 67 per cent on vehicle-related costs. The miles they walked increased by 93 per cent, and the miles they biked by more than 132 per cent. All the extra exercise resulted in weight loss for 47 per cent of participants; a total of 413 pounds was shed during the month, on average a pound or two per person. But the most relevant result of the experiment is that 61 per cent indicated that they planned to continue to live without an exclusively owned car, and another 31 per cent were considering that same commitment.[7] In just one month, alternative travel became a habit. One hundred people out of the 250 were resolute that they did not want their keys back. The car addicts had lost the urge to own. And as we shall show, once people dip a toe into one part of Collaborative Consumption, such as clothing swapping or car sharing, other behaviours gradually start to change, too.

Four Principles of Collaborative Consumption

When you look across an array of examples of Collaborative Consumption, you see that at the core they share four critical underlying principles – critical mass; idling capacity; belief in the commons; and trust between strangers. One principle is no more important than any other. In fact, in some instances, one is at the heart of making the system work and in others it is less important.

The first principle, critical mass, is a sociological term used to describe the existence of enough momentum in a system to make it become self-sustaining.[8] This concept is applied to an array of fields to explain everything from nuclear chain reactions to books becoming bestsellers to the widespread adoption of new technologies such as MP3 players. Malcolm Gladwell famously named the point of reaching popular critical mass the 'tipping point'.

Critical mass is vital to Collaborative Consumption for a couple of reasons. The first relates to choice. Specifically, when we shop, we seek satisfaction and convenience. Consumers associate shopping with going from shop to shop, aisle to aisle, rack to rack, to choose what they want. For Collaborative Consumption to compete with conventional shopping, there must be enough choice that the consumer feels satisfied with what is available. At clothing swaps, for instance, if a few people show up who wear different sizes and have different tastes, it's unlikely that participants will find items that they want and likely that they will walk away dissatisfied. Rachel went to a clothing swap hosted by My Sister's Wardrobe (part of the Clothing Exchange) held in a large and light-filled indoor amphitheatre in Melbourne. Kate Pears, who describes herself as a 'fashionista and a moderate greenie', started the exchange after studying consumption patterns and fashion waste as part of her master's degree. Rachel brought an unwanted black cocktail dress that she had worn half a dozen times and a pair of Cole Haan flats that were in great condition but which had never quite fitted. At the door her items were screened by the hosts for quality (the golden rule is don't bring things you would not want to receive), and she was given a button for each item to trade. Rachel entered the amphitheatre (doors open at the same time to ensure fair swapping) along with 150-plus stylishly dressed women of all ages and began perusing racks of clothing. Some items even had their original sales tags still on. Rachel used her two buttons to 'purchase' a green silk scarf and a black short-sleeved shirt that looked like it had never been worn. She was surprised not just by the quality of items she exchanged, but by the pleasure she got from seeing her unwanted dress and shoes leave with delighted new owners.

The Clothing Exchange is just one of thousands of clothing swaps happening around the world. When you Google 'clothing swaps', there are 12.7 million page views. Entries range from the

Swishing in London to the Pink Cow Clothing Swap in Tokyo to the Fashion Reloaded Clothing Swap in Berlin. This phenomenon has gone from private parties among a small group of girlfriends to high-fashion, big warehouse ticketed events with DJs, open bars and food vendors that can attract crowds of five-hundred-plus of all ages, sizes and fashion tastes. Some events don't even describe the trading as swapping but have invented a more aspirational name, 'swishing'. As the number of people (and items they bring) increases at these events, the likelihood of people walking away dissatisfied decreases. At some point the swap will reach 'critical mass': enough goods for all to find something they like and to feel that they have chosen well. The Clothing Exchange is able to reach this point more quickly by hosting specific swaps for different clusters of clothing sizes or tastes – for example, teenagers, pregnant mums, and people over sixty-five – and an Excess Baggage Exchange just for shoes, accessories and handbags.

A similar dynamic is at work with the bike-sharing schemes growing in popularity around the world, such as SmartBike in Washington, D.C., B-cycle in Denver and Barclays Cycle Hire in London. One of the most recent bike-sharing schemes, launched in May 2009, is Montreal's BIXI (coined from 'bike', plus 'taxi'). On taking office, Mayor Tremblay set clear goals to reduce the city's traffic and carbon emissions and to make the city more pleasant to live in. He decided he could not just build more cycling paths (Montreal in fact already has a network of more than twenty miles of bike paths); he had to make enough bikes available (and make them cheap enough) so that cycling would become the convenient and appealing choice for people to get around the city. To do so there had to be sufficient bike docking stations available 24/7 within a short distance from any rider's departure point and destination. If you go somewhere by bike and have to walk far to put your bike back in a station, the system breaks down. Indeed, cities that have started with too small a network of bikes, such as Rennes in France, have not been particularly successful.

BIXI launched with three thousand bikes with docking stations never more than one thousand feet apart. There are three hundred self-service docking stations across the city, many outside subway stops to ensure that people can hop off the train and complete the 'last mile' by bike. (Similarly in the UK, 5,000 bicycles were available at 350 bicycle docking stations across central London at the time of launch in 2010.) The docking stations are modular and removable. They can be broken down or set up in less than an hour. The stations are operated by solar power for logistical and environmental reasons. Because they do not need electrical sockets, they can be dropped anywhere. When snow covers the city, the bikes and docks can be packed up and moved. Real-time information about bike availability and station location is accessible from smart phones and on the Internet. BIXI also seems to be avoiding some of the theft and vandalism that have plagued other networks. The bikes are designed with sealed components to resist abuse and each bike contains a Radio Frequency Identification (RFID) chip. If rented and not returned, the bike will slow down and the brakes will lock automatically.

The design and planning team estimated that three thousand bikes were the 'critical mass' necessary to persuade enough people to switch from cars (and taxis) to bikes at first, enabling the city government to provide more bikes to get more people to switch. Within four months after the launch, BIXI had attracted more than seventy-seven thousand resident users, and more than 2.2 million miles had been travelled on the bikes, more than eighty-seven times the circumference of the earth. On 29 October 2009, the millionth ride was taken.[9] The city can now add two thousand more bikes over one hundred stations, a year earlier than was expected.

No universal magic formula can determine the right point of critical mass for different types of Collaborative Consumption. It varies depending on the context, the needs being met and user expectations. TechShop in Menlo Park, California, founded in the summer of 2006 by Jim Newton, sells itself as a fifteen-thousand-square-foot 'world-class workshop' where inventors, hobbyists, artists, automotive fanatics, mechanical engineers and model makers can access equipment, supplies and expert support to work on projects. Newton came up with the idea for TechShop when he realized that there are a lot of people who *want* to build things but can't afford to buy or do not have the space to store the required tools and equipment. Newton refers to his business as 'a community tinkering space'. Visit the workshop on any given day and you will see people working on projects from six-foot-tall robots to an electric car engine to wooden Christmas sculptures. For some of the five hundred members, who each pay $125 per month, it's a space to pursue their hobbies and have fun. For others, it's their workspace to engineer products, save on development costs and incubate new inventions. Regardless of their reason for joining, members expect to have access to everything from the latest laser cutters and plasma machines to engraving systems, welding tools, rapid prototyping equipment, industrial welding, sewing, plastics and casting machinery.

Approximately 150 miles from TechShop is Santa Rosa's tool-lending library for local do-it-yourselfers; it was started by Dustin Zuckerman, a library technician in his late thirties. His friends describe him as the 'giving type.' When Zuckerman was a teenager, a school career adviser asked him, 'If you could have any job in the world what would it be?' He replied, 'I would be a doorman. I like opening a door for someone, and the feeling of being thanked.' He now looks back and realizes this desire to engage in small acts of kindness pervades much of his life.

In March 2008, Dustin Zuckerman started a local tool-lending library from the back closet of his small one-bedroom cart shed in Santa Rosa. He first got the idea in 2005 when one of his clients asked him to put in a garden pathway. The task required a tool called a 'tamper'. The job paid $50, of which he spent approximately $35 for the tamper and $5 on lunch. 'I would not have seen it as such an expense had I known that I was going to use the tamper again,' Zuckerman explained. Realizing there had to be a better way to access tools he needed for one-off jobs, he later went online and typed 'borrow or lending tools'. He learned that the Oakland and Berkeley libraries had large tool annexes where you could check out the tool you needed. Re-creating the same idea on a smaller scale for the Santa Rosa community seemed to Zuckerman like 'such a simple but brilliant idea'.

Zuckerman began by gathering fifteen of his own tools he had lying around his apartment. In a Word document, he made a list of the tools he had and typed at the top 'Santa Rosa Tool Library Pilot Program'. He photocopied the document and handed it out to around thirty residents in his neighbourhood. People immediately loved the idea and started donating as well as borrowing tools. 'It was all very informal at first,' he remembers.

Today, routers, power tools, shovels, painting kits, saws and sanders are packed into every conceivable spot in his apartment and garage. In a camper van in his drive he keeps strimmers, power hoses and other bulkier equipment. He even has a fruit picker and a pole saw. The real turning point for the tool library happened in 2009 when a retired mechanic donated all his automotive tools. Zuckerman, who was now getting on average five borrowers on any weekday and upwards of fifteen people on Saturday and Sunday, realized he had a viable and prospering community resource.

The critical mass of tools and users for Newton's TechShop and Zuckerman's Santa Rosa library is different. TechShop needs thousands of the most up-to-date tools to enable its members to pursue complex projects. Zuckerman needs only a few hundred tools to help local residents with their home repair tasks, decorating jobs and gardening. But the principle is the same: the system will be successful if users are satisfied by the choice and the convenience available to them. If not, the system will probably be poorly utilized and short-lived.

Social Proof

The second reason why critical mass is such a vital ingredient to Collaborative Consumption is that a core group of loyal and frequent users will be attracted. Whether it's Barclays Cycle Hire users riding around the streets of London on distinct turquoise bikes or a clothing swap blogging about the deals they found, these early users provide a critical mass of 'social proof' that these forms of Collaborative Consumption are something others should try. It enables people, not just early adopters, to cross the psychological barrier that often exists around new behaviours.

Thirty years ago, Robert Cialdini, a psychology and marketing professor at Arizona State University, was one of the first social psychologists to study the role of social proof in motivating people to care for the environment. He has since investigated everything from how we respond to litter in a car park to public-service announcements about recycling. In 2007, Cialdini conducted a study in several Phoenix hotels comparing the effects of those ubiquitous hotel-bathroom placards that ask guests to reuse towels, testing four different messages to see how each appeal motivated guests' participation. All the signs were otherwise identical, instructing guests to 'place their used towels on the washroom towel rack or shower curtain rod'. Room attendants recorded whether guests participated in the programme on the first day that they stayed in the room.

First, Cialdini and his team of student researchers tested the traditional and most common pleas: 'Do it for the environment' and

'Help save resources for future generations'. The third said, 'Partner with us to help save the environment'. The two environmental appeals and the social responsibility message had similar rates of success, as 30 per cent of guests reused towels. The fourth message was based on the hotel's own interest: 'Help the hotel save energy'. Not surprisingly, this message was the least effective, eliciting a 16 per cent participation rate. The rate improved, however, when the research team conducted a second study injecting peer influence, with an invitation to 'Join fellow guests in helping save the environment' – including the statement that 'almost 75 per cent of guests in the hotel reused their towels more than once'. The outcome? Compared with the first three messages, the final peer-influence message increased towel reusage by an average of 34 per cent.[10]

Social proofing exists for a reason. It is a primitive instinct and a cognitive shortcut that allows us to make decisions based on copying the actions or behaviours of others. 'On some base level, it's survival recognition: these are the people who are most like me – we share the same circumstances,' Cialdini explains. He sees the power of this impulse 'less as peer pressure and more as peer information'.[11] Social proofing is crucial to Collaborative Consumption because most forms often require people to do something a little differently and to change old habits. In order for them to be convinced to make this change, most individuals need to see or experience a critical mass of consumers also making the switch. We will often decide what to do or what not to do based on what those around us are doing. It's the same force at play as the consumer desire gaps social scientist Alex Michalos says are created by the difference between 'what one has and what one thinks others like oneself have'.[12] The message that 'everybody else is doing it' sometimes works better than trying to appeal to people's sense of social responsibility or even to their hope of safeguarding resources for future generations. Ironically, the social phenomenon of pressure to 'keep up with the Joneses' could play a similar role in Collaborative Consumption as it did for hyper-consumerism over the past fifty years.

Power of Idling Capacity

If you are not an avid cyclist and own a bike, how many times do you use it? Not often, is most likely. The same is true of power drills. If you are like most people, you may use a power drill somewhere between six and thirteen minutes in its entire lifetime. And yet supposedly half of all US households have bought their own power drill.[13] There are approximately 50 million drills in homes across America gathering dust. Ownership of a product you use for just a few minutes makes no rational sense. There is the obvious cost of the money spent on the drill itself, but there are also the hassles of replacing those little screw heads that are always going missing; fixing it when it breaks; and then buying a newer version when the current one seems old or no longer works because the bit you lost is 'coincidentally' no longer made by the manufacturer. And when it comes right down to it, what most of us really want is, as legendary designer Victor Papanek put it, 'the hole, not the drill'.

The unused potential of those 50 million drills when they are not in use is referred to as idling capacity.[14] Even when you take a look around at your immediate surroundings, you'll be amazed by the amount of waste that exists – not just in landfills but in the stuff we own but rarely use: the 29 million personally owned vehicles that sit idle on average for twenty-three hours a day; the spare bedroom that is rarely used; the evening dress that awaits the right occasion; office space and equipment that are used for less than half the day; roads used only during peak times; extra belongings packed into storage units. In fact, in the United Kingdom and the United States 80 per cent of the items people own are used less than once a month. At the heart of Collaborative Consumption is the reckoning of how we can

take this idling capacity and redistribute it elsewhere. Modern
technology, including online social networks and GPS-enabled handheld devices, offers a multitude of ways to solve this problem. The
ubiquity of cheap connectivity that surrounds us can maximize the
productivity and usage of a product and mop up the surplus created
by hyper-consumption without creating costs or inconveniences.
Robin Chase, founder of Zipcar and the ride-sharing service GoLoco,
and one of the pioneering thinkers on maximizing idling capacity via
technology, says, 'This was what the Internet was made for, an instant
platform sharing excess capacity among many people.'

Ilan Bass, an old friend of Rachel's, started a new job in London.
He had never been a fan of the underground in rush hour. Although
the distance of his commute was relatively short, it involved two
Tube changes and a bus ride. A week into the job he realized that the
trip was going to take its toll. Bass went online and Googled 'lift
sharing in London'. The first site that came up was www.liftshare.
com. He created an account and entered his route into the system.
There was only one person, Susan Daniels, the chief executive of the
National Deaf Children's Society, offering a lift for his route. Daniels
had specifically requested a female passenger. Bass decided he would
contact her anyway. Susan replied the same day, asking for a personal description and a character reference, which he got from his
boss, who seemed bemused by the whole thing. For the next couple
of days, Daniels and Bass emailed back and forth getting to know
each other. 'Could you tell me a little more about yourself please?
Which company do you work for? And how long have you worked
there?' Daniels asked. Bass learned that Daniels was in fact deaf. As
she could not listen to the radio, she had decided she would like
some company on her daily commute. Being environmentally conscious, Daniels also realized that travelling to work with room for
four more passengers was a complete waste. In other words, her
spare seats had high idling capacity that could be utilized.

After eight emails, Daniels and Bass agreed to try a lift share together for the following week. She agreed to pick Bass up at 8:35 a.m. on Prince of Wales Road, just outside the old swimming baths, in her silver Prius. This was arranged by text. When Bass got to Prince of Wales Road, he realized that he had no clue where the old swimming baths were, so he looked them up on his iPhone. Running late, he ran down the road, where he finally saw a silver Prius waiting by the traffic lights with its hazard lights on.

Bass admits that he initially liked the idea mostly for selfish reasons. 'I wouldn't have to take the Tube or bus anymore and could glide into work while someone else gets stressed behind the wheel.' But since then he has discovered that driving to work with a woman who uses a mirror on the dashboard to lip-read him faultlessly unexpectedly starts his day with friendship and humour. 'I hear stories I would never have encountered, such as how Susan goes to salsa classes for the hearing impaired, with a gum-chewing sign language interpreter. All of the attendees basically dance to their own rhythm in utter chaos for an hour or so.'

Bass, like the millions of others who use ride-sharing services such as goCarShare, Liftshare and Catchalift, is a great example of how we can use the Internet to allocate resources where necessary. In the same way we can connect with friends and families through platforms such as Facebook, we can 'match make' the interests or needs of person A with person C (such as drivers and riders). We have entered an age when we can locate someone, or something, anywhere, in real time from a small device in our hands. According to a recent survey, 385 million mobile phones were in circulation worldwide in 2009. By 2013, that number is estimated to triple to 990 million.[15] And services such as Google's Near Me Now, Gowalla and Foursquare, where you can share location-based information with friends, are only just getting started. HearPlanet is an iPhone app that uses geolocation to determine where you are. It then feeds you information about the area's famous buildings, landmarks and historical sites. You can even listen to an audio tour guide that will give you real-time descriptions. Yipit, launched by Vincius Vacanti and James Moran in early 2010, is in their words 'a deep local search engine focused on Manhattan'. It uses your location and your preferences to send you the best daily deals for events, restaurants, shops, classes and so on, that best match your interests and habits. While this app largely feeds the consumer engine, it's only a matter of time before the same technology based on location signals will be used to pinpoint whatever we need to access and what is available to borrow, rent or share. Real-time technologies will be able to predict what we need, where and when; recommend the best options; and send special offers with sharing solutions. If you're travelling, for example, from Sunny Side in Denver to Cherry Creek Mall, an app will send you a discount voucher for the bike sharing scheme B-Cycle, and tell you that the fastest way to get there is to go to 345 St. Arthur Street, where there are three bikes available, and then drop the bike off at 2900 Cherry Creek Drive, where there are four docks available.

Idling capacity is related not just to physical products such as bikes, cars and drills but to less tangible assets such as time, skills, space or commodities such as electricity. A programme in the UK called Landshare and similar schemes in the United States called YardShare, SharedEarth, We-Patch and Urban Gardenshare connect gardenless would-be growers with unused spare land, as well as people with extra time or skills who want to help. The land available varies from spare acreage on farms to unused allotments to urban wasteland to small back gardens. The National Trust recently pledged to provide one thousand growing plots. Liz McLellan, founder of YardShare, explains, 'A lot of us would love to grow food, but we lack one of the more important things we need to do that. Some of us lack space, physical strength, time, or tools or even just have a "brown thumb," so it makes sense for us to group together.' The matches share the fruits and vegetables grown but often the unexpected benefits include friendships and community.

Without the social networking capacity of the Internet, such a scheme had little chance of matching 'want with need' and reaching scale fast. But now these programmes operate like a gardening 'dating agency'. A typical post from a landowner reads, 'I have a garden that is turning into waste land. Would anyone like to grow veg, etc., all I would ask is a share of the veg grown.' Or there is Philip, an experienced gardener, who posts, 'Can you help? I live in Edgworth, Bolton – do you have any land I could use? I have grown veg for years, new house is lovely, but no garden other than pots! Help!'

Adam Dell, a successful venture capitalist and brother of Michael Dell, started SharedEarth in January 2010. He first got the idea through his own experience of finding a gardener online. Dell posted a request on craigslist for gardening help for his land in Austin, Texas. The proposition was simple: 'I have spare land and would like to turn it into a vegetable garden. If you will tend to it, we will split the produce fifty-fifty. I'll pay for the seeds, soil, and equipment, you provide the labor.' Within forty-eight hours he received more than thirty responses. The experience was an inspiration to Dell, who began thinking about the amount of unused land sitting idle and the untapped gardening interest across the United States. 'How could I apply the basic ideas of social networking to create the largest community garden in the world?' he wondered.

SharedEarth launched in January 2010. Within three months, an estimated 25 million square feet of registered potential garden space was posted. The amount of land is expected to grow to 1 billion square feet by the end of 2010. Dell thinks it is growing so fast because 'People intuitively get the idea.' Landshare in the United Kingdom has experienced similar rapid growth. In October 2010, there were more than 55,000 members on Landshare, and there was a piece of land registered for every single postcode in the United Kingdom. The current ratio of landseekers to landowners is around 2:1.

'Like most marvellous ideas, it's simultaneously small and impressively vast in its reach. Pairing Mr Green's desire to grow leeks with Mrs Brown's need for an orderly garden may not sound earth-shattering, but similarly cumulative small actions are what keep the supermarkets at the centre of our food supply: landshare simply enables more people to step outside that chain,' the *Guardian* newspaper recently commented.[16]

Belief in 'the Commons'

The idea of 'the commons', a term applied to resources that belong to all of us, dates back to the Romans, who defined certain things as *res publica* (meaning 'things set aside for public use'), such as parks, roads and public buildings; and *res communis* (meaning 'things common to all'), such as air, water and wildlife, as well as culture, languages and public knowledge. The notion thrived, remaining relatively unchallenged until the fifteenth century, when undefined common grazing lands in England were 'enclosed' by thorn hedges and carved up among private owners. The concept of private property and enclosures accelerated across Europe and America throughout the eighteenth and nineteenth centuries. Privatization was justified by the rationale that shared resources were subject to overuse and misuse by individuals, who will always act in their own short-term self-interests, a scenario popularized by microbiologist Garrett Hardin centuries later in a 1968 *Science* article, 'The Tragedy of the Commons'. Hardin drew on the parable of a field used for grazing cattle. 'Picture a pasture open to all,' he wrote. 'A herdsman grazing his animals on the land will have an incentive to 'add another animal to his herd. And another; and another. . . . But this

is the conclusion reached by each and every rational herdsman sharing a commons. Therein is the tragedy.'[17] In other words, people
knowingly or unknowingly will take too much, even though it is
not for anyone's collective or long-term good. As Hardin posited,
'Freedom in a commons brings ruin to all.'[18]

Consider a traffic jam on a main road going into any big city. At
first, each person picks that particular road for the logical reason
that it's the fastest route. In the beginning, each additional car does
not slow the traffic down, as there is enough room on the road for
the additional drivers. At some point, however, each car reduces the
average speed and eventually there are so many drivers that the traffic slows to a crawl. All the people seeking to minimize their own
driving time add up to a longer commute for everyone.[19] Doing
what's rational results in a negative outcome to the collective interest
of all drivers, including you. On a global scale, Hardin's logic can
explain environmental issues such as overfished seas and rivers, air
pollution and water scarcity.

Since its publication, 'The Tragedy of the Commons' has become
one of the most reprinted articles to appear in a scientific journal
and is widely cited in hundreds of books. Indeed, individuals competing for resources are at the heart of one of the most discussed and
debated questions of economic theory and free markets: How can
we balance the interest of individuals and the interest of the group?
The typical response is that self-interest will always trump the collective good and thus oversight is required. But history is demonstrating that this is not always the best or only answer. And Nobel
Prize winner Elinor Ostrom's work debunks Hardin's claim that
'tragedy is inevitable'.

Tellingly, Ostrom's work has been recognized as the Internet,
the most robust commons in history, has emerged. David Bollier,
a renowned expert on the cyberspace commons, notes, 'Although
Ostrom has not written extensively about the Internet and the online

commons, her work clearly speaks to the ways that people can self-organize themselves to take care of resources that they care about.'[20] Stanford law professor Lawrence Lessig, like Ostrom, has dedicated much of his career to studying, researching and promoting the value of a commons of cultural, educational, and scientific ideas. Around a decade ago, Lessig, nicknamed the 'King of Internet Law', recognized the need to facilitate the sharing, remixing and reuse of creative content – songs, photos, knowledge, films. In 2002, Lessig launched Creative Commons, which provides free copyright licences to encourage sharing and collaboration, but which still restricts usages to which the creator does not consent. Since its launch, more than 100 million licences have been issued in fifty-two countries, and Creative Commons is used by the White House, the film director Ridley Scott and the musician Gwen Stefani, among others. In Lessig's words, Creative Commons was invented as 'a solution for failed sharing'. What Lessig and the Creative Commons have done is to create a significant culture of online socializing that encourages us to share.

Through our digital experiences, we are recognizing that by providing value to the community, we enable our own social value to expand in return. When we post photos on Flickr; our knowledge on the likes of Wikipedia, Open Street Map and Citizendium; our news on Public News and Slashdot; and our research on Bepress and NeuroCommons, we learn that we need to 'give to get' in these communities. As David Bollier writes in *Viral Spiral*, 'The commons – a hazy concept to many people – is a new paradigm for creating value and organizing a community of shared interests.'[21] Collaborative Consumption is tied to how these principles are being applied to other parts of our lives, beyond media or content, by tapping into an innate quest to be part of a solution or even a movement of people with similar interests. The experience is appealing as much for the 'collaborative' as for the 'consumption'.

A single phone is useless, but the more people who own telephones, the more valuable the telephone is to each owner as the total number of people on the network increases. Similarly, the more users who participate in programmes such as Landshare, Airbnb or bike sharing, the better the system works for everyone – there is a 'network effect'. Every single person who joins or uses Collaborative Consumption creates value for another person, even if this was not the intention.

Trust Between Strangers

The second intersection of Ostrom's research with Collaborative Consumption is her idea that 'commoners' can self-govern shared resources if they are empowered with the right tools to coordinate projects or specific needs, and the right to monitor each other. If this scenario sounds like a utopian dream, just think about the largely self-managed peer-policed systems of eBay, London Liftshare or Airbnb where, for the most part, disagreements are resolved among the community. In these highly successful 'marketplaces', top-down mechanisms of 'command and control' have been removed, along with layers of permission, decision making and middlemen. In their place, peer-to-peer platforms enable decentralized, and transparent communities to form and build 'trust between strangers'.

Most forms of Collaborative Consumption require us to trust someone we don't know to varying degrees. In ride-sharing programmes, just as with Ilan and Susan, we have to trust that the person is reliable and harmless; in markets such as eBay or craigslist, that the item a person is selling, swapping or giving is in the condition the seller describes; in landsharing, that it's safe to let the person into your back garden; Dustin Zuckerman must trust that local residents will return his tools; and so on.

In the hyper-consumer world, middlemen have always functioned as the 'actor in-between two other actors' bridging the gap
between production and consumption. We did not have to trust one
another because from sales assistants to traders, managers to brokers, negotiators to mediators, agents to distributors, there usually
were trustworthy agents in the middle to handle and control transactions. There were set rules in place. But Collaborative Consumption eliminates the need for these types of middlemen. With an
infinite marketplace for direct peer-to-peer exchanges, the role of
the middleman is no longer to police the trade. Just as Rob Kalin
recognized with Etsy and the founders of Airbnb envisioned, the
role of their companies is to act as curators and ambassadors, creating platforms that facilitate self-managed exchanges and contributions. This might involve developing the best possible gallery to
showcase photos of a space for rent, or an easy search engine to
enable people to find what they want, or a well-designed reputation system that enables us to get knowledge – interests, whom
users know, personal preferences, past actions – about strangers,
thereby taking anonymity out of transactions. A positive rating becomes equivalent to a firsthand reference from someone we've actually met, helping us to make better decisions about who to
exchange with.[22] The role of this new intermediary is therefore to
create the right tools and environment for familiarity and trust to
be built, a middle ground where commerce and community meet.
And companies can charge a service fee for providing that service
and playing that role.

Charles Leadbeater poses a provocative question in his book
We-Think: 'What will happen when the networks created by the
geeks combine with the traditions and habits of millions of people
who were until recently rural peasants?'[23] New online and off-
line marketplaces are forming where people can once again 'meet'
in a global village and form nonlocal trust. We have returned to a

time when if you do something wrong or embarrassing, the whole community will know. Free riders, vandals and abusers are easily weeded out, just as openness, trust and reciprocity are encouraged and rewarded. As we shall show over the next few chapters, when personal relationships and social capital return to the centre of the exchanges, peer-to-peer trust is relatively easy to create and manage, and most of the time the trust is strengthened, not broken.

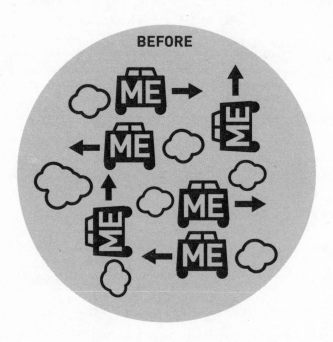

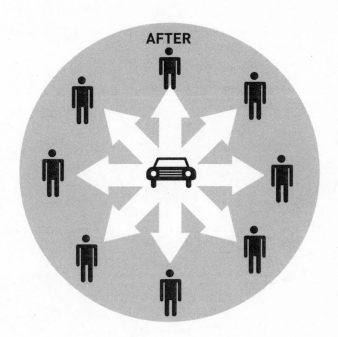

PRODUCT SERVICE
SYSTEMS

| **Better Than Ownership**

T he relationship between physical products, individual ownership and self-identity is undergoing a profound evolution. We
don't want the CD; we want the music it plays. We don't want
the disc; we want the storage it holds. We don't want the answering
machine; we want the messages it saves. We don't want the DVD; we
want the film it carries. In other words, we want not the stuff but the
needs or experiences it fulfils. As our possessions 'dematerialize' into
the intangible, our preconceptions of ownership are changing, creating a dotted line between 'what's mine', 'what's yours', and 'what's
ours'. This shift is fuelling a world where usage trumps possessions
and, as Kevin Kelly, a passionate conservationist and founder of *Wired*
magazine, puts it, where 'access is better than ownership'.[1]

We have constructed a large part of our freedom around our
'right to own' and our self-identity around what we do. But for the
Millennials, the first generation that writer John Palfrey describes as
'born digital', this powerful relationship with ownership is fractur-
ing. There are new channels emerging – channels that don't require
you to own anything other than a computer or even just an iPhone

– to share what we are doing (Twitter), what we are reading (Shelfari), what we are interested in (Digg), the groups we belong to (LinkedIn), and of course who our friends are (Facebook). As our online 'brands' define 'who we are' and 'what we like', actual ownership becomes less important than demonstrating use or use by association.[2] We can now show status, group affiliation and belonging without necessarily having to buy physical objects. Self-expression through objects will, of course, not become obsolete. We will, for instance, always treasure possessions that have high sentimental value, such as our wedding rings, relics from travels or family heirlooms. But our relationship to satisfying what we want and signalling who we are is far more immaterial than that of any previous generation.

When a song is downloaded from iTunes or we listen to a track on Spotify (a library of millions of songs hailed as the 'twenty-first-century jukebox'), we are experiencing the benefits of 'dematerialization'. We are turning products into services, even if we're not conscious of it. Chris Arkenberg, a regular blogger on technology and culture, wrote, 'For the past 20 years, millions upon millions of CDs, DVDs, cases and printed inserts have been consuming resources, fixing materials into unrecoverable or "downcycled" hard media and filling landfills. Apple has fundamentally rewritten this paradigm by dematerializing the content.'[3] But the benefits of dematerialization are not just convenience and choice. A recent study conducted by Intel and Microsoft comparing the environmental impact of various forms of music delivery showed that purchasing music digitally on the Internet reduced the carbon footprint and energy usage associated with delivering music to consumers by 40 to 80 per cent compared with buying a CD at a retail outlet.[4] Another instance of unintended consequences: most people's reason for downloading music isn't environmental friendliness; but nevertheless, downloading is environmentally friendly.

The debate rages about whether the 'digital way' is better or worse than what it is replacing, with critics pointing to serious implications in the areas of privacy, piracy and property. There will always be some bibliophiles who will want to hold and collect shelves of books and music lovers who revel in the pleasures of shuffling through old LPs. But, in many areas of our lives, the importance of owning stuff – actual physical stuff – is diminishing. The product is becoming just a means to an end. As Jeremy Rifkin wrote in *The Age of Access*, 'It is likely that for a growing number of enterprises and consumers, the very idea of ownership will seem limited, even old-fashioned, twenty-five years from now.'[5]

'Not Owning'

It would seem that an increasing number of consumers are realizing the merits of Aristotle's notion, 'On the whole, you find wealth much more in use than in ownership.' The idea of a service that enables us to derive benefit from a shared product is not new. Have you ever stayed in a hotel room, used a launderette or photocopy shop, rented a dinner jacket or fancy dress costume, or perhaps hired some tables and chairs for a party? The basic principles of 'not owning' can be traced back to ancient forms of commerce. During a dig in 1984, a team of archaeologists discovered clay tablets from the ancient Sumerian city of Ur that documented farm equipment leases from priests to agricultural workers in the year 2010 BC.[6] In the United States, leasing was first adopted in the 1700s, beginning with horses, buggies and wagons leased out by liverymen, and then expanded in the 1870s when transportation tycoons developed new and creative financing methods to lease barges, railway vehicles and locomotives as 'equipment trust certificates'. By the early 1900s, the concept of leasing commercial equipment was a common part of the fabric of day-to-day businesses. Today, commercial leasing of every-

thing from printing presses to power plants, office copiers to offshore
drilling rigs, telecom equipment to large-scale computer networks,
is a $225 billion-plus industry in the United States and amounts to
more than $600 billion worldwide.[7]

Not just companies, but also consumers have enjoyed the benefits of usage over ownership for years. Indeed, you can rent anything
these days from furniture to jewellery to plasma screens to sporting
goods and even artwork from more than twelve thousand rental
companies in the United States alone.[8] The similarity between these
traditional forms of consumer rental and leasing and current product service systems is that they both give people access to products,
tools and capabilities on a temporary basis. But with Web 2.0 platforms, an unprecedented opportunity exists for sharing a wide variety of products conveniently and cost-effectively to access items on
demand. These technologies create fresh relevance and massive opportunities to design systems of shared use that feel drastically different from traditional rentals.

If you have ever rented a car, you will be familiar with the
advance bookings, queues, paperwork and interaction with agents
explaining all the hidden costs and reminding you of your status as 'renter'. Sometimes you don't even end up with the car you
booked. And then there are restrictions around when you can pick
up the car, the minimum time you can rent it for and when you
need to return it. But the Internet and GPS technologies eliminate
these hassles, enabling car-sharing services such as Zipcar and
Streetcar to be almost 100 per cent self-service. Plus, car sharing is
often far more convenient simply because the cars are located in
residential neighbourhoods, close to where their customers live,
thereby removing the hassle of pickup and drop-off of rental cars
in branches often located in airports or remote underground car
parks. It's a great example of how modern product service systems
are changing the stigma and frame of reference of old-fashioned

renting, leasing or pooling into an experience far closer to the associations, convenience and control benefits of ownership.

There is considerable debate among academics and design experts as to how different types of product service systems should be categorized and defined, and what they should be called. We have simplified the array of PSSs into two models. In a 'usage' PSS, a product is owned by a company or an individual and multiple users share its benefits through a service. There are many scenarios where the market is ripe for this type of PSS, including when the product has 'high idling capacity' (cars or household tools); when the product has a limited use because of fashion (handbags) or it fulfils a temporary need (baby equipment and maternity clothes); when the product diminishes in appeal and value after usage (a film); and when high start-up or purchasing costs for products are the barrier to entry (solar panels).

The second model is an 'extended-life' PSS. Here an after-sales service such as maintenance, repair or upgrading becomes an integral part of the product's life cycle, thereby reducing the need for replacement or disposal.[9] Products that are expensive or require specialized knowledge to repair (electronic goods) or products that need to be updated or frequently maintained to preserve their appeal (furniture) are well suited to this type of product service system.

Revolutionizing the Way We Rent

Perhaps the most familiar example of a usage PSS is Netflix, the service that revolutionized the way we rent films and TV programmes, damaging industry giant Blockbuster along the way. Successful entrepreneurs Marc Randolph, Reed Hastings and Mitch Lowe founded Netflix in 1999, after Randolph and Hastings had made a fortune by inventing a debugging software tool called Pure Software. Hastings first got the idea for Netflix after going to Blockbuster one day and discovering that his family had been six weeks late in returning *Apollo*

13. The overdue video cost him $40 in late fees. It was later, on his way to the gym, that he had his eureka moment when he realized his fitness club had a much better business model: 'You could pay $30 or $40 a month and work out as little or as much as you wanted.' He reasoned that there had to be a similar way 'to make money renting movies without gouging customers on late fees'.[10]

Hastings, who is now in his late forties and lives with his wife and two children in Santa Cruz, likes films but admits he is no film buff. He is tall and slim and with his neatly trimmed salt-and-pepper goatee looks a bit like a younger version of another film industry pioneer, George Lucas. After his 'gym epiphany', he analysed the existing video rental business and learned that customers hated long queues, the familiar squabbles over choosing the video, and coming home empty-handed when the selection was poor. And then there was the hassle of returning the tapes – as he had experienced firsthand, it was easy to misplace, forget, or damage them – and the return penalties added up.[11] He sketched out his initial ideas, which were based on the simple premise of making it easy to rent films you want to see, without having to own them, and without ever having to leave your home.

Convinced he was on to a 'home-run' idea, Hastings was not fazed when some investors doubted this model. The naysayers questioned whether customers used to browsing store shelves and coming home with physical boxes would change their behaviour. Hastings did not mind if it took consumers a while to buy into the new system but, as it turned out, he did not need to wait long. In the first year after the Netflix launch, 239,000 film lovers signed up. Today it has more than 10 million subscribers (and it's growing by a staggering rate of around 25 per cent per year) who choose from more than 100,000 titles, from Hollywood hits to niche documentaries. Remarkably, if you stacked every film Netflix ships in a week (on average, 2 million DVDs a day) in a single pile, the stack would be taller than Mount Everest.[12]

Like other individual usage product service systems, Netflix attracts a mix of customers with different motivations – some like the convenience, some the selection, others the cost savings. Few consumers would say they use the service because it's 'greener', but, as with downloadable music, it is. Hastings would be the first one to admit that his motivations for starting Netflix were not to make his contribution to the battle against climate change.

It is amazing to think that to rent a video from a traditional store requires two round trips, usually done in a car, and often alone. This trip emits far more pollution than the addition of a paper envelope weighing less than 1 ounce to the mailbag of a postal worker who is walking past your house each day anyway. Plus, you use that same paper envelope to send the film back. It is estimated that if Netflix members drove to and from a rental store, they would consume 800,000 gallons of petrol and release more than 2.2 million tonnes of CO_2 emissions annually.[13] And when you consider how Netflix also spares the plastic cases used by stores like Blockbuster and the big promotional cutouts and merchandise they make and discard, you start to see how a system solution such as Netflix is far more sustainable than traditional video stores. As Netflix wades deeper into the world of online streaming, enabling consumers to watch films instantly, the dematerialized model becomes all the more environmentally friendly.

Collective Wisdom of Members

At the same time, Netflix has built a sophisticated platform to foster a community among its members, and to tailor recommendations to individual tastes. Talk to anyone who has ever used Netflix and they will tell you about how they 'discovered releases', 'learned about classics', and 'found rare gems' they never would have found on their own at a store. Approximately 60 per cent of members base

their selections on Netflix's Cinematch recommendations system.
Early on, people's willingness to share and rate the films they had
watched and to make suggestions to 'friends' surprised the founders.
The user community itself adopted the ethos of 'Millions of members helping you'. Impressively, there are now more than 2 billion
ratings from members, and the average member has evaluated approximately two hundred films. The result is an invaluable collective
wisdom impossible to replicate elsewhere. This same dynamic fuels
the success of Amazon, product reviewer site Epinions and enter-
tainment recommendations site Yelp. When you sign up, you become part of a hub that gives you access to the knowledge of millions
of other users. The notion that the collective intelligence of thousands, even millions, of people can produce the results and knowledge that smaller groups and individuals can't has been much
discussed, probably best in James Surowiecki's book *The Wisdom of
Crowds*. But what's new is applying collective intelligence to make
product service systems more attractive than individual ownership.

The in-depth knowledge accumulated through repeated consumer interactions presents a significant opportunity for businesses
to form deeper relationships with customers and manage their stock
more efficiently. Through the familiar 'My Queue', Netflix knows
what its members want to watch next. How many traditional shops
can say that they know what their customers will buy next? This
kind of knowledge is particularly valuable to sectors where consumers demand a lot of choice, such as fashion and toys. Retailers must
maintain a large stock of such products and, since the products are
dumped and replaced, environmental impact is significant. If you
have children, the chances are that your house is overrun with toys:
electronic toys that make irritating and loud noises; toys with a million pieces that turn up in the strangest places; toys from well-inten-
tioned relatives used once and then thrown to the back of a cupboard;
the latest gadget your children told you they 'must have', only to

utter the inevitable lament 'Mum . . . we're bored!' So there you find yourself, surrounded by expensive yet unwanted plastic, thinking, 'There has got to be a better way.' And there is.

The first toy library, called Toy Loan, appeared in Los Angeles in 1935, but the concept took off in the mid-1960s as a result of funding from former president Johnson's Head Start programmes. There are now thousands around the world. Historically this service, like many shared goods, carried the stigma of a welfare programme, intended for children with special needs or for low-income families. Now better-branded emerging companies such as MiniLodgers, Busy Bee Babies Scotland and DimDom France, which can be thought of as the 'Netflix for toys', are changing these negative associations. They all follow a similar model; you pay a subscription service between $25 and $65 per month and, in return, you receive between four and ten different toys on a monthly basis. (And yes, all the toys are sanitized after every shipment.) The service saves parents from having to concoct imperfect storage solutions and breaks the expensive habit of answering the familiar wails of boredom by purchasing yet more toys that end up gathering dust in the back of a cupboard a few weeks later.

In the typical transaction model around toys (and many other household and durable goods), you go into, say, a Toys 'R' Us and meander along the aisles feeling overwhelmed. Even if a salesperson extends himself, the person knows nothing about your family or what your child likes, and therefore blindly recommends the latest gadget. Product service systems are dependent on the opposite relationship with the user. By predicting needs, they create a smarter, more efficient consumerism. In the case of toys, the more the parent interacts with the service, the more user history and knowledge the provider attains to make recommendations for the child in terms of age, learning and skills.

Resources are still required to make and ship toys, but this system is clearly more sustainable. Not only does it reduce the number of toys a consumer needs to buy, if any, but the usage of one toy is maximized. Also, as these distribution channels become integrated with the product manufacturers themselves, it will be in their best interest to make their products as durable as possible to handle multiple users and heavy usage. And of course this service also prevents the toys your children outgrow or don't use from being thrown away and ending up as landfill, and perhaps becoming another piece of floating plastic soup in the Great Pacific Garbage Patch.

Peer-to-Peer Renting

Taking assets you don't use all the time and charging a fee for others to use them is the basis behind the numerous peer-to-peer sites emerging, such as Erento, Ecomodo, The Hire Hub and Zilok. These marketplaces enable people to lend and charge for sharing their own stuff. As with Landshare programmes that pair owners with growers – and Airbnb, which links hosts to guests – owners who have stuff to rent are matched with people who want those particular items on a temporary basis. That 'idling capacity' of underused goods is redistributed and individuals can make money from belongings that previously just sat idle.

On these peer-to-peer platforms everything from snow tyre chains to deep-fryers to sewing machines to Chassis the Drink Serving Robot are being rented out. You can even rent out artwork for as little as $2 per day. Peer-to-peer rental marketplaces are useful for people such as independent film producer Kestrin Pantera. Her high-definition camera is just one piece of equipment, alongside others such as amplifiers and lighting, that she does not use every day. On Zilok, a site launched in 2007, Pantera rents out her camera and sets the price, $150 per day. For Pantera, Zilok is about more than making money. 'With the limited resources we have on the earth, the next step for conservation is instead of just buying stuff, sharing stuff.'[14]

For consumers to overcome the culturally entrenched cult of possessions, we have to get to a point where sharing is convenient, secure and more cost-effective than ownership. These peer-to-peer
rental sites use digital platforms to solve two critical hurdles. They
create a centralized hub for sharing, reaching a 'critical mass of goods'
with consumer choice and easy accessibility. This is particularly important given that a large percentage of items rented are the sort we
use occasionally for spur-of-the-moment chores. As Liz Goodwin, director of the Waste and Resources Action Programme (WRAP),
points out, it's also important to give us 'the confidence that we can
get things when we need them, but we don't need to have them sitting beside us every day'.[15] Also, as these sites become hyper-local, we
won't have to travel long distances to pick items up or have them
shipped. Even though these marketplaces are still in their nascent
stages, critical mass is already forming. Zilok, launched in 2007, had
more than 100,000 items for rent in the United States alone at the end
of 2009. It is in five countries already: the United States, France, Bel-
gium, Luxembourg and the Netherlands. When we searched the site
for the availability of 'projector in Brooklyn, New York', there were
five available within a three-mile radius. This saturation is critical to
avoid negating the convenience and environmental benefits of 'possession on demand'. It is estimated that just shifting a fifth of household spending from purchasing to renting would cut emissions by
about 2 per cent – or 13 million tonnes – of CO_2 a year.[16]

The second hurdle facing peer-to-peer rental is security and
trust. Do you want to rent out your Nintendo Wii to someone you
don't know, even if it earns you, say, $25? Peer-to-peer rental sites
have several layers of security. Every transaction is backed up by a
contract that lays out the legal terms. Renters are also required to
leave a deposit and can opt for insurance in case the item is lost or
stolen in their care. And just as with eBay and Airbnb, review and
ratings tools enable the community to self-regulate who can be lent

to in good faith. For these services, the peer-to-peer rental companies charge about a 6 per cent commission on every transaction.

If you need to trim a hedge, do you buy a trimmer from B&Q for about £70 or rent one for £4? More and more consumers are renting, and when they rent, they experience firsthand that they don't need to buy and own to have what they want and get what they need. Access becomes the privilege and ownership the burden.

Removing Barriers to Entry

Another category of usage PSS removes a common barrier to entry, whether that obstacle is price, availability or even social status. Take public libraries, one of the oldest forms of product service systems. Many of the town libraries of the early 1600s were not open to the general public but were only accessible to scholars, who often had to review books in situ. The Boston Public Library in Massachusetts, opened in 1854, was the first large free municipal library in the United States that allowed people to borrow books and take them home to read. But this system was still the exception rather than the norm, making knowledge and greater literacy difficult to obtain. Scottish-American philanthropist and businessman Andrew Carnegie made public libraries available to people across the United States.

Carnegie was committed to the notion that education and information were the keys to a successful life, a lesson he learned while working for a local telegraph company in Allegheny City, Pennsylvania. He would borrow books from the personal collection of the company's founder, Colonel James Anderson. The colonel would open his library of four hundred volumes each Saturday afternoon so that any of his workers would have access to his books, a privilege that would have been impossible to obtain elsewhere. The colonel himself acted as the librarian, allowing each person to take out one book and exchange it for another the following Saturday.[17]

Carnegie's personal experience as an immigrant who worked his way into a position of wealth reinforced his faith in a society based on merit. This belief motivated his campaign of worldwide library building, earning him the nickname the Patron Saint of Libraries. He built more than 1,689 libraries in the United States in the late 1800s; many of these became civic centres, entertaining and educating hundreds of small American communities from Maine to California. The architecture of these buildings ranged from Spanish colonial to baroque, but they all shared the same feature – a beautiful doorway with a prominent staircase designed to welcome people and to symbolize a person's elevation by learning. Over the doors of the Carnegie Library of Pittsburgh, founded in 1895, carved in stone, are Carnegie's own words, 'Free to the People'. The stacks of books inside were open. Outside every library was a lamppost or lantern to symbolize the light of knowledge streaming in.

Fast forward to the twenty-first century and a memorable scene from the film *Sex and the City*. Louise from St. Louis shows up for her interview to be Carrie Bradshaw's personal assistant. She clutches a new Louis Vuitton patchwork denim handbag that costs more than $2,500. Carrie, who has recently been left at the altar by the show's infamous Mr. Big, is looking for an assistant to help get her life back on track. After interviewing a woman who shows up drunk and a man who arrives in a black suit and bright pink satin stilettos, Carrie thinks this sassy, straight-talking young woman with a degree in computer science is a godsend. Carrie, whose character is notorious for living for fashion, including an absurdly large wardrobe of Manolo Blahnik shoes, notices the bag immediately. After discovering that they both came to New York for the same reason, in search of love, Carrie tells Louise that she thinks she is perfect for the job. She just has one more question: 'So, Louise from St. Louis, tell me how does an unemployed girl from St. Louis with three roommates afford the Patchwork Bowly Louis Vuitton bag?' Louise retorts, 'It is

rented from Bag Borrow or Steal, Netflix for purses.' It turns out that
Louise fulfils her lust for designer bags by renting them at a fraction
of the price through the online service Bag Borrow or Steal (recently
renamed Avelle). The conversation ends with Carrie, amazed, asking, 'How did I not know about this?' The scene predicted a trend.
Luxury rental services satisfy consumers' ingrained desires for the
'latest and greatest' while at the same time avoiding that common
contemporary irony, 'a closet full of clothes but nothing to wear'.

The stories of Andrew Carnegie's commitment to building
libraries and Louise's rented Bowly Louis Vuitton handbag share
components critical to the concept of Collaborative Consumption.
Both are about access: giving people access to goods without the
need for ownership. In the case of Louise, Bag Borrow or Steal gave
her access to handbags – and the status they bring with them – once
out of her reach. And for Carnegie, libraries gave access to knowledge and community for people to better their lives.

'Green goods' such as solar panels suffer from the same problem
as luxury handbags. They are expensive and not affordable to many
people. If you ask people, 'Dollar for dollar, if you had the option of
using clean solar power or dirty power, which would you choose?'
the answer is almost always 'clean', but follow-up tends to include
lines like 'but it's too expensive' or 'but it's too complicated to install
and maintain'. Lyndon Rive, the CEO of SolarCity, writes, 'People
want to go green, but they won't do it if it costs them an arm and a
leg. Even the extreme environmentalists can't justify it.' Given that it
costs anywhere from $20,000 to $40,000 to install a solar panel system on the average home, it's easy to understand why the price tag
dampens interest. Plus, it isn't the solar panel itself that people covet.
It's the clean electricity and the immediate cost savings. Product service systems such as Citizenrē and SolarCity tap into this demand by
installing, monitoring and maintaining solar panels on a customer's
property but retaining ownership of the equipment, absolving hom-

eowners from the stress and costs of getting it fixed or replaced when it breaks down. These companies also overcome the lament 'it's complicated' because they handle state and local incentive and rebate programmes.

Service Envy

SolarCity customers, not surprisingly, talk as much about the service as the solar panels themselves. Indeed, Rive admits that most of his new business comes from customers who tell their neighbours not just about their 'electricity meters spinning backward' but the 'ease of the whole service and system'. This phenomenon is common among people starting to use product service systems. They are as proud of how they got the product as the product itself. Just like Louise, who didn't hide the fact that the bag was 'borrowed' or 'rented', they are proud of the statement using a PSS makes about them. The way people are accessing goods is bestowing social cachet and can create what designers from the company LiveWork refer to as 'service envy'.[18] According to David Townson, a strategic designer at LiveWork, service envy is about 'making people desire services more than products'. And to achieve this, 'We have to create services that enable people to tell each other who they are through the use of services instead of through ownership of things.'[19] If we could create service brands and systems that make us feel smart, safe and attractive, both the emotional and the functional need to own so many products would become obsolete.

A key to a product service system's success is its ability to satisfy our deep-seated need to feel like an owner for at least the time the product is in our care. Companies achieve this feeling of ownership through discreet branding of the service on the product itself (the Bag Borrow or Steal logo is never visible on the outside of the bag) or building common ownership quirks into the brand. Zipcar gives its cars affectionate names such as 'Simpson' the Volvo or 'Munselle' the Mazda. Technologies such as RFID (radio-frequency identification) membership cards that open the door to 'your' car also help reconfigure the relationship between products and services and destigmatize the notion of sharing. People are realizing that ownership for the sake of exclusive possession is less important than the sense of belonging that ownership imparts. In other words, ownership is becoming less about title and lease and more about the experience of autonomy and control.

When you think about it, there is no rational reason behind the notion that sleeping in a hotel bed or using a towel that hundreds of people used is acceptable, but sharing a vacuum cleaner with neighbours is abnormal. Naysayers, however, doubt that consumers will be willing to share certain types of items that carry a strong emotional attachment or products perceived as needing to be immediately accessible, such as cars. Yet car sharing is the most visible and celebrated form of product service systems.

Like many forms of Collaborative Consumption, car sharing has roots that reach back across the centuries. The concept of 'public transport for rent' was in place across much of Europe two hundred years before the car was invented, when horse-drawn carriages and drivers were available for hire. In 1891, the idea of the taxicab was born after German inventor Wilhelm Bruhn developed the taximeter, which measured the distance travelled (or the time taken) to determine an accurate fare. Shortly thereafter, a Nebraskan named Joe Saunders saw the opportunity to use a similar device to start the first rent-a-car business. He would lend out his Model T and charge ten cents a mile for its use. Saunders's first customer is said to have been a travelling salesman who needed transportation to impress a local girl he was taking out for dinner.[20] By 1925, Saunders had set up car rental depots in twenty-one states across America, perhaps becoming the first rental magnate.

The contemporary concept of urban car sharing has been around for more than sixty years. A cooperative known as Sefage initiated services in Zurich, Switzerland, in 1948. But it has become popularized and thought of as 'hip', 'financially smart', and part of an 'environmentally conscious lifestyle' only in the past couple of years. There are now more than one thousand cities in the world across four continents where people can share cars, through companies such as Mobility in Switzerland, ORIX Auto in Japan and Streetcar in the UK.[21] Launched in April 2004, Streetcar has become a popular alternative to car ownership in the UK, with a presence in more than 1,100 locations across eight cities and with more than 80,000 members. And if the growth of US-based Zipcar – membership is growing by more than 100 per cent per year – is anything to go by, it's clear that consumers will embrace alternatives to leasing or private car ownership if the service is delivered and branded in the right way. Robin Chase, founder of Zipcar, says, 'It's the car your mother said you could never have. When you are not using it, it is someone else's problem, and who cares.'

As with other forms of Collaborative Consumption, the rapid growth of car sharing is fuelled by increasing cost consciousness and environmental necessity. Social networks and wireless technologies have removed the obstacles involved with coordination. Consider what it would have taken in the 1940s to organize even just a couple of hundred car users. With such a large gap between effort and benefit, it's no wonder that people chose to buy their own car. But social networks make this problem obsolete by creating platforms that automate the coordination of users, making car sharing easy and convenient.

Making Car Sharing Sexy, Not Sorry

Our love affair with the car, from the first 1908 Model T, has elevated cars to symbols of individual independence and technological mastery. Entire generations have been raised on the dogma that 'Cars give us freedom.' But cars are a burden.[22] While for some people fiddling with engines is half the fun, for most of us the maintenance, cleaning, registration, repair, insurance and parking are an expensive headache. The American Automobile Association estimates that average Americans and Europeans spend approximately 18 per cent of their income (or $8,000 a year) for one person to drive a medium-size car. That is more money than the average family spends on clothing, health care and entertainment combined. That's a lot of money when you consider that the average car sits idle for twenty-three hours of the day.[23] What's more, an estimated 39 per cent of UK households own more than one vehicle.

Average car users save an estimated £380 per month when they switch to car sharing. Not only are all the peripheral costs of owning a car removed, but also when people car share, they think twice about whether a car is necessary for that trip. According to Susan Shaheen, an expert in Innovative Mobility Research at the University of California at Berkeley, car sharers report reducing their vehicle miles travelled by 44 per cent (addressing travel congestion) and surveys in Europe show CO_2 emissions are being cut by up to 50 per cent per user.[24] Can you imagine the cumulative environmental savings if even a quarter of the 600 million vehicles on the road were switched to car sharing?

Zipcar is getting people to change their car ownership habits by using the same psychological and sociological pulls of brand that got us to want to buy and own to get us to want to share. The white-and-green bus billboards for Zipcar with the messages '350 hours a year having sex. 420 looking for parking' and 'Today's a BMW day. Or is it a Volvo day?' highlight key benefits of car sharing: convenience and choice. Most people buy a car to meet the functional need of getting from A to B. But their choice of vehicle, as with most products, is influenced by the brand. With car sharing, drivers can pick whatever brand fits their mood that day. The service delivers not just 'wheels when you want them' (the Zipcar tagline) but the choice of 'wheels you really want'. And just like cult car and motorcycle brands such as Mini and Harley-Davidson, Zipcar embraces the need to create communities of members who feel connected to one another through some shared purpose or principle. Indeed, for some people, proclaiming you are a 'Zipster' is as important and carries as much cachet as having the latest iPhone.

Bruce Jeffreys, founder of GoGet, the largest car-sharing service in Australia, says that what he refers to as 'low product monogamy' and the 'consumer philandering' it produces are key factors in the growth of his business. The trend experts call this dynamic 'transumerism' and attribute its emergence to living in a consumer world with so many choices. The consumer culture of the last century has left us with a deep desire for choice. Product service systems can cater to the desire for 'just one more' but without the creation of waste. The 'what do we feel like today?' mentality makes the option of picking and swapping between a Prius, a Mini Cooper, a Toyota estate, and an eight-person people carrier appealing. As Paul Boutin wrote in *Slate*, 'Zipcar makes car sharing sexy not sorry,' and 'Car sharing turns members into automotive swingers, free from having to commit to one model.'

If one product can be used by multiple people, the need for the production and disposal of multiple, duplicative 'copies' of that product is reduced.[25] Every car-share vehicle on the road replaces seven to eight owned vehicles, as people sell their cars or decide against buying a second or third vehicle. Usage PSSs have the potential to disrupt traditional industries centred on exclusive ownership – electronics, durables, fashion, appliances, children's toys, household tools – and to turn on its head the concept of planned or perceived obsolescence. When we shift towards an economy based on maximizing units of usage rather than the amounts of units sold, eco-efficiency and business efficiency align. Business can generate new revenue streams from membership charges and micropayments. Zipcar charges $75 to become a member and then $8 per hour. In 2009, this fee schedule added up to a profitable year, with revenues of more than $130 million. In contrast, car sales declined by more than 40 per cent.

Bill Ford, automobile giant Ford's executive chairman, admitted in an interview with CNN in 2009, 'The future of transportation will be a blend of things like Zipcar, public transportation, and private car ownership. Not only do I not fear that, but I think it's a great opportunity for us to participate in the changing nature of car ownership.'[26] Car-sharing companies are not telling people not to drive; they are enabling them not to own.[27] Subsequently, a growing segment of society is reinventing the story we have been told about how we get around. Green guru Joel Makower commented in a recent article, 'Can you imagine when we reach a point where not owning a car becomes the ultimate luxury and its own kind of status symbol?'[28] This transition has started.

Reversing Take, Make, Waste

Ray Anderson, founder of Interface, the world's largest commercial carpet company, is a pioneer of extended-life PSS. Extended-life product service systems focus on after-sales services such as maintenance, repairs, upgrading or reuse that extend the life of a product as well as the user's relationship with it. Except for food and personal hygiene consumables, it's actually quite hard to think of a product for which the concept focusing on 'point of service' over 'point of sale' would not work.

Anderson founded his company in 1973, and for more than twenty years built it into the largest commercial producer of modular square carpet tiles for office buildings, airport lounges and other institutions. But this all changed in 1994 around his sixtieth birthday, when he had what he refers to as his 'conversion experience'. Anderson was advised that sales reps were for the first time being asked by customers, 'What is your company doing for the environment?' They did not have a good answer. His research department decided to convene a worldwide task force to determine Interface's environmental position and asked Anderson to give a speech to launch this initiative. As he later recalled in his book Mid-Course Correction, 'In my whole life I had never given one thought to what my company or I were taking from the earth, or doing to the earth. I did not have an environmental vision. I did not want to make that speech.'[29] But, fortuitously, two weeks before the speech, one of his sales managers handed him a book she had been given by her daughter, who worked for Washington's Environmental Protection Agency. The book was Paul Hawken's The Ecology of Commerce. That evening, Anderson thumbed through the book looking for inspiration and stopped at the page with the arresting heading 'The Death of Birth', an expression for species extinction. He kept reading. In his softly spoken Georgian accent, Anderson now tells audiences about how it was 'an epiphanic moment, a deep spear in the chest' when he realized he was the epitome of 'a plunderer of the earth'. He recalls, 'I wept.' The CEO was particularly struck by Hawken's argument that 'the only institution on earth that is large enough, powerful enough, wealthy enough, pervasive enough, and influential to lead humankind out of the mess it's making for itself is the same institution that is doing the most damage – the institution of business and industry, my institution.'[30]

Anderson made his speech, openly drawing on Hawken's material. He challenged his engineers to figure out how much stuff was required to manufacture the million pounds plus of synthetic fabric Interface produced. He was flabbergasted to discover that it amounted to more than 1.2 billion pounds of raw materials (most of it incinerated oil and natural gas) along with more than seven tonnes of air pollutants every year.[31] He decided that Interface would change the way it did business and become 'the first fully sustainable industrial enterprise, anywhere' by 2020. From the factory floor to the R&D lab, Interface made massive changes during the first few years, including switching exclusively to renewable power sources, reducing waste, using nontoxic materials and working out how to get carpet to stick to floor without glue. But Anderson realized that for his company to reverse what he refers to as the 'take, make, waste' cycle, he would need to change the way his customers thought about acquiring carpet. It would need to lease carpet, not sell it.

Reimagining the Larger System

The idea was simple in principle. Interface would offer a bundled service package that would include everything from 'soup to nuts': designing layouts and installing, maintaining and cleaning the carpet for customers. When a customer noticed that tiles had worn thin, not only would Interface come and replace them, but it would take the old tiles and use them as raw materials for new carpet. And so the process would continue over and over again. Anderson was creating what environmental designers refer to as a 'closed loop' system. Interface would produce zero waste and be responsible for reclaiming its own products from end to end. This virtuous circle incentivizes manufacturers not only to make better products but also to offer new services. In the hyper-consumption model, ownership of and responsibility for the product transfer to the consumer and the point of sale, creating a 'use and dump' culture and a lot of waste. With an extended-life PSS, the company's responsibility does not end when the product is manufactured or sold – it is accountable for the entire life cycle.

The foundation for moving towards a service economy (also known as the functional economy) is already being built.[32] Global giants across sectors have changed their business models and redefined what they offer, moving from being product sellers to being service providers. Xerox (photocopiers to document services), Steelcase (office furniture to office furnishing systems), AT&T (phone products to communication packages), Pitney Bowes (postage products to mail management systems) and IBM (hardware and software goods to business solutions) all have made the core purpose of their business to sell the function their products provide.[33] The risks of product commoditization are one reason for this shift; another is that the profit margins are higher in a product–service mix than in the 'pure sale of products'.[34]

Some companies may at first think that the extra responsibility of an extended-life PSS is too costly. But not only can manufacturers reuse the raw materials or components of goods; by supplying repair, maintenance and product upgrades, companies profit from the sale of additional services and keep in closer contact with customers. Anderson refers to this system as 'cyclical capitalism.' He points out that it's a more profitable business model. From 1995 to 1996, during the switch over to an extended-life PSS, Interface's sales grew from $800 million to $1 billion and the amount of raw materials used by the company dropped almost 20 per cent per dollar of sales.[35] The decline in the company's cost of goods more than covered for the transformation in systems required to effectively deliver the service. As Anderson comments, 'This dispels the myth of the false choice between the environment and the economy.'[36]

The greatest threat to the growing number of beleaguered consumer product companies such as the car and the domestic appliance industries is not the product service systems themselves but the influence they have to radically change how people think of ownership altogether. A similar story of disruption occurred in the music industry: iTunes did not change music per se but transformed the way we buy and experience music. Services such as Zipcar, Bag Borrow and Steal, SolarCity, and DenimTherapy are not reinventing their industry's product but reimagining the larger system within which their product operates.

BEFORE

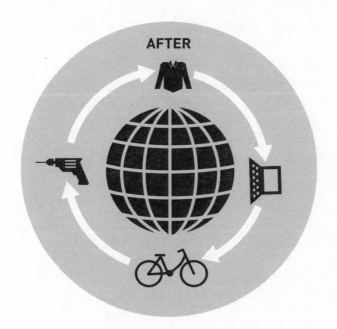

REDISTRIBUTION MARKETS

SIX

What Goes Around Comes Around

Deron Beal is a long and lean man in his mid-forties. During his career, among other things, he has been a finance manager with Procter & Gamble, a member of the US State Department diplomatic corps, a part of a theatre group and a student of literature in Germany. These days Beal spends much of his time running Freecycle, a massive reuse network often referred to as the 'eco eBay'. He works out of his former guest bedroom in Tucson, Arizona, and admits that he likes 'shuffling down the hall in his slippers to go to work'. Everything in his office – two laptop computers, a couple of desks, bookshelves, lamp, fax machine, filing cabinets, even his wastepaper basket – he got from Freecycle. But he does confess that he had to buy his high-back leather office chair. At six feet six inches tall, he found it hard to get one to fit his frame.

Beal started Freecycle in May 2003. At the time, he was director of Rise, a small nonprofit organization that picked up and recycled office supplies from computers to furniture for local businesses in Tucson. He was astounded not just by how much good stuff was given to the organization but by how hard it was to work out what to do with it. Beal would spend hours driving around and calling charities trying to pass on the goods they had collected. Around the same time he got married and moved into a bungalow home with his wife. Their newly merged household created doubles that they needed to get rid of, including a queen-size bed. 'Have you ever tried to get rid of a secondhand mattress?' Deron asks when recalling the beginnings of Freecycle. 'It can be just about impossible.' Most charity stores won't take beds, and none of his friends or co-workers needed one. Frustrated that there was not an easier way to find homes for his unwanted items, and reluctant to take a perfectly good bed to the dump, Beal thought, 'Why don't I just make up a mailing list on Yahoo! for the gifting of used items and open it up to anyone who wants to join?' Freecycle was born. It went from eighty to eight hundred members in just three weeks.

Today Beal admits he is amazed at 'just how big it has gotten.' Freecycle is now one of the fastest-growing grassroots movements in the world, with more than 7 million members across more than ninety-five countries from Australia to Russia to Singapore and Germany and even places such as the Occupied Palestinian Territories. In 2007, Yahoo! ranked Freecycle as the third-most searched environmental term on the planet, following only 'global warming' and 'recycling'.[1] Its appeal, however, reaches beyond the 'green' audience. Beal has appeared on popular television shows, was featured in Time magazine's 'Top 50 Most Influential Entrepreneurs', and has shared space with the celebrities in the pages of People magazine.

Freecycle.org is a virtual sidewalk where people can unload everything from half-used cans of paint to old sofas and carpets to fish tanks. It is based on the premise that there is 'No such thing as waste, it is just useful stuff in the wrong place.' The way it works is simple. From the main Freecycle site, members form local groups (in February 2010, there were more than 4,885 local groups) so that people never have to travel very far to pick up an item.[2] Users post short messages describing what they want to give away or items they may be looking for. Lists resemble a sample you might get if you did a big scoop at an urban dump. A recent posting for a New York City group that has more than 2,500 members reads: 'Offer: Rusty wheelbarrow. Old but works perfectly well.' 'Wanted: 24-foot+ Ethernet cable.' 'Offer: Huge pad of reflective paper . . . perfect for school art projects.' 'Wanted: 50-pound bag of cement for home building project.' 'Offer: fallen oak tree chopped into firewood; enough to last all winter.' 'Wanted: working clothes dryer.' According to Beal, 99 per cent of things get taken in a relatively short period of time, sometimes in just a matter of minutes. And this includes even stuff that charities such as Goodwill or the Samaritans would have to throw away (Beal later found out this is a staggering 50 to 75 per cent of things donated), or simply things they do not accept, such as broken appliances or piles of gravel. As Beal repeats the maxim, 'One person's trash is another person's treasure.'

Used goods have been exchanged for centuries. The first known handwritten notices listing goods people wanted or goods they had to give away were nailed to posts and walls and date back to fifteenth-century England. Some of America's and England's earliest entrepreneurs were the nineteenth-century 'peddler traders' or 'ragmen' who roamed collecting anything with resale value. Organizations such as the Salvation Army redistributed unwanted goods beginning in the 1850s and 'Waste as Wealth' or 'Don't Waste Wealth' were the mottos du jour during both world wars and the Great Depression that came between them. But the culture and age of throwaway living that arose in the 1950s narrowed our view of what stuff was good to reuse or pass on.

Despite the emergence of recycling programmes and the perseverance of scattered garage and yard sales, selling, swapping or gifting used or pre-owned goods are no longer second nature to most people. Such exchanges have not been particularly efficient through off-line channels, but in the Internet age, redistribution is becoming a way of life.

Collapse of 'Transaction Costs'

When we asked Beal which are the most commonly listed items on Freecycle, he explained that 'there isn't one particular thing' but instead massive categories of 'inconvenient things' (old pianos, sofas and televisions) and 'unusual items' (disco balls, fish tanks and even stuffed animals). These are the items that would have been a pain to lug to the dump (and sometimes you would even have to pay to dispose of them) or tricky to unload on a neighbour. The transaction costs to ensure they were kept in use, not in landfill, would have been high. In his paper 'The Nature of the Firm', economist and Nobel laureate Ronald Coase coined the term 'transaction costs' to refer to the cost of making any form of exchange or participating in a market.[3] If you go to the supermarket, for example, and buy some groceries, your costs are not just the price of the groceries but the energy, time and effort required to write your list, travel to and from the shop, wheel around your trolley and choose your products, wait in the checkout queue, and unpack and put away the groceries when you get back home. Your total 'costs' are greater than the dollar number on your receipt.

In the pre-Internet age, the transaction costs of coordinating groups of people with aligned wants and needs or even just similar interests were high, making the sharing of products tricky and inconvenient. Redistributing unwanted goods in and outside your immediate community was inefficient. Matching someone with something to give with another person who wanted that same item was not straightforward. Just think of what it took to find a new owner for a perfectly good desk you no longer wanted. You put an ad in the paper, drove around and posted signs in shops or community boards, asked your friends or co-workers if they needed a desk, and maybe visited local schools or charities. Not only was the likelihood of a match low, but the time and effort required were likely to be too high to make it worthwhile. Your best solution was to hire a van to haul it off to the dump, while someone else out there who would have been delighted with your desk went out and bought one.

We have grown attuned to leaping across indissoluble social boundaries by living in an age of what thought leader Peter Kaminsky refers to as 'ridiculously easy group forming'.[4] 'It's so easy,' he explains, to self-assemble groups, packs, pods, tribes, bands, mobs, crowds or whatever you want to call them that 'it happens without even thinking about it.' Whether it is a 'reply all' function in an email; an open community notice board such as craigslist; a global auction system such as eBay; a 'swaptrading' marketplace such as Swap; or an online registry network such as Freecycle, there is now a boundless marketplace for connecting pre-owned or secondary goods from where they are not needed to somewhere or someone where they are. Moving unwanted goods from nonuse to reuse is now practical, convenient and worthwhile. This development is fuelling the second model of Collaborative Consumption, redistribution markets, a system that brings together the four principles of Collaborative Consumption: trust between strangers, the power of idling capacity, belief in the commons, and critical mass.

Matching Supply with Demand

Marty Metro has an MBA from the University of Arizona, worked for a 'Big 6' consulting firm, and spent ten years specializing in building enterprise technology systems for Fortune 500 companies. Metro had to move around a lot for his career. With each move, he tried to avoid buying new boxes, partly because he refused to pay the exorbitant prices, but also to help save trees. Finding used boxes required spending a couple of days collecting them from work, the grocery store, the off licence, friends and neighbours. With every move, he was surprised at just how many he needed and how much time it took to collect enough.

In early 2002, after his fifteenth move, the business opportunity hit Metro. 'Why isn't there a single place we can go to get all these used boxes?' he recalls. With his supply chain background, Metro realized that with a little technology and a little marketing, 'We could pull everyone together and get the boxes for cheap and sell them for cheap.' Metro also figured that 'If there were an easy way to pass the boxes on, most of us would do it.' When Metro dug deeper into his idea, he discovered that 42 million people move every year in the United States alone. And moving boxes were nothing compared with the $120 billion worth of cardboard boxes around the world that flood businesses and retailers every day. He was also shocked to discover that cardboard recycling is something of a misnomer. In many cases, the used boxes Americans unpack are shipped to China, where the cardboard is recycled into pulp to make more boxes, which are then used to ship televisions, mobile phones, and other goods back to the United States and Europe. The ones that don't make it back to China often end up in landfill, in the United States. But regardless of the outcome, millions of cardboard boxes are used just once.

In late 2002, Metro launched UsedCardboardBoxes.com in a small warehouse in Los Angeles. Within one year, the space was not big enough to keep up with incoming and outgoing boxes. By 2006, with venture capital backing, Metro opened eight other distribution centres across the United States and Canada and was able to service any residential address in the continental United States.

Today, UsedCardboardBoxes.com 'rescues' boxes from big companies nationwide. Every box is inspected to check that it is not ripped, torn or soiled and then repackaged into moving kits. The 'Pack Rat' kit that comes with sixty-eight boxes, plus three marker pens, three box cutters, packing materials and six tape guns costs $161, including shipping. To buy the boxes alone new from a company such as Box Brothers would cost about $248. Metro admits that he is an entrepreneur who wants to make money but that he is also proud of the environmental impact his company makes. 'We now resell millions of boxes a year. Every used box we sell replaces the need for a box to be made.' The company also offers a free service (Freecardboardboxes.com) that matches people who have boxes to give with people who want boxes, city by city.

This simple example illustrates the potential for social networks to match supply and demand through a nearly instantaneous mass synchronization of wants or needs in which both sides always gain. The resulting linkage of people with disparate motivations is the definition of a vibrant marketplace. As with other forms of Collaborative Consumption, some people use the system for 'green' reasons or out of generosity, but there are also large numbers of people using these markets for self-interest, whether that is to make money or save money.

Unconsumption

The obvious environmental benefit of redistribution markets is that they keep stuff circulating, maximizing use and extending the life span of individual items. It is estimated that a staggering 24,000 items (amounting to 700 tonnes of stuff kept out of landfills) are passed on through Freecycle every day. But more importantly, redistribution reduces the waste and the carbon emissions and resources that go along with new production. Even if the reused goods have to be shipped or picked up by car, this transfer creates less impact than the materials and transportation required in the production of every new product or its eventual disposal into landfill. William McDonough, co-author of *Cradle to Cradle*, calculated that a product itself contains only 5 per cent of the raw materials used to produce it. And environmental thought leader Paul Hawken estimates that for every 100 pounds of product made, 3,200 pounds of waste are produced, a 32-to-1 ratio.[5] If you passed an old sofa to someone else, not only would you be keeping approximately 100 pounds out of landfill, but you'd also be saving the 3,200 pounds of waste that would have gone into making a new sofa. The EPA estimated that 98 per cent of all waste is industrial (and a large percentage is made manufacturing new products) and only 2 per cent is household waste. As much as we recycle our paper, bottles and plastic, the biggest way to help prevent waste is to buy less new stuff and reuse and redistribute more of what we already have.

The second benefit and unintended consequence of reuse is community building. As Deron Beal, Freecycle founder, explains, 'Unlike putting something on the curb where it just disappears, you actually get to pick who receives your item. Maybe it is a single mother or someone who is going off to college or a local non-profit organization, it is up to you. Eventually you meet that person face-to-face when they pick the item up from you.'[6] When Beal picked up a George Foreman grill from a family who happened to live one block from him, they handed him half a dozen fresh eggs. The family kept a chicken coop and had extra eggs that week. Rather than let them go to waste, they passed them on. Through these interactions a wealth of connections between people, neighbours, and strangers generates social capital. And unlike other forms of capital associated with hyper-consumerism, such as money or materials that become depleted after they are used, the social capital generated by Freecycle grows every time something is passed on – from families who have received baby gear they could not otherwise afford to schools that furnished gyms with free equipment to elderly people who have received wheelchairs or walking canes.

One of the most memorable stories Beal told us was about one-hundred-year-old Weldon Irby, who lives in Tucson with his wife, Jackye. Before he retired, Weldon had spent his whole life fixing machines as a mechanical superintendent at Pima Mine, a local milling factory. 'He's been mechanical since he was a little boy,' Jackye explained. When Weldon heard about Freecycle in 2005 (he was ninety-two at the time), he had been looking for ways to give back to his community. He realized that he could collect old bikes, fix them and give them to local families. Weldon says, 'A lot of those leftover bicycles just need a little TLC and they're ready to go again.' Weldon's work doesn't end when he gives away bicycles, though. He tells recipients to bring the bike back in if they have a flat tyre or for more serious repairs.

Beal himself has given a lot of stuff away, including a telescope, a table and a weight set. 'I got an email from the guy I gave the weight set to, and he told me he'd lost twenty pounds of fat and gained ten pounds of muscle in the past two months,' Beal says. 'I told him, well, that's great – I lost two hundred pounds of weight when I got rid of the thing.' He is under strict instructions from his wife, Jen, whom he affectionately refers to as the 'minimalist in the family', that 'he can give but he can't receive.' Indeed, she recently put the kibosh on his plan to get more stuff, including twelve land post poles to re-landscape their backyard.

Freecycle members say getting rid of old stuff can feel as good as getting new stuff. Some even describe the process as addictive and find themselves wondering, 'What else can I give away?' New York Times columnist Rob Walker labelled this experience 'unconsumption', explaining that 'what Freecycle has done is channel the same blend of utility and pleasure that motivates consumption itself.'[7] The moment when people thank you for giving them something you planned to throw away, behavioural economists would describe as the proverbial 'warm inner glow' you feel after performing an altruistic action. A team of leading neuroscientists at the National Institutes of Health recently conducted a series of brain scan experiments to see if altruism is hardwired. Nineteen participants were given a series of choices about whether to donate $128 to charity or to accept it for themselves. The scans revealed that when people took the money, the part of the brain normally associated with selfish pleasures like eating and sex lit up. But an entirely different part of the brain associated with bonding and attachment lit up for those who chose to give the money away.[8]

I'll Help You, Someone Else Helps Me

Anthropologists and socioeconomists have spent decades examining the principle of people responding to a positive action with another positive action, referred to as 'direct reciprocity'. The roots of the term are indeed *re* and *pro*, meaning back and forth, to and fro between people.[9] The well-known phrase 'You scratch my back, and I'll scratch yours' might sound cynical; another, 'Do unto others as they do unto you,' sounds more idealistic – but both capture the belief that humans have an innate propensity to reciprocate. We understand that it is in our long-term self-interest to do so. Robert Cialdini explains, 'The rule for reciprocation allows one individual to give something to another with confidence that it is not being lost. This sense of future obligation within the rule makes possible the development of various kinds of continuing relationships, transactions, and exchanges that are beneficial to the society.'[10] It's easy to see how cooperation worked in times when transactions took place between relatives, neighbours or members of the same small village, when the exchange was face-to-face, and when people could easily keep track of their interactions. But what happens in communities where the giving and taking are happening between people who don't know one another and who are geographically dispersed?

In social networks, the reciprocation becomes indirect (indirect reciprocity). No longer is it based on the simple premise 'I'll help you, if you help me.'[11] Now the cooperative dynamic becomes 'I'll help you, someone *else* helps me.' During the final stages of writing this book, Rachel's Twitter account was hacked. In the middle of the night, thousands of spam messages were sent to her followers saying 'hey. I lost weight and FEEL great . . . I did it with Free acai berry from here: http://z8.ro/4e2' When she woke up and opened her email she had emails from more than twenty-five people from her Twitter following. 'Rachel, if no one's alerted you, thought I'd let you know I suspect your Twitter was hacked. . . .' and 'You usually post useful links and insights but I just received a weird DM (direct message) about "acai berry" diets. I think you have been hacked.' When Rachel contacted Twitter, she was amazed to discover that several people from her Twitter community had already alerted Twitter about the problem and it had been fixed, all whilst she had been asleep. When she was asked to fill out a report form to help prevent others from getting hacked in the future, Twitter framed the request as 'sharing is caring.' Nowadays if Rachel sees that one of the people she follows has been hacked, she is motivated to return the favour by sending the person a message and contacting Twitter, even if it is not one of the same people who directly helped her.

A culture of 'indirect reciprocity' is often referred to as the 'gift economy', one where people give goods and services without any explicit agreement for immediate or future reward.[12] This model is at work in Freecycle. Unwanted items or boxes are given away with no written agreement but with the implicit understanding that givers may one day want to post something they want to receive. In many ways, Freecycle has the same motivational currency that is fuelling networks of open source projects such as Twitter or Flickr where you allow people to download your photos and vice versa. These systems require a new kind of trust and reciprocity, a behavioural dynamic that in turn reinforces sharing, collaboration, honour, sociability and loyalty.

Get Out of the Way

In the same way that shared commodities such as information, knowledge and media have become increasingly cooperative, the reusing or passing on of stuff is becoming a vehicle for forming trust between strangers. Beal has a passionate philosophy that 'you bring out that goodness in people if you create organizations that are fundamentally built on values of honesty.' Another pioneer in redistribution markets who shares this view is the person *Time* magazine referred to as 'the wizard of the local web', Craig Newmark, the founder of craigslist. As Newmark puts it, 'Trust is the new black.'

As most people know, craigslist is essentially a community marketplace devoted to serving the everyday needs of people – whether you're looking for furniture, a job, an apartment, a nanny or a pet. Beyond its community features that include 'discussion forums', 'lost and found', and 'job postings', craigslist functions like Freecycle, where members form local 'hubs' and post what they need or what they want to sell or give away. The key difference is that people generally charge for stuff on craigslist. It's not usually free.

Newmark, just like Beal, created one of the Internet's most popular sites almost by accident. He started it in 1995 by sending his friends and co-workers a list of cool art and technology events in San Francisco. Gradually, it spread into the wider community. 'People started sending me more and more stuff, such as job listings, stuff to sell, and apartment rentals to add to the list, and more and more people asked to be added to it,' Newmark says. Within two years, he had thousands of readers, most of whom he didn't know.[13] From there it has grown into the world's most popular website for classified ads, with more than seven hundred local sites across seventy countries from Romania to Kenya to Canada. The site has 47 million unique users every month in the United States alone – nearly a fifth of the nation's adult population.[14] Worldwide it receives approximately 20 billion page views per month, making it the seventh most viewed site on the Internet. Newmark observes, 'This all happened without my intervention and when I saw what was happening most of what I did was just keep out of the way.' Jeff Jarvis, author of *What Would Google Do?* refers to the strategy of 'Get Out of the Way' as 'Craig's Law'. As Newmark explained to Jarvis, 'If you make a great platform that people really want to use, then the worst thing you could do is to put yourself in the middle, getting in the way of what people want to do with it.'[15]

Beyond defining some basic underlying rules, both Beal and Newmark placed the control and decision making in the hands of members. On craigslist it is as simple as 'Treat other people as you want to be treated.' Freecycle groups around the world all adhere to this rule: 'Keep it free, legal, and appropriate for all ages.' Other than that, local groups designate their own moderators to resolve issues that may come up and to self-police the community. Of course, a small percentage 'cheats' the system with spam and false postings. Newmark himself dedicates much of his time to catching the 'bad guys out there'. Early on he introduced a flagging system where tens of thousands of users identify spam or inappropriate postings. Instead of sending offenders nasty emails, Newmark and Jim Buckmaster, the current CEO, have introduced a reproach that involves a Japanese form of poetry, haiku. If you try to double- or triple-post the same message, something like this might appear: 'A wafer thin mint that's been sent before it seems one is enough, thanks.'[16]

Considering the size and diversity of exchanges occurring within these networks, instances of fraud or misbehaviour are remarkable anomalies. Ori Brafman and Rod Beckstrom write in the *The Starfish and the Spider* about the 'unstoppable power of leaderless organizations' and say that 'craigslist members feel that the site is a community and tend to put more faith in a fellow craigslist user than they would in a person off the street. Members assume the best of each other, and generally that's what they get in return.' Both Beal and Newmark were revolutionary in thinking of their users from the outset as interconnected members or a community of stakeholders, not isolated consumers.

Freecycle and craigslist show how the Internet can be used to create vast decentralized systems of redistribution that are predominantly self-organized. Beal and Newmark both believe that their networks have grown so rapidly because they are simple enough to be self-managed. They provided the minimum infrastructure to empower members to work things out among themselves. To paraphrase a point made in an article in *Wired* magazine on craigslist, it's actually the lack of helpful features on these networks that 'signals us to activate our own methods of reassurance'.[17] As with so many other forms of Collaborative Consumption, by pushing power back out to its users, these redistribution markets encourage people to manage their own actions and the actions of the entire community. This in turn creates high degrees of trust and reciprocity to efficiently move surplus stuff from nonuse to reuse.

Our Inner Ledger of Fairness

Every second of every day, buyers and sellers trade $2,000 worth of goods, a majority of which are used, refurbished or vintage, on the grandfather of reuse marketplaces, eBay.[18] Every minute, a second-hand vehicle changes hands on eBay Motors, without ever being taken for a test drive. All this happens between complete strangers with no guarantees the goods they pay for will even arrive, let alone be in the condition they expect. And yet most buyers get what they pay for. 'To some economists,' writes Christoph Uhlhaas in his article for *Scientific American Mind*, 'this is a borderline miracle because it contradicts the concept of economic man as a rational, selfish person who single-mindedly strives for maximum profit. According to this notion, sellers should pocket buyers' payments and send nothing in return. For their part, buyers should not trust sellers – and the market should collapse.'[19]

In traditional shops, before we buy something new, we go through an in-person examination. Whether it's the fruit we pick up and squeeze, the labels we inspect or the fabrics we touch, these experiential tools allow us to determine the desirability of a product. We also get a good indication of the reputation and quality of the goods being sold just by walking through the shop door. Even in 'old-fashioned' secondhand marketplaces such as car-boot sales or flea markets, we can look a seller in the eye and ask, 'Does it work?' or 'How long have you had it for?' or even 'Why are you selling it?' And if you decide to make a purchase, it's usually a simultaneous action of handing over payment and walking away with the goods. In online markets such as eBay that sell secondhand goods, these 'tools of reputation' do not exist.[20] You can't physically inspect an item; you may be buying from a seller for the first time; users are free to choose a trader identity, even a pseudonym; and on top of all these points of doubt, you pay without any guarantee your goods will be shipped. How do I know you will actually ship the Tiffany bracelet in time for Valentine's Day? Yet even if you just go by sales volume alone ($100 billion over ten years), eBay follows what Harvard political economy professor Richard Zeckhauser coined as Yhprum's law: 'Sometimes systems that should not work, work nevertheless.' (It's the reverse of Murphy's law, the popular adage that 'Anything that can go wrong will go wrong.') How does a system that shuttles vast quantities of used goods among distant strangers work so well?

For decades behavioural economists wondered whether our sense of fairness is as much a part of human nature as is our obvious sense of competition. The answer to this question is critical to redistribution markets. People's ability to determine what is fair and what is not plays a big role in making these peer-to-peer reuse systems work. In the 'ultimatum game', the classic experiment in behavioural economics that attempts to understand how fairness works, two people are paired together. Player A, randomly assigned, is known as the proposer. He or she is handed a sum of ten $1 bills (the total amount is irrelevant). The proposer's job is to decide how the $10 should be split and to make an offer. No dialogue or negotiation between the players is allowed. Player B, the responder, is then given the chance to accept or reject the offer. The twist is that if the responder rejects the sum of money offered by the proposer, both walk away empty-handed.

Does the proposer lowball? Does he split the money evenly? Is he overly generous? When Werner Güth first played the game in the 1980s, he and his colleagues predicted that the proposer would offer the lowest possible amount – in this case one dollar – and the responder would always accept. Why? Player A has the control of the split, so the rational and selfish thing for him to do is propose an offer that gives him the highest amount, in this case $9. For Player B, a dollar is better than nothing, making it in his or her rational interest to accept whatever is offered. The game was played over and over all around the world, from Taiwan to Israel to Pittsburgh to France to Java. The degree of cooperation varied, but researchers observed two consistent outcomes. First, any lowball offers perceived as unfair were almost always rejected by the responder. People will turn down free money rather than let someone else walk away with too much. They don't care that they would be better off with something rather than nothing. They care about what is fair.[21] Second, proposers almost always made fair offers, close to a fifty-fifty split, to ensure the offer would be accepted. In most games, the average amount offered was $4.71. This scenario is like giving a child a packet of M&M's and telling him it's up to him to choose how to share it with a friend, with the caveat that he and his friend must both be happy with what they get, or no sweets. And the child tips almost half the bag of M&M's into his friend's hand. Behavioural economists later discovered that the primary reason a proposer makes a fair offer is that he or she can imagine how the responder will feel and anticipate rejection and anger. Jonah Lehrer writes in *The Decisive Moment*, 'That ability to sympathize with the feelings of others leads to fairness.'[22]

Our inner ledger of fairness is critical to why eBay works so well. For the most part, sellers offer their secondhand goods for a fair price based on what they think the item is worth. They can protect themselves by setting a minimum price, but regardless, buyers usually make a fair bid (whether it's through an auction or the 'Buy It Now' format) that they feel will have a good chance of getting an 'accept'. Economist Axel Ockenfels has spent years investigating patterns of trading, negotiation and cooperation. He explains that 'buyers generally will not accept unfair offers and sellers seem to realize that.'[23] The same applies to sellers, who for the most part won't accept offers when bidders are lowballing. 'It is not a question of doing something to benefit the other party,' notes Ockenfels, 'but a reciprocal behaviour: as you treat me, so I will treat you.'[24]

Shadow of the Future

Like so many other forms of Collaborative Consumption, eBay is successful because of the bottom-up community ecosystem that founder Pierre Omidyar calls an 'of the people, by the people, for the people' environment.[25] In February 1996, when eBay was just six months old, Omidyar wrote a letter to all users: 'Most people are honest. And they mean well. . . . But some people are dishonest. Or deceptive. . . . It's a fact of life. But here, those people can't hide. We'll drive them away.'[26] Omidyar was referring to what has become the most well-known Internet reputation system, which he first introduced to help members assess and share feedback from their selling experiences.

After any transaction, both the buyer and the seller have the opportunity to rate each other's performance. There are three types of feedback a user can leave: 1 (positive), 0 (neutral) or −1 (negative). Users also have just one line to write a short comment or to explain why they gave this rating. Typical comments are along the lines of 'Item received as described. Thanks.' Or 'Seller was extremely helpful. Would highly recommend.' On the flip side, if the buyers did not receive their goods or the goods were not as they had expected, they post comments such as 'Paid through PayPal but never received items. Seller is a rip-off.' Once users have reached a certain amount of points, they receive a star indicating their trustworthiness. The 'Red Shooting Star' is the very highest, for 100,000 points or more, and the 'Yellow Star' is the starting point, for 10 to 49 points. Just as we rate songs on iTunes or films on Netflix or write reviews on TripAdvisor and Amazon, these individual ratings are pooled. Pooling empowers users to take on the responsibility to self-manage the community. As Professor Ockenfels puts it, the reputation system on eBay 'functions like an organized rumor mill'.[27]

The striking thing about the feedback on eBay is that it is so positive. Studies have shown that sellers receive negative feedback only 1 per cent of the time, and buyers 2 per cent.[28] This would indicate that 99 per cent of the used goods traded on eBay are at the minimum satisfactory. So why do people behave so well? It's simple. Users know their behaviour today will affect their ability to transact in the future. People want to buy from sellers with positive ratings, and studies show that items sold by sellers with a strong track record fetch an 8 per cent premium over identical items sold by sellers with low or few ratings.[29] As a result, users will often go to great lengths to protect their reputation. Take Doug McCallum, managing director of eBay in the UK. He had sold without a hitch a car, hi-fi speakers and a fireplace on eBay and had clocked a positive feedback record of about 150. But when he sold his computer, a disappointed buyer wrote to him complaining, 'It's missing the dongle that connected it up.' McCallum explains how he 'scoured the universe for this thing to get it to him, finally finding one in America which meant I made practically nothing on the sale but I did avoid negative feedback.'[30] It's incredible customer service on a peer-to-peer level.

An online peer-to-peer exchange for used children's clothing, thred-Up, was started in the spring of 2010 by James Reinhart, along with his Harvard Business School classmate Chris Homer and former Boston College roommate, Oliver Lubin. The entrepreneurs successfully launched a similar model in September 2009 for women's and men's shirts. Four thousand shirts were exchanged in the first two weeks. But the founders quickly realized that shirts were a niche; the bigger hand-me-down market was in children's clothing. Young children grow out of clothes on average every three to six months, having worn outfits only a couple of times. 'Currently parents are spending upward of $20,000 just on the staples of children's clothing by the time their child is seventeen. And they're retiring some fourteen hundred items!' explained Reinhart.

The entrepreneurs discovered that the problems plaguing existing online children's swap sites were twofold: inconvenience and poor quality. The team had already solved the first problem with the original thredUp model, building an easy-to-use interface and prepaid envelope system that made the experience feel similar to Netflix. But ensuring quality was a big concern, especially for children's clothing. The challenge was to design a reputation system that would encourage members to send only what they themselves would want to receive. The team now refers to this benchmark as the 'Golden thredUp rule'.

Reinhart explained to us how most reputation systems from Yelp to Amazon don't seem to decipher the difference between what people actually care about and what they think they care about. They also seem to focus on building a high level of trust or loyalty but don't pinpoint the single most important behaviour the reputation mechanisms need to encourage or the most 'unforgivable thing'. 'For us it is about how you incentivize quality exchanges. Dirty or poor-quality clothes are not acceptable. Nothing else really matters,' explained Reinhart.

The thredUp founders also recognized that ranking systems were gaining traction on increasingly popular real-time platforms, such as Foursquare, where people are motivated to participate and socially obligated to behave in a certain way to accumulate points and earn reward 'badges'. It is part of a human's innately competitive behaviour to want to be at the top of the scoreboard.

The thredUP team ended up implementing three different tools in its reputation system: the first is a star rating similar to eBay where people are rated on a scale of four stars based on the quality of items sent; the second is 'Stylie Points', a subjective zero-to-ten rating users give, based on the stylishness of the items they receive; and third, users are reviewed based on the punctuality of their shipments. Each reputation mechanism is targeted at the core promises of the thredUp offer: quality, style and speed.

Even though the system is still in its infancy, clothes offered from members with a four-star rating and high number of Stylie points are the first selected. On the flip side, senders who break the quality 'golden rule' are being banned from the thredUp community as other members simply refuse to transact with them.

Both thredUp and eBay are examples of reputation systems that fill the critical trust gap needed to make secondhand product markets work. As with McCallum's 'missing dongle', it's in the seller's best interest to resolve the problem. In the case of thredUP, it's in the members' best interest to send high-quality clothes on time. Robert Axelrod, a political science professor at the University of Michigan, posits that 'people cooperate not because of friendship or trust in each other, but the trust in a promise of keeping a durable relationship that could benefit them in the future.' This tendency he refers to as 'the shadow of the future'.[31] That shadow creates good behaviour in the present, as there are clear incentives for honesty and trust about the price and condition of what they are selling.

The Value of Reused Goods

When Pierre Omidyar first started eBay, it was called AuctionWeb. He put a broken laser pointer up for auction. He was then a software developer, and he posted it on his own personal website as an experiment. He was shocked when the item sold for $14.83. Pierre contacted the winning bidder to make sure he understood that the laser pointer was broken. 'I'm a collector of broken laser pointers,' came the reply. In that moment, Pierre realized that not only did the unwanted stuff that he was going to throw away have value to someone else, but a used marketplace could be big business. Items that may have zero utility to one person may still have a market or usage value to someone else, even if the item is perceived as out-of-date or broken.

In just one year after Omidyar's laser experiment, eBay experienced mind-boggling growth. The value of goods sold in 1996 was $7.2 million. In 1997, it had reached $95 million, with 341,000 registered users. Today there are more than 221 million eBay members who trade more than $52 billion worth of goods every year. That's more than the gross domestic product of 125 of the world's countries.[32] Admittedly, eBay has now grown into a gigantic online store, with a significant percentage of exchanges involving new products. But it undisputedly provides a global infrastructure for the exchange of secondary goods, and the company recently estimated that this secondary market is worth $500 billion.[33]

I Give You This, and You Give Me That

From 1976 to 1982, a classic BBC television show called *Swap Shop* broadcast on Saturday mornings. Hosted by Noel Edmonds, Keith Chegwin and John Craven, it was the archetypal children's programme with a mix of music, celebrity interviews, cartoons and quick news segments. But the most popular aspect, to the BBC's surprise, turned out to be a fifteen-minute segment called 'Swaporama'. Each week Noel would shout from the studio, 'Where are you, Keith?' The camera would then cut to Chegwin, or 'Cheggers', as he became affectionately known, who would rove all over England hosting Swap Parties. Crowds of children, often more than two thousand, would show up with unwanted records, kites, puzzles, books and all other kinds of paraphernalia they wanted to swap for someone else's unwanted toys. They were allowed to trade anything, except pets or siblings. A producer named Rosemary Gill came up with the idea when she recalled how schoolchildren loved to swap things in the playground – stickers, baseball cards, trinkets – and regarded it as an 'eminently useful and practical exercise for children'. But before the show aired, the producers worried that the kids would not swap different items or big toys for smaller toys, as they would perceive this as unfair. They were wrong.

The swaps happened so easily among the children. To paraphrase moral philosopher Adam Smith, they could see 'gain in what they were trading for'. Adult viewers observed that not only did the children know precisely what they were looking for, but the value of a fair trade seemed intuitive. A six-year-old girl from Cardiff swapped her dolls house for a set of hi-fi headphones. A young boy from Northampton swapped his three LPs for a jar of twenty-five old pence coins.

In 2003, anthropologist Sarah F. Brosnan and primatologist Frans B. M. de Waal of Emory University conducted an experiment to determine whether behaviours around trading and fairness is innate. They trained capuchin monkeys to trade pebbles for slices of cucumber. If both monkeys got the same reward, there was never a problem. As de Waal observed, 'You can do it twenty-five times in a row, and they are perfectly happy getting cucumber slices.' But then the scientists changed the pay scale. They gave one monkey a grape – viewed by the other monkeys as more desirable – for the same pebble. The cucumber receivers got agitated and started throwing pebbles out of the cage. Things only got worse when a few monkeys were given a grape for doing nothing at all. Some of them rebelled by stopping eating and 80 per cent of the time they stopped trading. The monkeys had learned that the fair trade was pebble for cucumber. As Margaret Atwood writes in *Payback*, 'These animals have strong opinions about the distribution of goods and the fair rate of exchange – refusing to trade a cucumber slice for a pebble, when the neighbour is getting grape.'[34] Like capuchin monkeys, humans often become focused on what something is worth and what constitutes a fair exchange. And if we experience what researchers call an inequity aversion, we refuse to trade altogether, even if we would be better off taking what we can get.

Most of us also don't want to spend a lot of time searching for the right trades among large numbers of people. You know someone, somewhere will want what you have, but how do you find him? And as we've seen, it's an innate consumer reaction to want to choose from a range of many products rather than just accept the one item someone is offering. But new automated online 'swap trading' marketplaces solve these practical coordination and valuation challenges and overcome emotional barriers to trading used goods. Swap sites range from focusing on one specific category of goods such as children's gear (Kizoodle), books (ReadItSwapIt), clothes (Swapstyle), DVDs (SwapDVD) or video games (SplitGames) to diverse marketplaces where you don't necessarily have to swap like for like, such as Swap. All operate as vast infrastructures for matching what you 'have to swap' with what you 'want to swap'.

College friends Greg Boesel and Mark Hexamer started to think about online swap trading in 2004, a time when peer-to-peer precursor sites such as craigslist, Freecycle and Netflix were taking off. The pair had met while studying for graduate degrees at Boston College and had already created a successful legal software company together. As Hexamer recalls, 'The inspiration for their site was really a whole bunch of things, as opposed to one "a-ha" moment.' They began to notice that their nephews played a new $55 video game for a couple of weeks and then got bored with it. Their friends with children would watch videos such as Shrek and The Little Mermaid numerous times but would quickly move on to their next favourite film. Boesel's and Hexamer's mothers would swap books with their friends without thinking about it. And their own shelves were full of DVDs and CDs they would neither watch nor listen to again. The final impetus was when Boesel, like so many readers, devoured The Da Vinci Code in a matter of days. After he turned the last page he wondered, 'What do I with this book now?' He did not want to throw it away or go through the hassle of selling it for a few dollars on eBay. Boesel proposed to Hexamer, 'Could we create a site that would let people swap any product for the same value as what they're offering?'

The Six Degrees of Swap Trading

As maths whizzes, the two friends started to think about the algorithms that would enable trades to happen instantly. They realized the key would be to calculate an equal value of goods to automatically ensure an undeniably fair exchange. And not just for two-way direct trades but for three-way cross-media trades that would, as Hexamer put it, 'explode the system'. For example, in a three-way, user A would send a CD to User B, User B would send a DVD to User C, and User C would send a video game to User A. The problem Boesel and Hexamer had to solve was much aligned to Chris Anderson's Long Tail concept, the niche strategy of selling (or in this case, trading) large numbers of unique items in small quantities.[35] How would a person in Iowa who wants to trade an unwanted Wii Super Mario Galaxy 2 for a PlayStation Sims 2 find a match?

The site Boesel and Hexamer ended up launching in 2007, Swap-Tree, renamed Swap.com in 2010, solves this problem in sixty milliseconds. You enter the UPC (for Super Mario Galaxy 2 it's 045496900434) or IBSN on the back of the box (this code is used to identify the edition, release or version, and thereby determine the value) in a little green box. You then mark the condition of the item from 'worn' to 'never used'. When we tried this system out on Swap, 132,209 items popped up that could be traded for the Super Mario Galaxy, including 100,350 books, 20,349 CDs, 8,809 DVDs, and 2,701 video games. And at the time we experimented, there were two copies of Sims 2 to be traded instantly for Super Mario, one from 'Gwerd67' in Florida and the other from 'Ukfan64' from Kansas. If you decided to make the exchange, Swap generates the postage label, too (on average items cost $2.20 to send by post). The whole trip to the post office, including the weighing of the item, can be bypassed. From start to finish, swaptrading Super Mario for Sims 2 would have taken no more than two minutes.

In October 2010, there was an inventory of approximately 5.5 million items on people's 'have lists' and 9 million items on people's 'want lists', with more than 3.5 million swaps being made to date. To a certain extent, the multiway, multimedia trading system that connects these goods is leveraging the concept of six degrees of separation. Boesel explains, 'We have essentially created a social network for your media. When you tell us you have the movie *The Departed*, we connect you to all the people who want that movie, and all of the people who want those people's items.'[36] Cracking this challenge has enabled the founders to create two critical experience factors that can compete head-to-head with shopping for new stuff: choice and instant gratification.

The experience of swap trading sites is almost a mash-up between the technology of Amazon and the ideology of Freecycle or craigslist. Just like Newmark and Beal, the Swap co-founders have observed that the community (now more than 2 million), as Boesel puts it, 'adopts a certain set of values' based on trust between strangers. The whole system is self-policed, and the traders are rated using a reputation system just like eBay's. As Omidyar and Newmark believed, users who make false claims about the condition of an item or who don't ship an item promptly are weeded out and 'punished' (your account is suspended if you don't fulfil a trade). So far 99 per cent of all trades have received a positive rating and 1 per cent a negative rating for relatively minor reasons such as 'item arrived one week later than expected'.

Swap started with books, DVDs, CDs, software and video games. 'Every household contains hundreds of them. Furthermore, they are all of similar value and can be easily and inexpensively mailed,' Boesel explains. In the first month, the average number of such trades is around 4, in the second month it is 4.5, and by month three, it is 5. More importantly, six months after joining, the user is still making five trades a month, a strong indication that people fall into a habit of swaptrading in a relatively short period of time. As Boesel puts it, 'People quickly realize, "Oh yeah I can do this".' Once that habit sticks, it can be easily transferred to a multitude of other categories.

Just as we saw in product service systems, these types of redistribution markets work particularly well for stuff that we buy to fulfil a short-term need or products that diminish in appeal after use. These are items such as an overplayed video game that becomes worthless to one person but is of immediate value to another. Daniel Nissanoff, in his book *FutureShop*, refers to these items as things we 'want to have but not to hold'. He posits that in the future we will think of them in 'terms of temporary ownership'.[37] It's also possible that passing something on will become as second nature as buying something new.

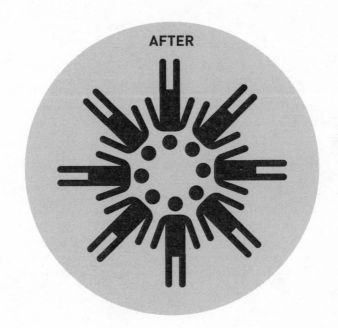

COLLABORATIVE
LIFESTYLES

| **We Are All in This Together**

At the age of nine, Annie Novak had her first bartering experience in her school cafeteria in Chicago. Every day her mum, Rita, would give her the same three things to take for lunch: a bag of pasta with cheese on top, a piece of fruit and a carton of juice. 'My good friend Emily Grimm,' Novak recalls, 'wanted my pasta, and I craved her fruit roll-ups and Chips Ahoy, so we swapped! This went on for several years.' As with most children, the act of trading something she had for what someone else wanted came intuitively to Novak – so much so that at the time she didn't even think about what she was doing.

Novak is now in her late twenties. She lives in New York City, and in early 2009 she started a 6,000-square-foot organic 'rooftop farm' that overlooks the Manhattan skyline, in Greenpoint, a neighbourhood in Brooklyn. Together with Ben Flanner, she oversaw the deposit of 200,000 pounds of soil onto the roof of a film warehouse, the installation of an irrigation system and the planting of seeds. In the summer of the same year, more than thirty varieties of vegetables, fruits, flowers and herbs were in full growth. Novak grew up

not in a farming family or even in the countryside but in Evanston,
a suburb of Chicago along the shoreline of Lake Michigan. Her
mother was an artist and her father worked for the Chicago Board of
Trade. 'I remember lying on his office rug at eleven years old as he
tried to explain his job. In no part of the conversation did it become
clear how the corn and soy he traded were, in the reality outside of
economics, actual crops and plants. They represented possibilities,
prices.' It was the nature of her dad's work that he would lose and
make terrific amounts of money on a daily basis. This meant that
even though Novak and her two sisters grew up in a beautiful house
with everything they needed, her family never felt financially
secure.

Novak first moved to New York to attend college. During this
time, she had frequent phone conversations with Brian, her father.
She became increasingly sensitive to the pressure he felt to support
his family and how much that pressure shook his daily moods. Trag-
ically, a month before she graduated in 2003, her father died in a car
accident and, to her family's surprise, he left no inheritance. 'So
much of who I am today and how I choose to live my life came from
that turning point. I wasn't worried about money, but having the
skills to support myself, so I learned about mechanics, construction,
and the most fundamental of human skills – farming.'

To help herself escape from her enormous grief, she travelled
through Argentina, Peru, Fiji and Ghana, working with farmers and
investigating the ways people grow and eat their food around the
world. In particular, she noticed how often people swapped and
bartered food in exchange for the other goods and services they
needed, such as tools, clothes and doctor's visits. When she returned
to New York in 2005, Novak began to apply the same trading principles to her own life.

Novak started farming with organic farmer Keith Stewart in Port
Jervis, New York, and then with Kira Kinney, who runs a small farm

in New Paltz, New York. She exchanged the surplus fruits and vegetables they grew for items such as milk, eggs, bread, butter, ice
cream and vegetables. These days she barters the produce from her
own Rooftop Farm. She still has to buy certain things such as grains,
tea, work boots, petrol and personal goods, and pays with cash for
certain services like medical bills, but bartering has become a significant part of her life. Her primary motivation is not to save money
– though that's a nice benefit – but because she relishes the web of
relationships and experiences that come with it. She borrows her
neighbour Susan's car, and in exchange Novak helps Susan and her
grandmother with their garden in Long Island. She barters vegetables for professional services including legal advice, accounting and
web design that she needs to run her latest venture, Growing Chefs.
And so the list goes on – bicycle parts, travel, favours, furniture and
books. Novak's favourite trade was for a trip to Peru. She gave a
series of cooking lessons to a friend in exchange for her spot on a
trip to the Amazon River. On her wish list to barter are petrol for the
car trips, health-care coverage and a piece of land.

When you meet Novak, you get the sense that she is more of a
passionate and ambitious entrepreneur than a Pollyannaish do-gooder.
She is not just full of ideas about how to get people to grow their
own food and eat more healthily. She is curious about the way markets work and the system of order that money brings to our lives, an
understanding gleaned from her father. 'I like money, as there are
lots of things I could not do or achieve without it,' she admits, but at
the same time she regards money as 'a middleman, a form of short-
hand language to get what we want. You pay what is asked and the
product is yours. The exchange doesn't require a relationship with
people, just a communication of agreed value.'

Product service systems and redistribution markets are two systems that lead us to rethink the reasons and way we consume products and services. But what about the less tangible and more personal

assets that make up our day-to-day lives? What about things like our knowledge, time, workspaces, creativity, money, homes, gardens and other social spaces? It's not just consumer goods that can be bartered, loaned, gifted or swapped. You can share a couch, a garden, an office, a carpool, a workspace, a meal, a chore, a skill or homegrown produce. These exchanges are thriving in a system we call collaborative lifestyles.

The idea of the exchange of goods or services for other goods and services without any money changing hands is the oldest form of economic trade. In the ancient world, people exchanged metals, crops and livestock with one another. The tribes of Mesopotamia and Babylonia evolved the system, exchanging goods of practical value such as weapons, spices, salt and cloth. Barter was used for thousands of years, before the notion of centralized coins and paper money was invented in the Renaissance. The idea of bartering resurges in financially strapped economies when people must find nonmonetary ways to get what they need. An extensive barter economy sprang up during the Great Depression. When President Roosevelt shut down the country's banks for a full week in 1933, many department stores accepted groceries for dresses; some doctors and lawyers were paid in batteries or oil; butchers took alcohol or tobacco for meat. But most Americans dropped the practice when a stronger economy returned.

Let's Do a Deal

The concept of using what you no longer need or want, or perhaps what you have a surplus of, to get what you do need makes perfect logical sense. We have all acquired some skills within our lifetime, whether we can fix a car, decipher a tax code, speak a foreign language or grow vegetables. Some people have more time than others, or have access to a space, a product or expertise that someone else does not. Similarly, most businesses have underutilized assets such as office space or employee time; there are unfilled rooms in hotels or empty seats on planes; hairdressers, accountants, dentists and other service professionals often have some open appointments in a week; and retailers have surplus stock. Nonetheless, most of us don't think of these skills as assets that we could use to pay for some of what we need or want. This may be because bartering requires a certain level of trust, respect and an honest vocabulary around what something is worth, often with a stranger. Novak explains, 'I opened my bartering network simply by offering people vegetables, and more often than not, I was offered something of value back. But most people find it emotionally hard to take this first step because of the social stigmas associated with it.'

It is one thing for a person like Novak to barter, but would it be possible for bartering to work on a larger scale? Caroline Woolard and four other artists from Brooklyn recognized that sometimes a physical space is needed for people to feel comfortable to start a barter network. In January 2010 the group turned a 350-square-foot former barbershop on Norfolk Street in the Lower East Side of Manhattan into Trade School. The narrow space has a long chalkboard on one side and a row of coat hooks on the other. The place is furnished with recycled objects such as modified tins of paint that have been turned into benches. A red flag hangs on the Trade School door with a hand-sewn old-fashioned white school bell representing a call to gather for class, and a crisscrossed blue fish and yellow ruler signifying the exchange of food and working skills. On offer at Trade School is an eclectic mix of lessons on everything from portrait photography to Web design to composting to salsa dancing. In return for free classes, teachers post what they want or need on the Trade School website and students agree to bring those items when they register for a class. Woolard herself has received running shoes in exchange for grant-making lessons. So far, more than eight hundred people have taken lessons and most classes are full (with waiting lists) of people coming from all over the city. The school itself is the physical counterpart to an online peer-to-peer bartering network called OurGoods that Woolard is also helping to launch.

The OurGoods team realized that the problem with barter is not just perception, but also the practical reality that to exchange one type of good or service for another, each side must want what the other is offering. This scenario is what economists call the 'coincidence of wants'. Let's say you're a plumber and you want to trade your services (goods A) for urgent legal advice (goods B). You would need to find a lawyer with an immediate need for plumbing help. The supplier of goods A must want goods B, and the supplier of goods B must want goods A at the same time (and, prior to the Internet, in the same place). The improbability of this coincidence occurring is what William Stanley Jevons, an English economist and logician, called the 'double coincidence of wants'.[1] But the Internet eliminates this inefficiency. It enables diverse and dispersed individuals and businesses to connect on a global scale and efficiently match their haves and wants without ever needing to know one another. Technology enables nonlocalized trust to be established and grow. The cyber bartering community is growing quickly, with approximately five hundred online barter exchanges in North America and Latin America, from smaller exchanges geared towards a specific community, such as OurGoods aimed at artists and designers, to massive open exchanges, such as ITEX, Bartercard, U-Exchange and Miroma Media Trading. More than $10 billion worth of goods and services were bartered by more than 400,000 businesses globally in 2008. ITEX alone handled more than 1,600 separate transactions every day of the year. Bartercard, the world's largest network, with more than 75,000 members across nine countries, exchanged

more than $2 billion worth of goods and services through its net-
work alone in 2009.[2]

The way these online bartering marketplaces work is pretty similar. They don't actually carry any products or services but are strictly
the brokerage or facilitator of transactions. Businesses or individuals
trade goods and services to earn barter dollars or pounds that become a credit within an account. Yvonne Hill, a fifty-nine-year-old
mother who runs a boutique hotel in Cornwall, accrued more than
£17,000 worth of trade on Bartercard from stays in her hotel. She
used this credit to pay for state-of-the-art dental work, haircuts,
clothes and even a holiday in the Caribbean.[3] With every completed
trade, Hill's account was debited – one trade pound being equal to
£1 – and the account of whomever she was trading with credited.
Bartercard charged a 6 per cent service fee for every transaction. The
power of these systems is that they efficiently overcome the problem
of the 'double coincidence of wants', as the trades do not have
to be reciprocated directly. Yvonne's dentist does not have to stay at
her hotel.

Banking on the Community

Barter exchanges use traditional currencies as a common measure of
value, but they may also use time. Thousands of other communities
in twenty-two countries across six continents are creating time
banks and local exchange trading schemes (LETS).[4] Edgar Cahn,
founder of TimeBanks USA, refers to the idea as 'a time machine
taking us back to an age when we knew each other and trusted one
another'.[5] From the SPICE Timebank in Wales to the Lyttelton Timebank in New Zealand to Estonia's Bank of Happiness, the way they
work is simple: for every hour you spend doing something useful

for someone in your community (grocery shopping, walking a dog, fixing a bike) you earn one 'time dollar' that you can then bank at an online portal and spend on things you may need done (such as computer advice, babysitting, plumbing). Tiina Urm, one of the founders of the Bank of Happiness, commented in an article in *The Times*, 'We call it a bank because we want to bring forth a new set of values.'[6] Urm started the bank in 2008 with Ahti Heinla and Rainer Nõlvak (the same team that created Estonia's Let's Do It campaign) to develop a repository of collective altruism that could spread all over the country. They create what social strategist Umair Haque calls 'Thick Value'. As he puts it, this is 'value that accrues to everyone and that can make people, communities, and societies better off'.[7] Research has shown that 72 per cent of people involved in time-banking experience a stronger sense of community as a result, and 86 per cent of people state they have learned a new skill as a result of participation.

These types of bartering currencies are being given many labels, including alternative currencies, community currencies, personalized currencies and complementary currencies. They are complementary because most people agree that they should sit alongside a national currency, and by no means replace it. Even though we don't give it much thought, we know that the coloured paper notes that we call money are a social and economic construct. The value of any currency is based on trust, and it works because we all agree it has a special value and governments guarantee it. 'The centralized currency was developed by monarchs in the 12th and 13th centuries to prevent peer-to-peer transaction and promote central authority transaction. What people want is the ability to transact,' Douglas Rushkoff, author of *Life Inc.* explains.[8]

One social entrepreneur who shares this view is Stan Stalnaker, founder of the co-working and social network Hub Culture and the first peer-to-peer currency, called VEN. Stalnaker would categorize himself as an optimistic entrepreneur rather than an idealist. His interconnected thinking is more closely associated with a Google or Facebook mind-set than with any specific religious, spiritual or political ideology. In early 2007, he started thinking about how he could formalize the way Hub members put a value on intangibles such as business introductions, talent trades, and the general exchange of soft favours and goodwill. Stalnaker also noticed the increasing buzz and growing comfort around virtual payment systems, especially in the gaming world and online communities. Second Life had invented Linden Dollars; the role-playing game World of Warcraft traded WOW Gold; and Tencent QQ, the most popular instant messaging platform in China, had introduced the Q coins, which people were using not just to pay for virtual goods such as avatars for their blog, but as currency for real-life goods and services. Stan wondered how he could create a currency that operated somewhere between a thank-you and a credible payment.

After reading about the broader economic view of currency as not just money but also time, skills and effort, he decided to start VEN, the first global peer-to-peer social currency to move from an online network into the real world. He got the name from an old Buddhist word that means 'sharing that comes from giving' and the symbol from a Venn diagram, the place of overlap that can increase value for unrelated groups or circles. The digital currency, which floats against the US dollar and other global currencies, can be used between members who buy and trade knowledge, goods and services. The currency is redeemable at any Hub Pavilion around the world. To date, approximately twenty thousand members have exchanged more than 1.2 million VEN.[9] 'I think there's a tidal wave of change coming in how we view finance and the very idea of money – and while it won't be replaced, we'll find lots of ways other than cash to get what we want. People will trade individually and independently among each other, all around the world,' says Stalnaker.

Social Lending Marketplaces

In one of the most famous scenes of Frank Capra's 1946 classic film *It's a Wonderful Life*, there's a run on the Bailey Building and Loan, a small bank owned by the tortured main character, George Bailey. As depositors clamour to get their money back, Bailey tells them, 'You're thinking of this place all wrong, as if I had the money back in the safe. The money's not here. Your money's in Joe's house . . . and in the Kennedy house and Mrs Macklin's house and a hundred others.' This scene eerily resembles what happened nearly seventy years later in the crash of 2008. As the banks tried to reassure customers that their assets were not in serious danger, customers withdrew billions of dollars. People no longer believed that their money was completely safe. A study conducted by Mintel at the end of September 2008 showed that only 16 per cent of adults trusted traditional big banks.[10]

Elsewhere in the financial world, a relatively new sector labelled social lending was going through extraordinary growth. The year 2008 marked a turning point for peer-to-peer social lending marketplaces such as Zopa in Europe and Prosper and the Lending Club in the United States. Giles Andrews, the current CEO of Zopa, heard repeatedly from new members, 'I trust you more than a big bank.' Even Andrews admits this was nonsensical, given that, at the time, Zopa was a start-up employing eighteen people in a small office in the West End of London. Social lending works within a network of lenders and borrowers, when people with spare cash they might otherwise put in their savings accounts or in the stock market lend it to people looking to borrow. They cut out the big bank as the middleman. In 2010, the average rate of return for lenders was 8.2 per cent and borrowers' interest rates were on average 20 per cent lower than rates at traditional banks. It appears that this is not a niche market. Many Internet users will consider taking a loan from their peers before they go to traditional lenders such as banks and lending institutions. In 2006, there were $269 million peer-to-peer loans, and in 2007, a total of $647 million. By 2013, it is estimated that social lending will rise at least 66 per cent to $5 billion of outstanding personal loans.

The basic premise of social lending has been around for centuries. People borrowed from relatives, friends, friends of friends, or wealthy moneylenders. For a loan to happen, three people were required – a borrower, a lender and a witness – and a handshake. This kind of lending was relatively easy when we lived in communities where everyone knew everyone else – and their reputations and needs. As global trade and commerce increased, a need arose for a central trusted conduit between large-scale suppliers of funds and borrowers, and the model of social lending disappeared. In its place, we saw the rise of financial middlemen – the asset managers, mortgage brokers, pension and mutual funds advisers, and the big banks themselves – who for the most part introduced faceless transactions and overheads, while removing the community loyalty that was the glue in person-to-person lending.

eBay + PayPal + Match.com

In 2003, Richard Duvall, a successful banking entrepreneur, turned forty and decided to take the summer off. He retreated to his home, a converted thirteenth-century house in the English countryside, with his wife and four children. Despite his successful career in finance, Duvall wanted some time to work out what he wanted to do next.

In the early nineties, he had been the head of IT at the banking giant Prudential. His close friends and colleagues, as well as passing acquaintances, described him as passionate, gentle and inspirational. Bill Gates called him 'one of the most dynamic people I have ever

met'. Duvall launched the first mainstream digital bank for Prudential, called Egg, which would simplify and personalize the experience of financial services. Duvall had tasted the power of technology
to create close customer relationships. By 2003, he was eager to rip
up the old rulebook again.

During his summer 'off', Duvall immersed himself in articles,
books and research on how digital tools and the Internet were disrupting industries. He believed that the 'twin forces of technology
and the will of the individual' would turn traditional business models upside down and radically transform the way people think and
live towards a more collaborative economy. Duvall was particularly
interested in the work of Carlota Perez, a leading economist at Cambridge University and an expert in technoeconomic paradigm shifts.
Perez posits that every seventy years, a disruptive technology emerges
that alters the foundations of the economy and the norms by which
society constructs itself – our homes, our workplaces, our education
system, the way we govern, how we spend our leisure time and so
on. The five ages of transformation that have happened to date: the
industrial revolution; the age of steam and railways; the age of steel,
electricity and heavy engineering; the age of oil, automobiles, and
mass production; and the age of information and telecommunica-
tions.[11] Duvall wanted to understand the socioeconomics of how
these shifts transformed people's lives. Why did customers change
their behaviour? Over what time period? How did businesses adapt
and succeed?

He was also intrigued by other social online ventures that were
attracting millions of users by the day, such as Skype, Friends
Reunited, YouTube and especially eBay. The words that founder
Pierre Omidyar had given at a graduation speech stayed with him all
summer: 'eBay wasn't a hobby. And it wasn't a business. It was – and
is – a community: an organic, evolving, self-organizing web of
individual relationships, formed around shared interests.'[12] Duvall

wondered, 'How could the same concept apply to personal banking?'

To work out the right opportunity and approach, he enlisted the help of James Alexander and Dave Nicholson, former Egg colleagues, and external expert Bruce Davis, a well-respected independent ethnographic researcher. After months of observing and talking to people about how they were earning, saving and spending money, they identified a widespread desire for more control, freedom and self-expression. As Duvall explained, 'We used to define ourselves by what we consumed, the brands we wore, the cars we drove and the consumer electronics that we stuffed under the TV set. Now we're defined much less by brands and more by the things we do, the choices we make, our values and beliefs, our self-expression.'

The team also noticed during the research that most people spoke of their existing banks as a necessary evil. As Alexander told us, '"Normal people" with good jobs and decent credit histories were describing going into a bank like going into a shoe shop asking for a pair of men's black leather shoes in size 42 and being told to come back in three weeks to be handed a pair of women's red suede shoes in a size 40 for twice the price.' The customer experience, satisfaction and trust generated by traditional banks set a low bar for competition beyond their actual capital.

The team individually dispersed to develop ideas. It was Dave Nicholson, the youngest on the team and the 'techie geek', who first came up with the concept that he dubbed at the time a 'bond market for consumer lending'. 'If companies don't need to borrow from banks but can go to a market (the bond market), why can't consumers do something similar?' he wondered. Nicholson realized the Internet enabled what communities had been. 'We began to clearly see the idea like an eBay for banking: a "meeting place" for borrowers and lenders to get together,' Alexander explained. It is an auction-like process in which the lender willing to provide the lowest interest rate wins the borrower's loan.[13] The formula for the concept that Nicholson first scribbled down was 'eBay + PayPal + Match.com = an online money matchmaking service.' They realized that the appeal behind this idea was that by cutting out the traditional banks and sidestepping the middlemen, they could give people a better return for their money, even if they charged a small, say 1 per cent, commission for 'matchmaking' the loan.

Notably, the default rate on Zopa is low, about 0.7 per cent. This rate is even more impressive when you consider that the average default rate on credit cards in mid-2009 was more than 10 per cent.[14] Zopa reduces the risk of peer-to-peer lending by using the established trading logic known as hedging your bets. If a farmer plants an entire crop of just tomatoes, a fungus can wipe out the whole harvest in a matter of days. This is why most farmers follow the principle of mixed crops. Fund managers apply the same logic when investing in a range of stocks and mutual funds. Based on this principle of not putting all your eggs in one basket, peer-to-peer lending sites such as Zopa minimize risk by dividing a loan into small amounts and spreading it over a wide range of a dozen or more borrowers. But why is the default rate *so* low? After all, major credit card companies don't put all their eggs in the same basket, either.

In Zopa, money moves from Person A to Person C (without the need for Big Bank B in the middle). This path follows the basic economic law of disintermediation, the removal of middlemen from a process or supply chain to create more efficient markets. But it's not the concept of the efficiency behind disintermediation that is important in collaborative lifestyles. It's the significant shift the transparency creates in generating new levels of peer-to-peer trust, even between strangers. 'Ten years ago some people thought it would be mad to send money to someone in the post in the expectation that they would receive a parcel in return, but that collaboration led to the development of the largest retailer in the world,' current CEO Giles Andrews says.

Borrowers often tell him that they would rather pay interest to Zopa lenders than to a bank. They feel invested in rather than taken advantage of. Lenders enjoy finding out what their money is used for and being in control of setting their rates. Some even say it's addictive and fascinating seeing who's borrowing what and why, and will check their Zopa account several times in one day. As Rob Forshaw, a Zopa lender, puts it, 'It makes me feel like I am part of something bigger and seems to trigger a sense of belonging. With belonging comes pride and passion.'

Working Alone and Together

In 2005, Brad Neuberg was a thirty-one-year-old freelance open-source software programmer living in San Francisco. He had just left a tech start-up to work for himself. Neuberg enjoyed working from home, yet the experience was also isolating. He tried the de facto techie office, a coffee shop, but found it too noisy and distracting and devoid of meaningful interactions. Despite his complaints about the monotony and conformity of the nine-to-five cube-working culture, Neuberg discovered that he missed the social camaraderie of an office. To his surprise, watercooler conversations served a purpose. 'It seemed I could either have a job that would give me structure and community,' he recalls, 'or I could be freelance and have freedom and independence. Why couldn't I have both?'

Neuberg had been inventing collaborative software systems since 1998, including Web software named Open Portal and a distributed Web browser named Paper Airplane. He started thinking about the key ingredients that made these platforms work so well – community, creativity and structure – and how he could apply these elements to his current working dilemma. He wondered, 'How could I have the

kind of community and the cool people around me that I would
have at a place like Google without having to join a big company?'
He rallied three fellow techies who had also been talking about the
solitary tensions of working independently. They rented a space
called the Spiral Muse for two days a week in the Mission and set up
a few folding tables, wireless Internet and a printer, and created a
basic meeting space. Neuberg had no idea he was starting what
would become a global movement he called 'co-working'.

After the friends hosted a co-working Meetup, word of the concept spread. Soon other free-agent techies, researchers, writers,
filmmakers and entrepreneurs began dropping in wanting pay-as-
you-go usage of the space for a few hours or a few days. All these
people were working for themselves and had sworn never to return
to a traditional office and the politics that go with it, but they also
yearned for some form of working community where they could
cross-pollinate ideas face-to-face. As Stephen Humphrey, a professor
of management at Florida State University's business school, who
spent more than forty years researching social interaction at work
and telecommuting, says, 'We suddenly start to realize, we miss socializing – and we need it.'[15]

Eventually Neuberg left the Spiral Muse group and, ironically,
took a job at Google; but with some of the original participants,
including Chris Messina and Tara Hunt, he went on to start another
successful co-working space called the Hat Factory. Today, co-
working 'offices' are being set up across the United States (Sandbox
Suites, Citizen Space) and the UK (Le Bureau, Cube London, Hub
King's Cross), and the phenomenon is rapidly spreading around the
world. 'I urged people to steal the idea,' Neuberg says.[16] The growth
of this movement is not surprising, given that it's estimated that
one-fifth of the workforce, or 30 million people, are working on
their own in some form or another in the United States alone.[17] And
many of these people, including Stan Stalnaker (who as part of Hub

Culture runs a collection of co-working pavilions around the world), are, as Stalnaker puts it, 'global, heavily wired, eco-conscious and cost-cutting workers who were looking for a hip yet conscientious temporary co-working environment in their home cities as well as on the road.'

Co-workers describe what their shared workspaces mean to them not in pragmatic terms but with emotional expressions such as 'hubs of interactions' or 'fraternities of mutual interests'. The spaces themselves vary in terms of perks and culture, but they are all based on combining the best elements of a coffee shop (social, energetic, creative) and the best elements of a workspace (productive, functional). As Dominique Cardon and Christoph Aguiton, French social science researchers on communications and cooperation, say, co-working creates a 'third place'. 'Something which is neither a desk in a company nor the domicile of the person; it is a kind of public place you can join when you want, with the guarantee of finding some social life and the chance of a useful exchange.'[18] Go into one of The Hub network's spaces, such as the one Rachel visited in an old, beautifully designed, light-filled warehouse-type building located in the heart of King's Cross, London, and you will find it buzzing with independent workers. Half the people may be working on laptops alone (many with headphones on) and the other half may be found huddled together in the kitchen and lounging alcoves, having, as Neuberg would put it, what looks like meaningful interactions. They are working both alone and together.

Integral Part of Culture, Not a Counterculture

In the same way we constructed fences to establish our hyper-individualism, we need new kinds of boundaries to create the magic of a shared belonging. In opposition to the adage 'Good fences make good neighbours,' we now need to formalize fenceless relationships.

There is also a need to combine old sound ideals with design and experiences that lean more towards hip dot-com than the tie-dyed communalism of the sixties.

Stephanie Smith, a Harvard-trained architect, charismatic designer and social entrepreneur in her early forties, embraces this idea. The worlds of architecture, design and culture have identified Smith as one to watch with her ideas on low-impact design, mass production and alternative forms of community. She talks passionately but with authority about archetype typologies, connected lifestyles and tribal solutions. Smith proudly admits that she is heavily influenced by the thinking of the legendary designer and pioneer of sustainability Buckminster Fuller, sharing his passion to work out the question: 'How we can make the world work for 100 per cent of humanity in the shortest possible time through spontaneous cooperation without ecological damage or disadvantage to anyone?'[19]

Smith was sitting in her offices at Ecoshack, a Los Angeles-based experimental design studio, when she realized that she could no longer afford to be green. It was early in the economic crash of 2008. Everything seemed uncertain. 'How can it possibly be that I need to keep buying to be green? I have to buy a Prius, I have to buy fluorescent lightbulbs, I have to buy a solar panel. . . .' Wasn't there a better way, she thought, to be more sustainable?

She started to look back in history for ideas. Convinced that the collapse was a deeper symptom of an isolated consumer society, she began researching the different ways people come together and share resources. The main problem with what we're calling collab-orative lifestyles, she realized, was not the concept in itself but the stigma attached to sharing. Smith decided to apply her design and Web skills to rebrand an old sharing idea: communes. As she com-mented in a recent NPR interview, 'In the past, the people that started utopian communities really insisted that the best way is to leave your old community and start over. . . . It often led to failure.

What we are interested in doing is making them an integral part of culture, not a counterculture.'[20]

Wikipedia's definition of a commune is 'a community where resources are shared'.[21] When you think of the commune concept through this wider lens, every single neighbourhood in America and around the world could be a commune, as can every apartment building, school, church group, college dorm or office building.

Ariel Schwartz wrote in *Fast Company*, 'Communes aren't just for hippies anymore.'[22] In 2008, Levi's featured 'Wanna Start a Commune?' T-shirts in its flagship stores during the holiday season. The shirts appeared on the mannequins in the front windows, after a Levi's executive apparently told his staff, 'Consumers are ready for this.' These hip black-and-white tops with big bold type that were in fact advertisements for Stephanie Smith's venture sold out within a week all over the country.

These days, everyone from teachers to truck drivers, from busy professionals to stay-at-home mums, from designers to doctors, is starting to explore different forms of communal living. Ecovillages, co-housing, cooperatives and other forms of intentional communities (the label now favoured over communes) are sprouting up all around the world. Smith wants to play a big part in this resurgence.

To start her project, Smith decided that she needed to pick a relatively small and contained community where she had a good relationship with someone who could help her get the project off the ground. Her good friend Scott Vineberg lived in a cul-de-sac in the bluff of Topanga Canyon in western Los Angeles. A cul-de-sac seemed like 'an automatic community waiting to happen', with many houses clustered together around a dead-end street. It has an immediate and obvious shared context. It was only later that Stephanie discovered that she had picked the exact spot on which Topanga Canyon's commune once resided in the 1970s.

The goal of the first 'cul-de-sac commune' pilot was to help work out what kind of tools and support the residents would need to facilitate collaborative and more sustainable living, whether that involved sharing a car, dividing up tasks, exchanging goods or services, or simply sharing space, chores and time. Was the answer a more elaborate online posting board along the lines of craigslist? Perhaps an iPhone app that would help residents come together? Or was the requirement not technology-based at all but a designated neighbourhood leader? In the answer to these questions, Smith believed, were the clues to a bigger question: What *stops* people from sharing and living cooperatively?

At first, Scott needed some persuading to help in the endeavour, but he agreed to give it a go. It seemed like a way to get permission from his neighbours to build the water well he wanted. He knocked on the doors of his neighbours and invited them all around to his house on 25 January 2009, at 8 p.m. for drinks and a chat about the project. Some seemed sceptical, but to his surprise, and Stephanie's delight, everyone showed up. What happened next shocked them both. Most of the neighbours didn't know each other, so much so that the first twenty minutes were taken up with the awkward and obligatory 'My name is and I live at number 4'-type introductions. Smith was puzzled. 'How can you all live in such close proximity to one another and not even know each other's names?' she asked. One resident's response summed it up: 'Well, we see each other fleetingly most days, say when we go outside to pick up our papers, leave for work, or take out the rubbish. I might give a quick wave or nod, but we never stop for a proper chat or even a hello.'

After the Topanga residents had a few drinks and relaxed a bit, the 'big reveal', as Stephanie puts it, took place. People started to talk about their hectic lifestyles and how isolated they felt living hundreds of miles from their families. They agreed that not only could elements of a more collaborative lifestyle save them precious time and money, but, as one resident put it, 'We could be each other's safety net.' From the outset, people's primary motivation for getting involved differed. Some wanted to save money or time. Some professed more altruistic motivations such as a stronger neighbourhood fabric. Specific reasons cited for participating included cost savings, coming together, convenience and being more socially conscious/ green, in that order. Not surprisingly, these are almost identical to the reasons people have given us for engaging in different forms of Collaborative Consumption across product service systems, redistribution markets and collaborative lifestyles.

As the evening wore on, more and more people admitted to wanting to feel part of a community again. Smith jotted down notes as residents talked through the more obvious initiatives such as ride sharing to work, improved recycling, and a shared compost pile and community garden, and then started throwing out more innovative ideas such as buying solar power en masse, a common chicken hutch, Scott's community well, a pizza oven and even shared rodent control.

What Smith discovered in Topanga – and is now on a quest to make us all realize – is that coming up with ideas or getting people receptive to communal living is not the issue. The residents of Topanga had so many ideas that they had to decide where to start. The challenge the residents experienced was coordination. This barrier has historically prevented most people from attempting to 'share nicely', as the perceived effort and energy needed to make it work negate the value in return. The apparent transaction costs have been too high. They were happy to carpool, but how could they easily be aware of each other's schedules? They wanted to share chores such as grocery shopping, but how would they know who wanted what and when? Meeting to decide these things would defeat the purpose of making life easier. And they didn't want to create any kind of committee or nominate a leader to organize the effort, as that would

be resorting back to the kind of centralized authority they were trying to avoid. As James Surowiecki writes in *The Wisdom of Crowds*,
'How can people voluntarily – that is, without anyone telling them
what to do – make their actions fit together in an efficient and orderly way?'[23]

With this need in mind, Stephanie launched the online version
of the venture, WeCommune.com, in early 2009. A simple yet innovative platform, it makes it easier for people to come together and
share resources in ways that fit into modern lifestyles. 'WeCommune helps build deeper, smarter forms of community,' Stephanie
explains. It is still in beta stage, but the programme includes specific
management features to meet these challenges, including a Facebook
app that helps users post and manage a 'share', barter or group barter (e.g., a dog-walking club or childcare co-op), and a digital bulletin board tool that people working in cafés and co-working
environments can use to post real-time resource-sharing opportunities. Smith is also working on a 'surplus reallocation tool' designed
for urban districts that allows anyone to create a 'free' shelf, box,
table or room, and add it to a map so that others can find and use it.
They can take something, leave something, or both.[24]

WeCommune Inc. is not a not-for-profit venture. Smith saw the
opportunity from the outset that businesses will pay for the privilege of offering goods or services to groups of people with specific
needs. A commune with a focus, such as improving food quality,
may get an email from Whole Foods offering special discounts.[25]
Some sceptics have derided the idea as nice but 'too Californian' to
take hold in other parts of the United States. Yet within just eight
weeks of the launch, Smith estimates that more than three hundred
communes have been created, from Toronto to Texas.

When we asked Smith what her ambition was within the next
two to three years, she answered, 'I want to be on *Oprah* sitting on
the sofa with Mark Zuckerberg (one of the founders of Facebook)

talking about the sharing revolution.' Her goal is driven not by arrogance but by a down-to-earth vision of wanting people to embrace communal behaviours to become resource efficient and connected.

In an article in *The New York Times*, 'Saving the Suburbs', Allison Arieff commented about the growth of Smith's cul-de-sac projects. 'This tendency – let's call it extreme neighborliness – is so old-fashioned as to seem innovative. Startlingly basic and wholly actionable, it's a bright spot in a dark time.'[26] Other projects with similar intentions are emerging. They include Ecomodo, Thingloop, Neigh-Borrow, Bright Neighbor, NeighborGoods, rBlock, GoGoVerde, Share Some Sugar, DaveZillion and Skillshare, all of which help build a reciprocal and more sustainable community. The stories you hear of through these communities all follow the same simple principle: 'Give a hand, get a hand.' A recent post on DaveZillion (named after a friend who was known for helping his neighbours) reads, 'Thanks to the JT, Shane and Jamie for helping with the installation of the light fixture in my dining room and for help with some demolition. Anytime you guys need help, count me in.'[27] In this way online networks can create what media guru Tim O'Reilly calls 'Architecture for Participation',[28] with the coordination problems of neighbours, self-organizing eliminated. They also create anchors of commonality that break down the emotional barriers we often have around sharing or asking for help.

Have you ever noticed that lots of people stand around in a crowded bar but talk only to the people they know? In contrast, when you go to a house party, many people talk to one another, especially after a few drinks. A house provides a shared context or an anchor of commonality. You are in a house belonging to someone you know or a close friend knows, and this intimacy creates a higher sense of togetherness and trust. The same principle applies to successful virtual peer-to-peer communities where there is a simple yet compelling organizing ideal – share photos, share knowledge, share code – that gives lots of diverse people a sense that they fit in and a reason for co-creation.

In collaborative lifestyles, anchors of commonality give people permission to collaborate, form new social bonds, and break down the emotional barriers and stigmas we often have around sharing or asking for help. Anchors of commonality can be formed by a physical space such as Smith's cul-de-sac, Neuberg's co-working spaces or a hip storefront such as Trade School, or they can be built by an online platform such as Swap or Bartercard, bringing together people with similar interests. But often a set of appealing values embodied by a brand creates the commonality we need to draw us into new behaviours and collaboration. It's the transition Smith witnessed when neighbours who had lived next door to one another for years went from stilted introductions to genuine offers of support when they had a name, a structure and a common reason to do so.

Pushing Virtual Communities into the Real World

WeCommune and other neighbourhood sharing sites illustrate how our social networking behaviour is bleeding into the physical world. Perhaps the most prominent example of how we are pushing virtual communities into the real world is CouchSurfing, 'a worldwide network for making connections between travelers and the local communities they visit'.[29]

In April 2000, on the spur of the moment, Casey Fenton bought a cheap airplane ticket to Reykjavik, Iceland, for a long weekend. At the time, Fenton was twenty-two years old and finishing his degree in film and video production at Hampshire College. He had been raised in Maine in a small town of about two hundred people. 'I did not know anyone around me who liked to travel or who was inquiring about the world in the same way that I was,' he recalls.

Fenton had no place to stay in Reykjavik, and he didn't want to pay for an expensive hotel or play Mr Tourist in a youth hostel. He searched the online student database of the University of Iceland; extracted names and email addresses of fifteen hundred students; and sent messages like 'Hey Bjorn, I am coming to Iceland. Can I stay on your couch and hang out with you for the weekend?' Within twenty-four hours he received fifty invitations saying, 'Hang out with me.' Fenton had to choose whom he wanted to stay with. He picked a female socialite and a rhythm-and-blues singer who he later learned was relatively well known in Reykjavik. 'She played guide, showing me the things that were touristy, such as the lava fields, but also taking me to bars and music clubs I would have never found.' After that trip, Fenton decided he wanted to travel this way every time, 'living with locals, living their life'.

Shortly after Fenton got back, he started programming a website to enable others to have the same experience. He recruited Dan Hoffer ('a strategy kind of guy' with a degree in philosophy from Harvard and an MBA from Columbia), Sebastien Le Tuan (a Vietnamese interface designer who had spent half his life in Paris and the other half in San Francisco) and Leo Silveira (a Brazilian-born graphic designer) to cofound CouchSurfing.org with him.

By October 2010, there were 2.28 million plus CouchSurfers in more than 79,273 cities across 241 countries worldwide.[30] According to site analytics portal Alexa, it is currently the most visited hospitality service on the Internet, averaging more than 35 million daily page views in November 2009. And now other similar sites are emerging, including HospitalityClub.org, GlobalFreeloaders.com, and Place2Stay.net, which all serve as neutral middlemen matching travellers who want to sleep on a couch for free with people who are willing to serve as a temporary host and who have a couch to spare.

The concept of CouchSurfing has reached critical mass in terms of amassing enough willing hosts to support the 'surfers'. But it has

also reached critical mass in terms of being big enough to disseminate
its deeper message of 'building meaningful connections across cultures'. And of course the scale also provides social proof that the idea
is safe and really works. As cofounder Dan Hoffer puts it, 'The more
we network and the more we understand each other, the better
chance we have of this world being a better place.'

CouchSurfing is an excellent illustration of how peripheral relationships created through collaborative lifestyles can powerfully
bind us together. Mark Granovetter, a sociologist at Stanford University, named this force 'the strength of weak ties',[31] social relationships of people whom we don't know that can bolster an individual's
prospects and well-being.[32] It is estimated that more than 111,186
close friendships have been created through CouchSurfing and approximately 18 per cent of visits are reciprocated directly.[33] When
you talk to CouchSurfers, they regale you with stories of kindness
and of meeting people they otherwise would not have met as a regular tourist. Steve Savage, a forty-year-old from Australia, has Couch-
Surfed all over the world. 'Besides the obvious benefit of not having
to pay for accommodation, CouchSurfing allows travelers to experience a country and its culture from within instead of just as an ob-
server. . . . Basically, you can become part of their life for the time
you're visiting.'[34] And on the flip side, hosts, even if they choose not
to surf themselves, gain from the experience of sharing their culture. As Fenton told us, 'People use CouchSurfing for different reasons, whether just to travel or to connect with people in a strange
place, but I think most participate to learn as much as they can about
other cultures – and about themselves.'

People often ask Fenton, 'Isn't staying with a total stranger
dangerous? How can people go into each other's homes when they
have never met?' There is an old Russian proverb, '*Doveryai, no proveryai*,'
that translates as 'Trust, but verify.'[35] Just like on peer-to-peer systems
such as eBay, craigslist or Swap, CouchSurfing has reputation

mechanisms to enable a high degree of trust between strangers. 'Right from the beginning, we wanted people who had never met each other (and who lived far away) to be able to trust one another. The question we tackled was, "How can we create that trust via the Internet?" It's not a perfect translation from how we would create trust in the real life,' Fenton explains.

The founders were not exactly sure what would work, so they implemented four different trust features in the site. People pick and choose which features they want to pay attention to and which features work for them. At the most basic level a user's name and physical address are verified for a small credit card charge (it's treated as a donation to help keep the system running). The second level is the prompts on the profile section of the CouchSurfing website for the user to describe him- or herself. 'On most websites you have one box where you have to fill in a description. The majority of people are not able to describe themselves accurately; they are like a deer in headlights when they see this kind of question,' Fenton explains. The founders came up with different open-ended questions that anyone could answer but that would also prompt people to share something deeper about themselves. 'Where did you grow up?' or 'What are some of the most interesting things you have seen or done in your life?' These were questions that hosts and travellers could read to get a sense of who that person really was, his or her 'personal philosophy', as Fenton puts it. After a stay, the host rates and leaves a reference for the guest and vice versa (more than 4 million people have rated that they have had positive experiences, a staggering 99.794 per cent of all member experiences). Last, members have the opportunity to reach the highest level of verification available, called vouching. Users can vouch for others only if at least three other CouchSurfers have met them face-to-face and have vouched for them already. 'The trust features combine together to give a holistic view on trust, which is probably how it works in real life, too, where you combine different points to make decisions on who you trust and who you don't,' Fenton told us.

Just like co-working, skillshares, bartering, social lending and co-housing, CouchSurfing is a new idea with an old ethos. But these behaviours don't feel like stale or stigmatized answers from the past. Instead the values that tie them together – openness, community, accessibility, sustainability, and, most importantly, collaboration – come straight out of the digital culture. In most instances it is technology that is the differentiator reshaping the appeal of these solutions. Just as smart cards and GPS-locatable pods, instead of keys, locks and garages, are making car and bike sharing a facet of the future, and smart design and complex algorithms make sites such as Swap compelling and effective, collaborative lifestyles take ideas rooted in old values and reinvent them into a modern paradigm.

While social capital is created across all forms of Collaborative Consumption, it is heightened when we share our nonproduct needs (skills, time, space), building and strengthening relationships with family, neighbours, friends, co-workers and total strangers. To participate in collaborative lifestyles, all you need to do is 'reorient your personal compass a little bit', as Bill McKibben comments in *Deep Economy*. Collaborative lifestyles require you to 'shed a certain amount of your hyper-individualism and replace it with a certain amount of neighbourliness. . . . If we let go a little bit of our individualism (at the moment, we have plenty to spare), we recover something we have been missing.'[36] And sometimes we don't even realize what we have been missing until we experience the bridge back from some form of isolation to some form of community.

Unfortunately there is no simple data extrapolation to plot the precise future of Collaborative Consumption. No one knows how big, far and fast it will grow. Nor is it a scientific development with an easily identifiable beginning and end. But we can see striking characteristics and growth trends that indicate how this socioeconomic phenomenon could evolve by 2015 and what sort of opportunities lie ahead.

These final chapters address critical questions about the implications of Collaborative Consumption for you, your products and services, and your businesses. Collaborative Consumption is by no means antibusiness, antiproduct or anticonsumer. People will still 'shop' and companies will still 'sell'. But the way we consume and what we consume are changing. As we move away from a hyper-individualist culture that defines our identity and happiness based on ownership and stuff towards a society based on shared resources and a collaborative mind-set, fundamental pillars of consumerism – design, brand and consumer mind-set – will change, for the better.

3

IMPACT

EIGHT | Collaborative Design

In 1953, the US Air Force Office of Scientific Research charted the growth curve in speed technology for fighter jets. The scientists plotted a graph starting with the Wright brothers' first flight in 1903, which reached an airspeed of 6.8 kilometres per hour (kph); jumping to 60 kph two years later; and going all the way through to the fastest flight time clocked, 1,215 kph, by the F-100 Super Sabre. If it could find a pattern to speed progress, the US Air Force figured that it could extrapolate which planes it should be funding for the future.[1] 'It told them something preposterous,' wrote Damien Broderick in *The Spike*; 'They could not believe their eyes. The curve said they could have machines that attained orbital speed . . . within four years.' Sure enough, four years later, within weeks of the predicted date, the USSR launched *Sputnik*.[2]

Egyptian-born Karim Rashid is one of the most prolific and acclaimed designers of his generation. His works are held in the permanent collections of fourteen museums worldwide, including MoMA in New York. He is the winner of hundreds of international design awards. Frequently jet-setting around the world, dressed in a white or pink suit, Karim has a messianic belief in beautification. He currently has more than three thousand designs in production in thirty-five countries. One of his latest products is the Slice Precision Cutter, a ceramic blade that lets the user 'cut and peel just about anything'.[3] At $6.99 it feels like a bargain. Although the Slice Precision Cutter is billed as the ultimate cutting device, you can also buy the Slice Ceramic Letter Opener, the Slice Ceramic Safety Cutter, the Slice Veggie Peeler and the Slice Ceramic Blade Y-Peeler. Admittedly, each product is quite striking, encased in fluorescent green plastic and eschewing minimal material usage to create large tactile and ergonomic shapes. The methodology and thinking behind these products can be found online in his Karimanifesto: 'Now design is not about solving problems. . . . Every business should be completely concerned with beauty – it is after all a collective human need.'[4]

Karim's Precision Collection is a symbol of flamboyancy and, many would say, arrogance, of design trends that have given us some of our most ridiculous – if interesting – objects. This design intent exists in dramatic contrast to the evolution of 'design thinking', a way of thinking at the centre of Collaborative Consumption. It is possible to look back at the examples and arguments in this book and think they mark the death of design. After all, product service systems, redistribution markets and collaborative lifestyles are about dematerialization, reducing and reusing products, using less, and seeking alternative sources of fulfilment such as group participation. But the truth is, from BIXI bikes to Interface Carpets to Swap or thredUP, design is more vital than ever, with expanded responsibilities for designers that cross a multitude of disciplines. It's not just about the bright colours of logos or the slickness of products, and it's about more than producing nicely packaged green products or cool-looking hybrid cars. Today, design must continue to shape our everyday actions, reconfigure our spaces and influence our consumer desires, just not through materialism and the production

of more stuff. Designers must help find a healthy balance between
the needs of consumers and companies and the collective interest of
society.

In 2006, future-thinking design guru Bruce Mau with the Institute Without Boundaries created an exhibition called 'Massive
Change: It's Not About the World of Design. It's About the Design of
the World'. The exhibition started in Canada and travelled to the Museum of Contemporary Art in Chicago. As visitors entered the show,
they confronted gigantic black and white type with the question,
'Now that we can do anything, what will we do?' It's a question that
designers face every day. What's their role in the choices consumers
make? How can they 'culturalize' people to share and behave more
collaboratively? How can design change our world for the better?

Cameron Tonkinwise is currently the chair of design thinking
and sustainability at Parsons The New School for Design in New
York, and stands at the forefront of understanding the role of design
in Collaborative Consumption. Tonkinwise's PhD in philosophy
from Sydney University is, perhaps, a testament to what he describes
as a move away from compartmentalized 'thingification' towards
design as systems thinking. To 'thingify' is to create a product from
scratch and to release it into the consumer space – a practice fundamental since the genesis of the design profession. It is also to ignore
the complex social and biological process behind the production of
goods.

For the past couple of decades, the sustainability movement has
pressed designers to stop focusing on 'thingification' and address the
ecological impact of the products they design. As Paul Hawken
points out in *Natural Capitalism*, about 80 per cent of the environmental impact of a product, service or system is determined at the design
stage. Design drives the raw materials required, the way a product
needs to be shipped and stored, and what happens after a product's
'useful life' reaches an end.[5] Architect William McDonough and

chemist Michael Braungart, authors of the influential book *Cradle to Cradle*, write, 'One organism's waste is food for another and nutrients and energy flow perpetually in closed-loop cycles of growth, decay and rebirth, or, in other words, flow from cradle to cradle, instead of cradle to grave.'[6] Cradle-to-cradle thinking marked an important move away from isolated product creation towards life-cycle design, which considers how a product exists within an interconnected web of biological processes. McDonough and Braungart were influential in getting designers to reconsider how everything is connected and pioneers in thinking about the relationship between business, sustainability and consumption.

The age of networks combined with increasing environmental pressures and consumer demands for business to design experiences over stuff has created what design leaders describe as the crucial jump from design *creation* to design *thinking*. Design thinking means taking the process of intentional creation and applying it beyond discrete products to solving big problems using systems and experiences.

Putting Systems First

Design thinking intersects with Collaborative Consumption in several ways. For starters, the design becomes more focused on facilitation than object creation, on transitioning from consumption to participation. As Tim Brown, CEO of innovation powerhouse IDEO, puts it, 'The consumer moves from being a passive receiver to an active participant.' When design is conceived this way, the designer's role is to think about human experiences first, rather than just the thing itself.

The designers of a bike-sharing scheme such as Montreal's BIXI had to take into consideration everything from how people would feel riding in traffic to how to ensure the bikes would not get vandalized or stolen to how the system would need to respond to the specific challenges posed by Montreal's extreme weather. And then when the system launched, the designers observed and gathered feedback from riders and modified accordingly. The locking mechanism, the designers discovered, needed to be more robust and each station needed more empty docks to enable riders to drop the bikes off wherever they wanted when they were done. In other words, they had to do far more than create a bike to create a successful product service system.

Designers can't only be concerned with making their distinctive, final mark; they must be engaged in an ongoing process of collaboration with not just users but other creators. Notably, the design of BIXI required the collaboration of six design firms with different skill sets: 8D Technologies created the solar-powered terminals; Michel Dallaire designed the physical bike components; Cycles Devinci manufactured the actual bikes; Robotics Design created the bike dock; Michel Gourdeau suggested the name; and Morrow Communications developed the overall brand. As John Thackara writes in In the Bubble, 'Designers are having to evolve from being the individual authors of objects, or buildings, to being facilitators of change in large groups of people.'[7]

Even businesses such as IBM, Xerox, Sony and Dow have signed up for new collaborative avenues between businesses and users. They have all joined a new venture called Eco-Patent Commons, which pledges environmentally beneficial patents to the public domain, with the intention that 'anyone who wants to bring environmental benefits to market can use these patents to protect the environment and enable collaboration between businesses that foster new innovations.'[8] These new forms of open-source collaboration may prove to be as revolutionary to design as the leaps and bounds of the industrial revolution. 'Open source is doing for mass innovation what the assembly line did for mass production,' commented Thomas Goetz, executive editor of Wired magazine.[9]

Going forward, designers must also adapt to consumer needs and find new ways of delivering value in ways that set these experiences apart from simply buying products or traditional rental services. Netflix's initial innovation of renting DVDs through the Internet was only the beginning – and one that consisted of rethinking our relationship to existing products and services. The company's first task was building its customer base by improving the usability of its site. It designed its rankings system, then recommendations and peer-to-peer support, and finally an easy way to download films straight to the user's computer. This gradual evolution of experience was managed in a way that didn't lose or frustrate the user. To work within ever-changing sectors (and every business operates in one), the designer needs a holistic understanding of technology, behavioural science and marketing. Designers can and must play a critical role in uncovering what people need and want from systems of Collaborative Consumption, ensuring that they gain enough critical mass to continue to improve and grow.

Ezio Manzini is a professor of industrial design at Politecnico di Milano and a thought leader on strategic design for sustainability. He breaks down the process of designing what he calls collaborative service systems into four critical design components: fluidity of use, replication, diversified access and enhanced communications support.[10] Manzini is passionate about *strategic* design – finding solutions that work for consumers and can achieve widespread levels of use. How can designers make collaborative systems so easy that they will be adopted instantly and intuitively?

For Manzini, collaborative service systems vary across the different levels of effort required to participate in them. Systems that require more effort require more willpower, whereas systems that require less effort require less willpower. If you have flown into a large city and stood in a long queue for a taxi, you may have thought, 'Why don't people share rides?' Perhaps it's because people feel uncomfortable asking strangers about where they are going or it's just an added hassle to find someone going in the same direction, with luggage in tow. Virgin Atlantic is currently working on an initiative to solve this problem, in partnership with taxi2. You enter a few details about your flight and your final destination on the website, and the system matches you with other 'suitable travelling companions'. You then accept or reject the match (women can opt to be paired only with other women) and arrange a convenient place to meet. The site prints out a sign with the name of the passenger you are meeting and also provides maps to compare destinations, instructions for the taxi driver in the local language and three options for how to split the cost. The role of the designer, Manzini says, is 'to reduce the threshold of effort so that regardless of the amount of willpower a given user may have, the system can achieve its purpose'.

BlockChalk is a virtual community bulletin board for neighbourhoods in nearly nine thousand cities. In function, it is like a hyperlocal version of Twitter. From your mobile phone, you can leave a message for someone on your block or street, whether it is to report something you found, announce something happening in your neighbourhood, ask to borrow an item, warn people of something to watch out for or just chat. A typical 'chalk' (BlockChalks's word for a message) reads, 'Found dog while running last night @River Bank De & Poppy Way in Edgewater . . . Please post on here if he's yours, or you know who he belongs to.' It was created by Josh Whiting, who was formerly a senior engineer for craigslist and Del.icio. us, to make it easy for neighbours to interact with each other. Recognizing that some users will want to keep their identity and location anonymous, you can reply privately or respond publicly, 'chalkback'.

When Shelby Clark founded RelayRides in early 2010, he realized that apart from insurance to cover renters, there were two hurdles to overcome to make peer-to-peer car rental an appealing idea. The first was being able to ensure security of sharing a valuable possession with strangers. The second was eliminating the hassles of booking and using a neighbour's car. There were plenty of existing technologies to build the online reservation system, but how could RelayRides design a system that would make it easy to access a car during authorized periods without the hassle of constantly having to meet renters to exchange keys?

The RelayRides team designed a GPS device – resembling a taxicab meter – that is installed into every owner's car. The device can unlock the doors for an authorized renter; immobilize the engine, making it impossible to start the vehicle without a reservation; track how far the vehicle has been driven so that the renter can be charged if included mileage is exceeded; and locate a vehicle's whereabouts, so if it's not returned where and when anticipated, RelayRides will find your car and automatically assess a penalty.

RelayRides and BlockChalk are examples of Manzini's 'fluidity of use', the idea of removing barriers to use so that the solution is attractive and seamless to take up. Fluidity of use could be applied more widely to Collaborative Consumption. The postage system on Swap that automatically calculates the United States Postal Service shipping costs and provides users with the option of printing postage directly from the site removes the hassle of not knowing shipping costs and waiting in a queue for stamps. But design thinking could help us eliminate the need to find the right box and postage altogether. What would an efficient delivery system look like between neighbourhoods that exchange and swap goods?

Car- and bike-sharing systems are proliferating around the world because the idea can be replicated across multiple contexts, from college campuses in the United States to small towns in Europe, and now Asia and South America, with little adaptation. It's the design of the systems (easy sign-up, swipe cards, GPS tracking, automatic billing) that has facilitated their replicability. And the continual design innovation to improve these systems and integrate more user benefits only increases their appeal. In October 2009, Zipcar launched an iPhone app that lets users unlock their rental cars direct from their iPhone. No swipe card is even needed. And when drivers can't find their cars in the parking lot, they can use the app to honk the car's horn. The London Cycle App, which locates Barclays Cycle Hire Docks directly from the iPhone, had more than 100,000 downloads in the first four months of launch. Each bike in B-Cycle, the bike-sharing programme that launched in Denver, Colorado, in April 2010, is outfitted with computers that track mileage, calories burned and amount of carbon offset. This information is collected and available on your personal B-cycle web page. B-Cycle demonstrates how cutting-edge design is being used not just to meet the basic need to get around but to make the bikes in the shared system more attractive than a bike you might own.

There are so many different aspects of Collaborative Consumption in need of this user-driven design. How could co-housing concepts similar to WeCommune be made appealing and viable for different urban and suburban contexts? What would a system look like whereby local governments or councils gathered ideas from citizens on how to better use underutilized assets (empty buses, churches, playgrounds)? What would the design of the 'Zipcar of laundry services' look like?

Diversified access, the third critical design component for Manzini, is another way in which designers can contribute to the rise of Collaborative Consumption. Manzini describes diversified access as creating a system whereby users can enter in a number of different ways and get similar results. Dim Dom, a French toy-sharing company, achieves this access by allowing consumers to participate through a number of different entry points – in this case, prices and the period of subscription. The company satisfies a range of needs, from one-month packages such as the Cherry, aimed at grandparents, where you pay a onetime fee of 49.95 euros for five toys, to longer-term monthly subscription rates for parents, such as the Maxi, where you pay 25 euros for six toys every month.

Different ways of receiving a service are another way to think of diversified access. Consider food networks between farmers and urban dwellers. Some urbanites may choose to get their local food from farmers' markets or get it delivered via a community-supported agriculture scheme; others may choose to join a land-share or yard-share programme; still others might work at a co-op in exchange for discounted prices. Either way, a system of local food production is enhanced. Diversified access creates different *degrees* of participation for consumers, as with toy rentals, or different *kinds* of participation, as with local food systems.

The fourth ingredient in Manzini's design thinking is 'enhanced communications support'. Part of the power of Collaborative Consumption is that we possess many of the resources – from actual goods to human talent – to meet our needs. We just need to find ways to coordinate and derive value from them. Skill-sharing networks such as Trade School, Brooklyn Skillshare or the School of Everything, where people who have something to teach are connected with people who want to learn, demonstrate how communications platforms can allow simple forms of collaborative lifestyles to take off. What's more, the act of designing a system for sharing makes otherwise invisible connections visible. 'Until now,' Manzini told us, 'the main effect of the diffusion [of new information technology] has been to destroy traditional forms of social organizations. . . . Now this kind of connectivity can help to organize and renew new forms of community.'[11]

As Manzini's principles demonstrate, designers should be thinking more and more about the *system* in which a product or service is being used – all of the physical and cultural interfaces that intersect to create the context of usage. Although system design will become ever more important, products do still exist in Collaborative Consumption. Whether they are shared bicycles, toys, cars or handbags, or easily disassembled furniture and fittings that find their way from consumer to business and back, designers will continue to make things. What are the characteristics of an ideal Collaborative Consumption product?

One for Life

One obvious key factor is longevity. Across redistribution markets and product service systems in particular, profits are driven by units of usage and not the number of units sold. Designers must create products with the potential for dynamic longevity, not built-in obsolescence. While longevity can mean designing with durable materials that can withstand continual wear and tear, longevity may also mean making goods – computers, clothes, phones, cameras – that can be seamlessly updated, as well as easily broken down for future reuse, resale, or repair.

When designers build in a capacity for disassembly, they address a critical environmental inefficiency – currently 80 per cent of all products are one-way products, and 99 per cent of the material contents of goods will become waste within six weeks.[12] By making products that can be either returned to the producer or passed on to other consumers, designers can close the loop of material waste and redirect valuable resources. Furthermore, designing product service systems that enable infinite upgrades from just one product allows consumers to fulfil a desire for newness and enhancement. And it also enables businesses to maintain an ongoing relationship with their customers.

To attempt such a goal, Timberland has designed an extended-life product service system with its new Earthkeepers 2.0 footwear. These

boots and shoes have longevity in many senses of the word – classic
durability, easy disassembly and reusable components that close the
recycling loop. Timberland footwear has always been known for its
eco-consciousness and resilience. Now, if and when your sole does
wear out, you don't need to throw the whole product away. Send it in
and Timberland will replace it. Instead of buying a new model, consumers can replace the piece they want to update: for example, by
adding a different colour leather, new metal rings or a different in-
sole. This guarantee provides consumers with more options for personalization, as well as a capacity for ongoing 'newness' and change
over time. The Timberland shoes and boots are becoming a 'one for
life' product that can be upgraded or repaired to last a lifetime.

Modularity can also extend a designer's involvement beyond
the product itself to the interaction between the company and the
consumer around the product. The furniture company Steelcase, for
instance, has designed chairs so they can be disassembled in minutes. When consumers want to get rid of their Steelcase chairs, the
company asks them a series of questions about the age, condition,
amount and location of the furniture, as well as what they'd like to
accomplish with the items. Based on those answers, Steelcase suggests one or more of four scenarios: refurbish the chair, sell it to a
third party (through a redistribution market), donate it to a charity
or recycle its component parts. Every time a consumer is offered a
chance to recycle, redistribute, repersonalize and reinvent a product,
the designer is manufacturing a new touch point and collaboration
between the company and consumer. As John Thackara writes in *In
the Bubble: Designing in a Complex World*, 'Designing the context of innovation and learning is therefore about fostering complex interactions,
not about filling up spaces with gadgets.'[13] From carpets to electronics to clothes, companies are beginning to design goods with the
simple premise that the longer a product can last in the system, the
stronger the system will be as a whole.

The reality is that most consumers get bored with owning the same car, computer, phone or even chair for too long. Boredom leads to the purchase of tons and tons of unnecessary 'latest and greatest' things, along with the disposal of last year's model. We want innovation and variation. We crave newness and change. Scolding people – 'You must not do this' – does not change self-interested behaviour. Designers must reimagine and reinvent not just what we consume but how we consume. As designer Bruce Mau points out in a recent issue of *Wired* magazine, the next wave of design thinking can't be about denial. Indeed, designers should strive to infuse Collaborative Consumption with a cool cachet. Ironically, we must learn to covet sustainability.

• • •

In the end, the role of designers has diversified. Their responsibility has magnified as they influence more and more parts of the Collaborative Consumption system. If you visit an online job postings site today, you'll find listings for the following positions: software designers, innovation designers, brand designers, experience designers, communications designers, interactive designers, information designers, product and sound designers . . . to name a few. Furthermore, more and more businesses are hiring so-called right-brainers and MFA graduates, realizing that insight into the creative, collaborative process is necessary for understanding and nurturing such a process for consumers.

Like a curious child, talented designers are good at observing, exploring and asking 'Why? Why? Why?' The role of the designer has always been to see patterns and make connections between random things, decipher the right problem to solve, discern why people will use something and why they will not, discover what we want and need, shape the way we think, and imagine the future. The design world reinvents assumptions and recombines ideas to turn

'What if?' and 'How might we?' into 'What we can do'. Design thinking will be critical in taking the world of Collaborative Consumption out of the realm of possibilities and into real workable solutions, solutions that fulfil our consumer whims, desires and unarticulated needs, but in a way that is not dependent on more stuff. Designers won't leave their mark by engraving autographs on products in a Karim Rashid kind of way. Rather, they will find themselves participating in a living, breathing process long after their initial creation, whatever that might be, is complete.

NINE | Community Is the Brand

n 1943, Abraham Maslow, an American psychologist, published 'A Theory of Human Motivation'. In this groundbreaking paper he mapped out a hierarchy of needs, a pyramid with the basic physiological needs – such as food, warmth and water – and safety needs at the bottom, and esteem, belonging and self-actualization at the top.[1] More than sixty years later, it remains the strongest model for understanding what is meaningful to consumers and explaining what they do and why. Brands such as craigslist, Zipcar, Zopa or WeCommune satisfy many of the basic needs in the lower parts of Maslow's pyramid (they help feed us, house us, transport us and so on), but at the same time, they tap into higher needs of belonging and esteem. In contrast to the 'me' brands of hyper-consumerism, 'we'-based relationships are built into Collaborative Consumption.

In the same way that brands have manipulated us to want more and more stuff by connecting advertising campaigns to deep fundamental human needs and motivations, brands can make us want more of the sustainable values and benefits attached to Collaborative Consumption. These values include relationships, respect, support, skills, happiness, new habits, space and even time. We became hooked on the likes of Apple, Volkswagen, and Abercrombie & Fitch because these brands helped us create self-esteem and identity. Now we are latching onto the rising brands of Collaborative Consumption for similar reasons but through interactions and community, not mere shopping. Collaborative Consumption helps feed what Marilynn Brewer, a social psychologist at Ohio State University, refers to as our 'social self', the part of us that seeks connection and belonging.

Even mega consumer brands such as Nike are shifting their brand focus and advertising away from products and towards building collaborative communities. Nike is spending 55 per cent less on traditional advertising and impressive celebrity endorsements than it was ten years ago.[2] Instead, Nike is investing in nonmedia social hubs such as Nikeplus, co-created with Apple, where runners around the world post running routes, map their runs, offer advice and encouragement to one another, track their progress towards goals, upload running songs and arrange to meet up with other runners in the real world. Nikeplus is indeed in many ways a cultural commons, a shared community of people creating a knowledge hub devoted to running. By the end of 2009, Nike had aggregated more than 1.2 million runners who had collectively clocked more than 130 million miles.[3] As Nike's brand president, Charlie Denson, described in a recent speech to investors, 'Consumers want to be part of a community, whether it's a digital community or a virtual community, or whether it's a physical community. They want to feel like they're a part of something. They want to be engaged.'[4]

Yes, people who participate in Nikeplus are more likely to buy Nike products (admittedly, it is estimated that 40 per cent of community members who previously did not own Nike ended up buying a product),[5] but what is critical for the growth of Collaborative Consumption is that we are moving beyond an era of defining ourselves just by the swoosh on our T-shirts or sneakers. Now we express who we are by what we join, in this instance the world's largest running club. Brands are realizing that they need to offer experiences, not just products. And now it's not all about Nike, the sportswear company, but more about you, the athlete, meeting your own needs through the facilitation of the brand. Power is shifting to consumers. This dynamic is critical for Collaborative Consumption, as it means we can start to decide which products and services matter.

The role of brand is far from dead in the world of Collaborative Consumption, but the way brands are built, managed and spread has changed. The path that many emerging brands of Collaborative Consumption follow is similar to well-known Web 2.0 household names such as Flickr, Skype, and Facebook. They are based on empowering communities (often using the Internet as a platform to give consumers a voice) and the realization that it takes a community, not a campaign, to create a brand.

Skype went live in August 2003. Within two years there were more than 100 million user accounts. By the end of 2008, Skype had hit 405 million users and people made more than 2.6 billion minutes of SkypeOut calls.[6] Not a dollar had been spent on traditional, expensive advertising campaigns. Hundreds of thousands of early users spread the brand through discussing a new service called VoIP, whereby you could call people anywhere in the world for free on blogs, Facebook and forums. Skype made it easy for the brand to go viral by providing users with items they could easily share, such as Skype buttons for personal websites. Within a couple of years, the verb 'to Skype' was being used almost as often as 'to Google'. The network effect was in play. Given that any Skype user can call any other Skype user, it was in the early adopters' self-interest to get their friends and relatives to sign up to Skype, not Vonage or Go2Call or any other VoIP service. But awareness of Skype grew at a rapid rate primarily because people felt that they had made a discovery of something new and valuable and immediately wanted to talk it up. The same is true of Collaborative Consumption.

Airbnb has received an array of top-tier traditional press plaudits, from *Time* magazine to CNN, but founder Brian Chesky admits it's the 'viral thing' that has enabled Airbnb to build a critical mass of more than 210,000 users in more than 157 countries in less than three years. 'People want to go to work on Monday and when asked what did you do over the weekend to be able to say, "Well, I hosted this brother and sister from Sweden".' Users want to declare their collaborative, nonowning or sharing status. 'People approach Airbnb all the time with ideas on how they can help us. They will start forums, host their own Meetups, and more than 80 per cent will write a review after their stay,' Chesky explains. An early fan even came up with Airbnb's tagline, 'Travel like a Human', which the founders agreed perfectly summed up their ethos: 'It's an understanding about who we are and a loyalty you can't fabricate.' And as the brand grows, these early evangelists feel a sense of satisfaction in their role in its success. Their 'payback' is in the social reinforcing dynamic – people join because their friends have already done so.[7] In other words, one traveller picking where to stay on Airbnb rather than booking a cheap hotel on Expedia makes Airbnb a more attractive choice to others.

Brand Evangelists

If glossy ads and slick television campaigns defined twentieth-century consumption, an average British consumer looking for a loan for a used car is part of a movement of peer-to-peer branding in Collaborative Consumption that could spell its demise. If you type in 'Zopa' on YouTube.com you'll encounter 'Dyfedpotter', the pseudonym of an unassuming young man in a plain white T-shirt and chinos. He has made a home movie of himself extolling the merits of low-interest loans from this social lending network. Sitting on his living room floor, Dyfedpotter explains to a slightly wobbly camcorder, 'I wanted to borrow £4,000 for a secondhand car. First I was going to borrow money from a bank, but then I heard of Zopa.' For the next three minutes, using only a packet of Skittles and his laptop, he explains the simplicity of Zopa, describes his own personal experiences and encourages others to join.[8] His zero-budget advertisement, with its air of authenticity and credibility that no advertising agency could replicate, has received thousands of hits. Dyfedpotter is an evangelist who will engage with a new product, service or system, spread the word, and influence a critical mass of other users to follow. Erik Qualman, in his book *Socialnomics*, highlights why people such as Dyfedpotter are so important to brands. Only 14 per cent of people trust advertisers, yet 78 per cent of consumers trust peer recommendations.[9]

For decades, companies have spent billions of dollars building 'brand communities', a group of people interacting with one another based on their shared love of a product or service. The ones that succeeded − Harley-Davidson, Virgin, Apple and Starbucks − embraced the idea of moving a brand from something you want to something you love to something you can participate in.[10] Conversely, failure often resulted from community being an afterthought strategy or an artificial add-on tactic developed by a marketing department, not by the users themselves. In 2007, retailer Target encouraged selected college students who were regular customers to sing Target's praises on social networks such as Facebook in exchange for discounts, CDs and other prizes. The students were told, 'Keep it a secret.' Unfortunately, the covert marketing plan backfired. Some students felt Target was essentially asking them to lie for rewards. They blogged about the request on the same Facebook page that was set up for students to sing Target's praises, and the story ended up in the mainstream media.

But as with many Web 2.0 brands, community is in the DNA of Collaborative Consumption brands, so much so that users are not referred to as consumers but embraced as members. Members are given all the traditional benefits of joining a club: status, identity, shared interests and ownership. The website for BIXI, the bicycle-sharing service in Montreal, announces 'We are BIXI,' and this announcement is followed by a manifesto declaring what the members believe in: 'Because we know that being part of the solution means knowing that great changes can arise from the smallest of actions done together. Because we're thinking and behaving differently. Because we see the big picture. WE ARE BIXI.' Community is the brand, and a brand is owned by the community.

Just as sports fans celebrate when their team wins, members of strongly branded collaborative communities have even held self-organized parties when the product or service they love hits a milestone. Take Zipcar, a poster child of a Collaborative Consumption brand built from the bottom up. On 17 May 2007, 'Zipsters' organized a party for Zipcar's seventh birthday at City Hall Plaza in downtown Manhattan. The invitation on Yelp declared, 'Zipcar was born right here in your own backyard. And what was once just a cool idea now has 25,000 members in Boston and over 90,000 around the world. Oh, they grow up so fast! So come out and sing "Happy Birthday", grab some free grub and test your skills at any one of our birthday party games.'

From day one, Collaborative Consumption brands invest in the community. And instead of talking at users, collaborative brands first listen and then encourage a multiway conversation. For many organizations, customer service is less about a top-down approach of responding to complaints and more about establishing communities, entwining the reputation of the user and the organization. This is particularly important because the relationship with users is often decentralized and peer-to-peer, so it cannot be directly controlled.

Zipcar can't control the way someone leaves a car. Bartercard can't control the quality of goods and services exchanged. Airbnb needs to maintain a high quality of traveller experiences because, as Chesky admits, 'Everything about our company is our brand.' Airbnb's founders see the company's role as empowering the host to create the optimal experience. From advice on the types of photos to post and descriptions to leave, to a kit of suggestions of the little things hosts can do, such as place a mint on the guest's pillow, their goal is to make the user, and thereby the company, look as good as possible.

Founders of Collaborative Consumption companies spend a lot of time greeting the first wave of core users and then, on an ongoing basis, introducing them to other members. This approach has proved successful with Web 2.0 brands. When Caterina Fake cofounded Flickr, the social networking site for photo sharing, she handheld each new user. 'We would spend twenty-four hours, seven days a week,' she recalls, 'greeting every single person who came to the site. We introduced them to people, we chatted with them. This is a social product. People are putting things they love – photographs of their whole lives – into it. All of these people are your potential evangelists. You need to show those people love.'[11] CouchSurfing's Casey Fenton, Freecycle's Deron Beal, craigslist's Craig Newmark, and almost every other entrepreneurial leader mentioned in this book have fanned out across social media platforms to interact with users. The leaders view themselves not as brand rulers but more as hosts of a party helping to integrate new members with the rest of the community.

Letting Go

Land of Etsy, Indiepublic and We Love Etsy are just a handful of social networks for people who love Etsy. The sites were not created by Etsy and are not managed by their employees. We Love Etsy was

created by Lis Kidder, a twenty-eight-year-old associate at a law firm
in Washington, D.C. In her spare time, Kidder is a glass-jewellery
designer. She wanted to create a dedicated place for fellow Etsy users
to blog, swap tips, share photos, and post reviews and ideas for selling on Etsy. In January 2010, We Love Etsy had more than 8,460
members who share advice on everything from getting noticed by
search engines to creative ways to market their items. In a recent
Wall Street Journal article, CEO Rob Kalin commented, 'I'm not interested in controlling [members'] conversations, just in giving them
more personalized space to have them in.'[12] Users want the freedom
to express association with the brand as they choose. For this to happen, collaborative companies have to let go, actively encouraging
people to make their own homemade video tutorials and providing
forums for how-to-help, ideas and complaints. They can't pick and
choose what gets spread or try to control the way advocates choose
to advocate.

Zopa encourages members to 'chew the fat', even if it has nothing to do with what they are offering. Posts on the Zopa community
board are as diverse as table tennis, crop circles, sociological principles and the financial industry.

Equally impressive is the degree of participation and how much
members help each other. In December 2009, there were 45,940
replies to the discussion post on lending. Someone by the name of
'CloudBreak' recently wrote: 'Hi there, I am not sure this is the right
place to ask this question but I am running out of ideas and thought
maybe here might have a solution. . . . My brother and I have been
working on building a business over the last five years . . . we are in
a position where the money we owe, 75,000 pounds, is strangling us
because we owe it in so many different places, so many different interest rates. We want to consolidate into one payment. . . . Do you
know if it is possible to borrow 75,000 unsecured from anywhere or
whether anyone will consider this? Thanks in advance.'

'Adelows', a longtime Zopa member, replied to this post, 'Welcome to Zopa, you have misunderstood the situation. Zopa makes loans up to 15,000. Click here.' He then goes on to explain what Zopa does and why. Zopa CEO Giles Andrews points to this sort of exchange as a key factor in Zopa's success. 'Not only is Adelows doing a marketing job for us,' he comments, 'but rather than writing one line, saying, "No, you cannot have seventy-five grand you can have fifteen," he has gone on to explain Zopa and then given CloudBreak some advice on how he might use his property as equity and signed off, "Good luck". To me that is amazing.'[13] Adelows is acting as part of the Zopa team, yet he has greater credibility with other members because he is not an official employee. Brand evangelists can play a powerful role for a brand, if they are given the autonomy and space to do so.

Andrews says that even 'criticism is helpful. In every critical posting there's something of use.'[14] For new companies, proactively soliciting feedback on ways the products and services can be improved is invaluable. Zopa members have helped reinvent the way risk rating is done, getting away from the traditional credit ratings banks use, a system 'that denied their own CEO a mobile phone account!' Zipcar observed that users wanted to modify or extend an existing reservation by texting, and so they added it as a service. Vélib' riders gave feedback on the availability of bikes, helping optimize how they were distributed throughout Paris. This two-way feedback dynamic reinforces the investment members have in the brand.

Brand of No Brand

A vibrant collaborative community of brand evangelists does not necessarily require a sexy or even nice-looking brand. Just like many Web 2.0 brands, such as Wikipedia, Digg, PlentyOfFish or Tumblr, the 'brand of no brand' can become the brand. Take craigslist, the poster child of the antibrand. It is undesigned and unmarketed, and it has a no-frills bulletin board that dispels style in favour of functionality. It does not have any kind of logo, icons, special fonts or tagline. Its name, presented in plain text, is a portmanteau of its founder (Craig Newmark) and what it is (a list). From a design perspective, the site itself is far from a visual masterpiece. At first glance it appears like a messy shop window, confusing and jumbled. Links appear to be in random places, there are no consistent typographic standards, everything is in the same colour, and there is no navigation menu directing you to where you should go or what you should do first. And yet in 2006 it was nominated by Brandchannel Readers Choice Award as the seventh most popular brand in the world after Apple, YouTube, Google, Starbucks, Wikipedia and Target.[15] Craigslist beat Oprah Winfrey, Amazon and even brand giant Coca-Cola. How does a company that skips the usual visual vocabulary and breaks other rules of traditional branding achieve such status?

One of the reasons that people love a bare-bones brand such as craigslist is that it is built on nothing but usefulness to the user. In a world full of spin, frills and agendas, users find the functionality refreshing. Just like Swap, CouchSurfing, eBay, rBlock (a neighbourhood sharing site) and Freecycle, craigslist is intentionally built in a utilitarian way so that it can grow fast, adapt and improve based on what users want. The system was designed from day one to be in a state of perpetual beta. These utilitarian brands generate strong emotional associations and loyalty. You only need to look at the section on craigslist called 'What People Tell Us' to get a sense of the emotional attachment users have to the community. 'I have built my entire life from craigslist since moving to the Bay Area. All of my apartments (4), my current job (as an attorney) . . . I also have gotten help moving from some craigslisters, given away furniture and other assorted items, and even bought some things. People have given me recommendations and I have reciprocated on a myriad of issues. I check craigslist several times a day, so I must be a junkie. Hell, I even wanted to date Craig at one point!'

When people look at companies such as craigslist that sidestep the usual brand vernacular, they might assume that the brand is not cared for and managed. But in fact nonbrands require strict rules to remain so simple and to maintain their original vision. Often the founders become the grand guardians entrusted by the community to do the right thing and to protect the image and reputation of the brand. Craig Newmark won't allow paid splashy advertising on his site, and he fends off repeated suggestions from outsiders to improve the design of the site. Newmark spends his days policing the reputation of the site against matters of fraud, spam and trolls. He won't let extras or options be added unless a critical mass of members ask for them. Notably, he has publicly dismissed selling the company, out of loyalty to its community.

Whether it was Deron Beal's need to get rid of a queen-size bed, Greg Boesel's desire to swap his *Da Vinci Code*, Marty Metro's need to find moving boxes or Casey Fenton's wish to find a place to stay with a local, many examples of Collaborative Consumption are born out of real need. Because the passion is authentic and embedded in the product or service, the relevance and desirability of what these enterprises are offering does not need to be manufactured or manipulated through clever advertising. As successful venture capitalist Fred Wilson (an early investor in the likes of Etsy and Twitter) said, 'In the end of the day, many of these new collaborative-based brands such as Meetup are just tools . . . but they are tools with a soul and mission and rallying cry — and that's one of the reasons they will continue to thrive.'

TEN | The Evolution of Collaborative Consumption

We are all familiar with the drawing depicting the great evolutionary theory of ape to man. On the far left is the hunched-over *Pliopithecus*, a now-extinct ancestral ape. On the far right is the upright modern *Homo sapiens*. And in between are usually thirteen gradually evolving species showing measured progress across approximately 2.3 million years. It's an image in many classrooms around the world not just because it's educational but because it's comforting. Gradual change means that an ape didn't one day wake up as a human, naked and bewildered. This soothing theory of gradual evolution existed until 1972, when two palaeontologists, Dr Stephen Jay Gould at Harvard University and Dr Niles Eldredge at the American Museum of Natural History, proposed that fossil records showed that evolution happened in rapid bursts.[1] This theory became known as punctuated equilibrium and continues today to be a source of fascination not only to scientists but to business management theorists and philosophers as well.

It's hard not to feel that in the last fifteen years we've been living in a world of punctuated equilibrium on steroids. Every day, it seems, we wake up and feel that the world has changed overnight and go to sleep wondering what the world of tomorrow will bring. Just a few centuries ago, one of the most important revolutions of our time – the industrial revolution – took almost one hundred years to take root. The words 'Industrial Revolution' were first used in a letter written by French envoy Louis-Guillaume Otto on 6 July 1799. But the idea did not become popularized nor come into use until more than eighty years later when Arnold Toynbee, an English economic historian, began giving detailed lectures in which he painted a vivid portrait of how the system had created a major turning point in modern history, affecting almost every aspect of our daily lives.[2]

Now, life-altering technological and social advances are happening within a few years, if not months. Do you remember thinking that you were cool because you had a car phone? Were you amazed when the first iPod came out and you could store a thousand songs in your pocket? Well, today the car phone is a relic and the iPod is an iPhone with the capacity to store more than 7,000 songs and more than 100,000 other apps. Just fifteen years ago there was no mass adoption of the Internet. We thought this thing called the Web would be some kind of television, but better.[3] In an article in *Newsweek* in 1995, Clifford Stoll wrote, 'Visionaries see a future of telecommuting workers, interactive libraries and multimedia classrooms. They speak of electronic town meetings and virtual communities. Commerce and business will shift from offices and malls to networks and modems. . . . Baloney.'[4] We could simply not imagine the way the Internet would redefine our lives and the opportunities it would create.

To explain this hyper-evolution, of which Collaborative Consumption is a part, we can look at the range of communication platforms that are changing our world. The Internet and mobile technology are allowing movements to become self-conscious and identifiable in real time and, in turn, spread and grow. In the same way that individuals reflect on and report their daily activities and thoughts on Twitter or Facebook – and, in turn, have those contributions reflected on, mimicked, edited and disseminated – society is undergoing a constant process of reflexivity and adaptation. We are able to put a name to things and get a sense that we are part of a greater movement. This awareness of community momentum and purpose spurs further explorations and growth into new economies and innovations. We have become increasingly adapted to change. And because Collaborative Consumption is based on natural behavioural instincts around sharing and exchanging that have in fact been suppressed by hyper-consumerism but that are innate to us, it has the potential to grow notably fast.

Changing the Consumer Mind-Set

The ideological debate between those who believe in self-interest as the purest way to maximize production and those who believe that it operates as an affront to the collective good and equality has dominated our political, economic and philosophical discourse for centuries. But while we've debated, the world has continued undistracted down a path of self-destructive growth. It is through the fog of anxiety that Collaborative Consumption has emerged with a simple consumer proposition. It meets all the same consumer needs as the old model of mass consumption but helps address some of our most worrying economic and environmental issues. While it is complex to audit and project its entire environmental impact, Collaborative Consumption does reduce the number of new products and raw materials consumed and does create a different consumer mind-set.

When Jonathon Porritt was chairman of the Ecology Party in the UK (1978 to 1984), he and his colleagues struggled with what became known as the Great Washing Machine Debate. Porritt, a leading environmental thought leader in the UK, serves as an adviser to many entities, from Marks & Spencer to Prince Charles to the sustainability think tank Forum for the Future. In the 1980s, when he was still active in the Ecology Party, which would later be renamed the Green Party, he was faced with the problem of what to do with the deterioration of one of the first mainstream product service systems: the launderette. At the time, masses of people were going to shopping centres to purchase washing machines, either for the first time, for upgrade or for replacement, resulting in what Porritt calls a 'staggering increase in the number of personally owned machines'. Between 1964 and 1992, the proportion of homes in the UK alone with washing machines rose from 53 per cent to 88 per cent.[5] At the same time, 50 per cent of all launderettes closed. Given that the average home washing machine was used only four or five times a week, that it consumed more than 21.7 per cent of our personal water usage and that each year around 2 million used washing machines were being discarded, Porritt and his colleagues were concerned.[6, 7] The move away from collective services and towards a self-service society had serious environmental implications.

The Ecology Party considered two choices: lobby for some form of governmental taxation and incentives, or launch a powerful campaign to change the consumer mind-set back towards using launderettes. Neither option was attractive. Government was slow and infatuated with economic growth over sustainable causes. And a strong anti-washing-machine campaign would only alienate the consumer. 'By being over-prescriptive you become your own worst enemy and force people into even more defensive and negative behaviour,' Porritt said.

The Great Washing Machine Debate was just one example of a larger struggle taking place in the environmental movement. How do you address the public and inspire sustainable behaviour without being negative or dogmatic? According to Porritt, this issue is still huge in the environmental movement today, which recognizes the inefficacy of trying to shame people into a more sustainable choice but nonetheless struggles to find an alternative.

Fast-forward twenty years and there is a different answer to the Great Washing Machine Debate and the conflict between enticing self-interest and ensuring social good. It exists at 122 Folsom Street in San Francisco. Brainwash is a launderette founded in 1999 by Jeffrey Zalles. Zalles admits that his primary concern isn't being green. What he's done is worked out how to make launderettes cool again. Brainwash woos customers with additional offerings of a café, happy hours, live music, stand-up comedy nights, pinball machines, free Wi-Fi and even a place to do your homework. The space is bright and modern with indoor and outdoor seating, cool music playing, funky artwork on the walls and helpful friendly staff – a little different from the dark and dingy experience associated with most launderettes.

A big part of Brainwash's success is based on a simple insight: customers need something to do while waiting for their laundry to finish, and it needs to be better than what they would do at home. That's why the sense of community that Zalles has built through cultural events and Meetups is so smart and critical. 'Everyone who comes here could afford to get their own home washing machine . . . but where is the fun in that!' says Zalles. Indeed, the demand for Brainwash is so overwhelming that he is looking to open more franchises this year.

The idea behind Brainwash is simple, but the behavioural impact is significant. And Brainwash achieves seemingly opposing outcomes: clean clothes, fun, friends, affordability and environmental responsibility. Instead of forcing consumers to sacrifice personal convenience and comfort for doing the right thing, Jeff makes the right thing more attractive. By diversifying the motivations and putting the emphasis on consumer experience over a prescriptive sense of obligation, Brainwash achieves Porritt's goal with barely a whimper of activist politics. Brainwash hardly identifies itself with its purpose. Does it exist to provide a cheap alternative way to get your clothes washed? Is it a cool café and culture club where you can hobnob and hang out? Or is it a powerful green statement? The answer, of course, is all of the above.

The key difference in Brainwash's approach to the Great Washing Machine Debate is that instead of trying to change consumers, the system itself has changed to accommodate needs and wants in a more sustainable and appealing way, with little burden on the individual. In this respect, Collaborative Consumption actually enables an entitled, self-interested consumer who is so well served he doesn't even realize he is doing something different or 'good.' By taking an indirect, open-ended approach, Collaborative Consumption enables consumers to break down the stereotypes of collectivism or environmentalism and simply do what works best for them. It is so intuitive about our basic needs that consumers often fall into it by accident. One could argue that it doesn't matter whether the system leads to a change in mind-set as long as it converts our consumption into positive outcomes – fewer products, more efficient usage, less material consumed, reduced waste, and more social capital.

Throughout the book, we've seen certain consistent and specific motivations for participating in Collaborative Consumption: cost savings, coming together, convenience, and being more socially conscious and sustainable. The fact that it attracts new consumers based on traditional self-interested motivation, including money, value and time, and that it converts this into positive social and environmental outcomes, should not detract from its overall impact on consumer behaviour.

When people enter Collaborative Consumption through one particular door – a clothing exchange, a car-sharing scheme or a launderette – they become more receptive to other kinds of collective or community-based solutions. Over time, these experiences create a deep shift in consumer mind-set. Consumption is no longer an asymmetrical activity of endless acquisition but a dynamic push and pull of giving and collaborating in order to get what you want. Along the way, the acts of collaboration and giving become an end in themselves. Collaborative Consumption shows consumers that their material wants and needs do not need to be in conflict with the responsibilities of a connected citizen. The idea of happiness being epitomized by the lone shopper surrounded by stuff becomes absurd, and happiness becomes a much broader, more iterative process.

Reputation Bank Account

Reputation is one of the most salient areas where the push and pull between the collective good and self-interest have real impact. Reputation is a personal reward that is intimately bound up with respecting and considering the needs of others. Undeniably, almost all of us wonder and care, at least a little bit, what other people – friends, family, co-workers, and people we have just met – think about us. But this question of social reputation did not often affect our consumer behaviour. There was no central place where all these soft perceptions, opinions and ratings accumulated; but also, as consumers operating in a hyper-individualistic world, we considered our credit rating far more important than any kind of peer-to-peer review. Now with the Web we leave a reputation trail. With every seller we rate; spammer we flag; comment we leave; idea, comment, video or photo we post; peer we review, we leave a cumulative record of how well we collaborate and if we can be trusted.

Sometimes people are not conscious of their reputation capital or have to experience a loss to realize how important it is. Others are at first cavalier and don't see the connections or ramifications of their actions. As Casey Fenton, founder of CouchSurfing, described it to us, in everyday life you might have a disagreement with somebody and go your separate ways. That person may speak badly about you to someone else, but is unlikely to damage your reputation in the long term. 'But in CouchSurfing somebody cannot just tell one person, but tell everybody about it. So the consequences are vastly different. It means you really have to go the extra mile in the way you interact with people.'[8]

Reputation has always functioned as a form of reward for humans. The striatum at the centre of the brain is our monetary reward processor. Give a guy a buck and the striatum lights up. In April 2008, Professor Norihiro Sadato of Japan's National Institute for Physiological Sciences added one other critical function to the striatum: a reputation award processor. Professor Sadato explains, 'Although we intuitively know that a good reputation makes us feel good, the idea that a good reputation is a "reward" had long been just an assumption without scientific proof.' Sadato developed this theory by conducting a series of MRI scans of the brains of nineteen subjects while they engaged in two different exercises. The first was a basic game. Participants had to choose one of three cards in the hope of winning a cash prize. The second exercise asked participants to have their characters appraised, based on the results of personality trait questionnaires. The researchers found that the striatum activated as expected when the participants won money. But they also found that it responded to high and low appraisals (but did not perk up to more neutral comments).[9] Online rating systems, as well as other examples of immediate and simple forms of community feedback, provide these forms of appraisal that motivate people to behave in a responsible way.

Today, reputation serves not only as a psychological reward or currency, but also as an actual currency – called reputation capital. We have already seen how people build their reputations by playing within the rules, helping others and touting their accomplishments. Reputation capital has become so important that it acts as a secondary currency — a currency that claims, 'You can trust me.' As Andy Hobsbawm writes in *Small Is the Next Big Thing,* 'Online reputation systems are a new mechanism for trust between individuals anywhere in the world and could become a cornerstone of the modern economy.'

The more you participate in Collaborative Consumption, the more reputation capital you earn, and the more you earn, the more you can participate. This dynamic manifests itself in tangible ways; for example, the more hours you bank with a local time bank or LETS scheme by doing things for other people, the more hours you have to spend on things you need. It also operates in softer ways; for example, the better the review and feedback you receive, the more choices are made available to you, whether it's places you can stay, what and whom you can barter with, or who will lend money, tools or a car, and so on. Reputation capital becomes a currency with which to build trust between strangers and helps manage our belief in the commons.

It is only a matter of time before there is some form of network that aggregates your reputation capital across multiple forms of Collaborative Consumption. We'll be able to perform a Google-like search to see a complete picture of how people behave and the degree to which they can be trusted, whether it's around products they swap and trade or money they lend or borrow or land or cars they share.

But isn't it in each company's best interest to design a system that is based on the actions performed within a single community? If you have invested time building your reputation on thredUP, why would you want to start from scratch on a new clothing exchange? Reputation systems that are confined to a specific context therefore help companies sustain loyalty and lower attrition because your reluctance to jump to a new entrant or competitor means you are locked into that community.

But we believe it will be possible to design a platform that aggregates your reputation trail and contributions across various types of communities. Joe Smith, for example, might show he is an eBay power seller, has a thredUp 'stylie' rating of 8.6 out of 10, has uploaded fifteen hundred photos under a creative commons licence on Flickr, is a five-star member on RelayRides, has a 100 per cent loan repay rate on Zopa, and so on. In the same way that we can move our credit history from one credit card to the next, our repository of trust and reputation will carry from one community to another.

Your reputation bank account, so to speak, will determine your access to forms of Collaborative Consumption and could become a more influential and valuable asset than your credit history. 'By the end of this decade, power and influence will shift largely to those people with the best reputations and trust networks, from people with money and nominal power,' Craig Newmark, founder of craigslist, recently commented.[10]

Redefining Value

Collaborative Consumption may be consumer and community oriented, but its benefits are shared across businesses. Thousands of new opportunities have already emerged under Collaborative Consumption, with successful revenue models based on memberships (Zipcar, Bag Borrow or Steal), service fees (Airbnb, Zopa) and micropayments for usage (BIXI, BabyPlays) being established. Also, as companies start to redefine themselves as acting as the bridge between individual users and the community, we will trust them more, and as a result interact with them in different ways. This broader and deeper relationship provides an opportunity for the company to offer more ancillary services such as personalization, workshops and community support. Etsy is an example of this model. The net result is that while we may see a downturn in the number of products consumed and the amount we shop, we won't necessarily see a decrease in the overall revenue of the company. This democratization and flowering of new companies will not necessarily be to the detriment of existing businesses. Companies such as Interface and Netflix show that it is possible to reposition from an old vertical retail model to an integrated collaborative one with huge cost savings and increases in consumer loyalty.

We believe Collaborative Consumption is part of an even bigger shift from a production-oriented measurement system that just gauges the amount we sell to a multidimensional notion of value that also takes into consideration the well-being of current and future generations.[11] Just as individuals are beginning to rethink the dichotomy between self-interest and collective good, some governments and businesses are starting to rethink their own metrics that have prioritized certain forms of progress. The consideration of a more holistic understanding of well-being and success is now taking place on a macroeconomic level, leading to a global movement away from what has been labelled 'GDP fetishism'. Gross domestic product (GDP) allows economists to plot and compare our national economy's growth, disparities, ranking and power. Today the GDP of the world is a little more than $60 trillion. The United States and the European Union account for approximately one-third of this amount.

The simplicity of the measurement of GDP is also its downfall. The argument against GDP fetishism is that we are more than what we make. Even the inventor of the GDP, the late Russian-American economist Simon Kuznets, was aware that the model of GDP had significant shortcomings. 'The welfare of a nation can scarcely be inferred from a measure of national income,' he said in 1934. Imagine walking into a cocktail party and instead of making casual conversation everyone asked, 'How much money do you make?' At the very least you would find it embarrassingly gauche, but you probably would also be somewhat offended. Most of us would like to be valued on account of more than just our salaries. What about our creativity? Our family? The volunteer work we do and books we read? But GDP doesn't merely ignore the positive nonfiscal elements of our contributions; it also values negative and harmful productivity.

Consider this allegory. Someone steals a truck filled with toxic waste. As the thief passes through a red light, the police start to chase the car, and the thief takes a corner too quickly and topples the vehicle. Out pours the waste and the entire community is affected. A massive rescue operation is put in place, ambulances rush in, hospitals are inundated, and it's going to cost millions of dollars to clean up. While the headlines cry catastrophe, the GDP calculates only the extra money being generated: increased ambulance and hospital revenue, more overtime for state services, lodging and travel for foreign correspondents, and a big contract to clean up the mess. It doesn't measure the personal devastation of the father whose child is horribly ill; or the impact on the soil, air and animals; or the psychological stress on the community.

In February 2008, the president of France, Nicolas Sarkozy, commissioned a report on alternative methods for measuring growth. 'We're living in one of those epochs where certitudes have vanished . . . we have to reinvent, to reconstruct everything,' Sarkozy announced.[12] 'So many things that are important to individuals are not included in GDP.'[13] Leading economists and scholars, including Amartya Sen and Nobel laureate Joseph Stiglitz, were summoned to help find a methodology to measure quality of life. 'It is time for our statistics system to put more emphasis on measuring the well-being of the population than on economic production,' Stiglitz declared.[14] In the three-hundred-page report, Stiglitz uses the example of traffic jams to show that more production does not necessarily equal greater well-bring. Even the authors of the report admit that it is not a complete solution. Sarkozy wanted to start a debate and create a first step towards creating an empirical methodology for evaluating growth in terms of its impact on society as a whole.

Momentous Time of Change

Author and thought leader Thomas Friedman wrote, 'Often in the middle of something momentous, we can't see its significance.'[15] We wrote this book because we believe we are in an optimistic and momentous time of change around our consumer system. We hope this period will be regarded as the transition away from consumption for consumption's sake, and away from the fear of what will happen to the economy when this ethos is abandoned. But in the nascent stages of this transformation, it can be hard to grasp what kind of movement it is. A revolution? A phenomenon? A new new economy? It will be exciting to see how Collaborative Consumption evolves. What unimaginable things will become shareable? What will become the 'Google of exchange'? What will become the American Express of social currencies?

In the space of a little more than a decade, we have seen the evolution of traditional banks to social lending marketplaces to completely new forms of peer-to-peer virtual currencies such as VEN. In the food sector, retail food cooperatives have surged in popularity, community-supported agriculture programmes have more than tripled, and now through SharedEarth and Landshare, we are seeing people share their own gardens. Even in a specific sector such as car sharing, there has been rapid progress in how we are cooperating. Companies such as Zipcar and Streetcar, where there is a trusted intermediary to orchestrate the sharing of cars we don't own, have been thriving. Over the past three years, we have seen growth in the number of ride-sharing companies (goCarShare, Zimride, Liftshare) and the number of users. And now we are seeing the emergence of peer-to-peer car rental, such as WhipCar, Spride and RelayRides, whereby owners can directly rent out their vehicles when they're not using them. The degree of peer-to-peer collaboration is evolving at an astonishing rate, creating new sharing models and business opportunities every day.

Based on the evolution of Collaborative Consumption to date, and the socioeconomic context the phenomenon is emerging within, we believe certain behaviours and ideas will take hold over the next decade in a significant way. People will have 'reputation bank accounts' alongside their normal bank accounts, and a reputation rating that will measure contributions made to various types of collaborative communities. Peer-to-peer marketplaces where people 'sell' their idling capacity (cars, energy, spaces, products, food and skills) will be viewed as a second source of income. Redistributing and swapping goods will become as much second nature as throwing stuff away. The consumer preference for handmade or locally produced goods will become the norm. Neighbourhood networks will explode and enable local crowdsourcing between residents on their creative and social projects together. Our possessions will have intelligence that allow us to share their stories with their future owners. Car companies will see themselves in the business of mobility, not in vehicles or in transportation. There will be an explosion in services that enable you to repair, upgrade and customize owned or secondhand products. Instead of automatically paying with cash for many products and services, we will offer to barter talents, skills and ideas, and virtual social currencies will have become a normal way to exchange. There will be a whole ecosystem of apps and software for our phones and computers that will enable us to share any kind of product, skill, time or service. A collaborative and sharing culture will be the culture.

We believe we will look back and see this epoch as a time when we took a leap and re-created a sustainable system built to serve basic human needs — in particular, the needs for community, individual identity, recognition and meaningful activity – rooted in age-old market principles and collaborative behaviour. Indeed, it will be referred to as a revolution, so to speak, when society, faced with grave challenges, started to make a seismic shift from an unfettered zeal for individual getting and spending towards a rediscovery of collective good.

ACKNOWLEDGEMENTS

First and foremost we would like to thank Gillian Blake. We are enormously indebted to her for the dedication and extraordinary editorial talent that pervade every aspect of this book. With warm encouragement and steadfast support, she has been with us every step of the way. Special thanks go to our agents, Ed Victor and William Clark. We are grateful for their wise counsel and insightful guidance on what this book should be about.

Most authors are lucky to have one great editor; we were fortunate to have two. Ben Loehnen at HarperBusiness pushed and prodded us on every flabby generalization and bloated comment with unflagging patience and good humour. Ben, you are a wonderful editor and we appreciate the indelible marks of excellence and insight that you brought to this book. Thanks to Leda Scheintaub for polishing and checking this text. We'd also like to express our appreciation to HarperCollins US, our publisher, for championing the idea from the outset and for being so open to trying new ideas to start a movement around Collaborative Consumption. Special thanks to the team at Collins UK, including Helena Nicholls, Sam Robinson and Katherine Hassett for their belief in the importance of this book for readers in the UK.

We are extremely grateful to Nicholas Blechman for designing the cover and internal artwork, and to Armin Vit for designing the Collaborative Consumption logo and website that so wonderfully convey the spirit of the idea. Many thanks to Andrew Zuckerman for taking the time to take our author photos.

Finally, we are grateful to the thought leaders, the entrepreneurs and the community pioneers that we have had the privilege to write about. They are each acknowledged on pages 231–33. We regard this book as just the beginning of a phenomenon pointing towards a better collective future. We hope it sparks conversation, debate and a swarm of positive endeavours.

From Rachel Botsman

For me, this is a book about the possibilities and powerful reconnections that can help reshape our future for the better. I am indebted to the brilliant thought leaders whose ideas have inspired me to think in this way. These include Yochai Benkler, Robin Chase, Jeff Howe, Kevin Kelly, Lawrence Lessig, Bill McKibben, Elinor Ostrom, Robert Putnam, Jeremy Rifkin, Clay Shirky and James Surowiecki. Personal thanks to Gillian Blake for transforming the way I write, and to Ben Loehnen for masterfully shepherding this project. This book would not have been possible without my coauthor, Roo Rogers. I am deeply grateful to him for his belief in me and for continually pushing to make this the best book possible in so many different ways. Thank you, Roo.

I am grateful to all the people who have taken the time to teach me what they know about work and life. These include Cindy Gallop, Marshall Ganz, Jordan Harris, Robert Harrison, Michael O'Keeffe, Ben Machtiger and Ira Magaziner. Special thanks to Tamara Giltsoff for introducing me to Roo and for being an understanding friend. I thank Dana Ardi for teaching me that hard things are hard for a reason but are worth fighting for. Thanks to Neal Gorenflo at Shareable for starting to build a community around many of the ideas in this book, and to Maria Popova and Tina Rothberg for their early blog support.

Thanks to the team at NESTA, especially Philip Colligan and Helen Goulden, for helping launch the ideas within this book in the UK.

I feel privileged to have such creative and kind friends who have all helped in their own ways. They include Alan Barr, Ilan Bass, Bree Dahl, Lydia Gilbert, Hannah Hewetson, Gareth Miles, Robert McKinnon and David Needleham. Special thanks go to Ben Yarrow, who edited my first shoddy sample chapter, and Amy Globus and Joe Silver for helping me with presentation visuals and our wonderful animation. Lauren Anderson deserves an extra large credit for her passion and wisdom in helping building Collaborative Consumption from a book into a global movement. Thank you for your patience, loyalty and willingness to do literally anything to make our work a growing success. Thanks to the people I follow, and those who follow me, on Twitter, who have expanded my peripheral vision.

Warm thanks go to my family, who are a constant source of support, good humour and hollers of 'Go Rach!' – Cathy Alexander, Nicole Botsman, Tony Botsman, Wendy Botsman, Luc Bondar, Natalie Simmons, and our newest member, Mr. Finn. I am indebted to my parents, Ruth and David, whose love, intelligence and encouragement I can always rely on. I am most grateful for my deep roots and big wings! Heartfelt thanks to my brother Dan, who offered innumerable insights to half-baked ideas that significantly improved the intellectual rigour of this book. He has also offered wise counsel at all times in taking the ideas of Collaborative Consumption beyond words and into a movement. Special thanks to my nana, who taught me an early lesson in life: love and laughter are a daily gift, even during difficult times. I dedicate this book to her.

Most of all, I want to thank my brilliant husband, Chris. This book would not have been possible without his unwavering patience, love and selflessness. Everyone needs an honest sounding board and loyal best friend; I am tremendously lucky to be married to mine.

It was a privilege to write this book. I hope it inspires you in some way.

From Roo Rogers

My personal thanks go to Gillian Blake, Ben Loehnen and Jonathan Burnham for believing in this book from the start. While we have already thanked Ed Victor for being a fantastic agent, I must thank him and Carol Ryan again here for thirty years of unwavering support, friendship and guidance. My personal thanks to Mikaela Bradbury for her tireless research and for motivating me to find the right words when I felt blocked. Special thanks to Tamara Giltsoff, who introduced me to Rachel and who inspires me with her commitment to walk softly on this planet.

Debates, discussions and living examples – the following people, friends all, influenced the ideas in this book: Jordan Harris for once again opening my mind and helping me connect the seemingly random dots; Steven Johnson for turning a small college classroom into a lifelong journey; my brothers and sisters – Audrey, Bo, Zad, Ab, Ben, Sophie, Lucy and Harriet – for modelling the very behaviour this book looks to inspire; and my parents, Richard and Ruth Rogers, whose rigour and way of life have given me the purpose required to write this book.

Of course this book would not have been possible without Rachel Botsman, my collaborator and partner, whose sharp and prolific mind frequently left me breathless with admiration during our work together. Working with her brilliance has been exciting and inspiring. Being able to call her a great friend is even better.

This book is dedicated to Bernie Huang and our daughter Ruby Re Rogers. Together we create the greatest collaboration I know. As always, what's mine is yours.

INTERVIEWEES

We are grateful to the entrepreneurs, thought leaders, designers, politicians, community organizers and artists we were fortunate to meet and interview during the course of researching and writing this book. Their stories, insights and lessons are reflected on the pages of the book. We would like to thank them for their time and ideas, but mostly for being pioneers of Collaborative Consumption.

James Alexander – Cofounder of Zopa and CEO of Do the Green Thing

Giles Andrews – CEO of Zopa

Deron Beal – Founder of Freecycle

Yves Behar – Designer

Jeff Bennett – CEO of Swap.com

Nathan Blecharczyk – Cofounder of Airbnb

Greg Boesel – Cofounder of Swap

Piers Brown – Founder of Fractional Life

Robin Chase – Cofounder of Zipcar and CEO of GoLoco

Perrry Chen – Cofounder of Kickstarter

Brian Chesky – Cofounder of Airbnb

Shelby Clark – Founder of RelayRides

Casey Fenton – Founder of CouchSurfing

Cindy Gallop – Founder of IfWeRanTheWorld

Neal Gorenflo – Cofounder of *Shareable* magazine

Vinay Gupta – Cofounder of WhipCar

Clive Hamilton – Author and public intellectual

Chris Hughes – Cofounder of Facebook and founder of Jumo

Bruce Jeffreys – Cofounder and CEO of GoGet

Steven Johnson – Author

Micki Krimmel – Founder of NeighborGoods

Meriel Lenfestey – Cofounder of Ecomodo

Chris Maggio – Cofounder of the Stranger Exchange

Ezio Manzini – Author, designer and professor of industrial design

Sarah Matthews – Marketing director of Zopa

Marty Metro – Founder and CEO of UsedCardboardBoxes

Brad Neuberg – Founder of Coworking

Steve Newcomb – Founder and CEO of Virgance

Annie Novak – Cofounder of Rooftop Farms, founder of Growing
        Chefs

Sarah Pelmas – Cofounder of the Compact Group

Jonathon Porritt – Author and former chair of the Green Party

John Prescott – Politician and former deputy prime minister of
        the UK

James Reinhart – Founder of thredUP

Brent Schulkin – Founder of Carrotmob, cofounder of Virgance

Clay Shirky – Author and associate teacher in New Media

Stephanie Smith – Designer and founder of WeCommune

Nathan Solomon – Founder of SuperFluid

Stan Stalnaker – Founder and CEO of Hub Culture

Yancey Strickler – Cofounder of Kickstarter

Cameron Tonkinwise – Chair, Design Thinking and Sustainability,
        Parsons The School for Design

Oliver Dudok van Heel – Cofounder of Lewes Transition Town

Fred Wilson – VC and principal of Union Square Ventures

Jeff Wilson – Cofounder of the Stranger Exchange

Caroline Woolard – Cofounder of Trade School

Tom Wright – Cofounder of WhipCar

Jeffrey Zalles – Owner of Brainwash Launderette

Alan Zimmerman – Spokesman for ITEX

Dustin Zuckerman – Founder of Santa Rosa Tool Library

SELECTED BIBLIOGRAPHY

Akerlof, George A., and Robert J. Shiller. *Animal Spirits: How Human Psychology Drives the Economy and Why It Matters for Global Capitalism* (Princeton University Press, 2009).

Andersen, Kurt, and Tom Brokaw. *Reset: How This Crisis Can Restore Our Values and Renew America* (Random House, 2009).

Anderson, Chris. *The Long Tail: Why the Future of Business Is Selling Less of More* (Hyperion, 2006).

Atwood, Margaret. *Payback: Debt and the Shadow Side of Wealth* (Bloomsbury, 2008).

Axelrod, Robert. *The Evolution of Cooperation* (Basic Books, 1984).

Barabási, Albert-László. *Linked: How Everything Is Connected to Everything Else and What It Means* (Plume, 2003).

Barber, Benjamin R. *Consumed: How Markets Corrupt Children, Infantilize Adults, and Swallow Citizens Whole* (W. W. Norton & Company, 2007).

Barnes, Peter. *Capitalism 3.0: A Guide to Reclaiming the Commons* (Berrett-Koehler, 2006).

Benkler, Yochai. *The Wealth of Networks: How Social Production Transforms Markets and Freedom* (Yale University Press, 2006).

Blau, Melinda, and Karen L. Fingerman. *Consquential Strangers: The Power of People Who Don't Seem to Matter . . . But Really Do* (W. W. Norton & Company, 2009).

Bollier, David. *Viral Spiral: How the Commoners Built a Digital Republic of Their Own* (New Press, 2009).

Bonabeau, Eric. *Swarm Intelligence: From Natural to Artificial Systems* (Oxford University Press, 1999).

Brafman, Ori, and Rod A. Beckstrom. *The Starfish and the Spider: The Unstoppable Power of Leaderless Organizations* (Penguin, 2006).

Brown, Tim. *Change by Design: How Design Thinking Transforms Organizations and Inspires Innovation* (HarperBusiness, 2009).

Carroll, Lewis. *Through the Looking-Glass* (Macmillan, 1871).

Cheal, David J. *The Gift Economy* (Routledge, 1998).

Christakis, Nicholas A., and James Fowler. *Connected: The Surprising Power of Our Social Networks* (Little, Brown, 2009).

During, Alan. *How Much Is Enough?* (W. W. Norton & Company, 1992).

Friedman, Thomas L. *Hot, Flat, and Crowded: Why We Need a Green Revolution* (Farrar, Straus and Giroux, 2008).

Gershuny, Johnathan. *After Industrial Society?* (Humanities Press, 1978).

Gladwell, Malcolm. *The Tipping Point* (Little, Brown, 2000).

Glickman, Lawrence B. *Consumer Society in American History* (Cornell University Press, 1999).

Greenberg, Eric, with Karl Weber. *Generation We: How Millennial Youth Are Taking Over America and Changing Our World* (Pachatusan, 2008).

Haidt, Jonathan. *The Happiness Hypothesis: Finding Modern Truth in Ancient Wisdom* (Basic Books, 2006).

Hamilton, Clive. *Growth Fetish* (Allen & Unwin, 2003).

Hammerslough, Jane. *Dematerializing: Taming the Power of Possessions* (Da Capo Press, 2001).

Hawken, Paul. *Blessed Unrest: How the Largest Social Movement in History Is Restoring Grace, Justice, and Beauty to the World* (Penguin, 2007).

————. *The Ecology of Commerce* (HarperBusiness, 1993).

Hawken, Paul, Amory Lovins and Hunter L. Lovins. *Natural Capitalism: Creating the Next Industrial Revolution* (Back Bay Books, 2008).

Homer-Dixon, Thomas. *The Upside of Down: Catastrophe, Creativity, and the Renewal of Civilization* (Souvenir Press, 2007).

Howe, Jeff. *Crowdsourcing: Why the Power of the Crowd Is Driving the Future of Business* (Crown Business, 2008).

Howe, Neil, and William Strauss. *Generations: The History of America's Future, 1584 to 2069* (HarperPerennial, 1991).

————. *Millennials Rising: The Next Great Generation* (Vintage Books, 2000).

Hunt, Tara. *The Whuffie Factor: Using the Power of Social Networks to Build Your Business* (Crown Business, 2009).

Hyde, Lewis. *The Gift: How the Creative Spirit Transforms the World* (Canongate, 2006).

James, Oliver. *Affluenza* (Vermilion, 2007).

Jarvis, Jeff. *What Would Google Do?* (HarperBusiness, 2009).

Johnson, Steven. *Emergence: The Connected Lives of Ants, Brains, Cities, and Software* (Scribner, 2001).

Kasser, Tim. *The High Price of Materialism* (North-South Books, 2002).

Klein, Naomi. *No Logo* (Picador, 2002).

Lane, Robert E. *The Loss of Happiness in Market Democracies* (Yale University Press, 2000).

Laszlo, Ervin. *The Chaos Point: The World at the Crossroads* (Hampton Roads Publishing Company, 2006).

Lawson, Neal. *All Consuming* (Penguin, 2009).

Leadbeater, Charles. *We-Think: Mass Innovation Not Mass Production* (Profile Books, 2008).

Lehrer, Jonah. *The Decisive Moment* (Canongate, 2009).

Lessig, Lawrence. *Remix: Making Art and Commerce Thrive in the Hybrid Economy* (Creative Commons, 2009).

Lipovetsky, Gilles. *Hypermodern Times* (Polity Press, 2005).

Mauss, Marcel. *The Gift: The Form and Reason for Exchange in Archaic Societies* (Routledge, 2002).

McDonough, William, and Michael Braungart. *Cradle to Cradle: Remaking the Way We Make Things* (North Point Press, 2002).

McKibben, Bill. *Deep Economy: The Wealth of Communities and the Durable Future* (Times Books, 2007).

————. *Enough: Staying Human in an Engineered Age* (Henry Holt, 2003).

Nissanoff, Daniel. *FutureShop: How the New Auction Culture Will Revolutionize the Way We Buy, Sell, and Get Things We Really Want* (Penguin, 2006).

Orsi, Janelle, and Emily Doskow. *The Sharing Solution: How to Save Money, Simplify Your Life, and Build Community* (NOLO, 2009).

Ostrom, Elinor. *Governing the Commons: The Evolution of Institutions for Collective Action* (Cambridge University Press, 1990).

Packard, Vance. *The Status Seekers* (David McKay, 1961).

————. *The Waste Makers* (David McKay, 1960).

Patel, Raj. *The Value of Nothing: How to Reshape Market Economy and Redefine Democracy* (Picador, 2009).

Pearce, Joseph. *Small Is Still Beautiful: Economics as if Families Mattered* (ISI Books, 2006).

Pink, Daniel. *Drive: The Surprising Truth About What Motivates Us* (Penguin, 2009).

————. *A Whole New Mind: Why Right-Brainers Will Rule the Future* (Cyan, 2005).

Pollan, Michael. *The Omnivore's Dilemma: A Natural History of Four Meals* (Penguin Press, 2006).

Porritt, Jonathon. *Capitalism as if the World Matters* (Earthscan/James & James, 2007).

Putnam, Robert. *Bowling Alone: The Collapse and Revival of American Community* (Simon and Schuster, 2000).

Putnam, Robert, and Lewis M. Feldstein. *Better Together: Restoring the American Community* (Simon and Schuster, 2003).

Qualman, Erik. *Socialnomics: How Social Media Transforms the Way We Live and Do Business* (John Wiley, 2009).

Rheingold, Howard. *Smart Mobs: The Next Social Revolution* (Perseus Books, 2002).

Rifkin, Jeremy. *The Age of Access: The New Culture of Hypercapitalism, Where All of Life Is a Paid-For Experience* (Tarcher/Putnam, 2001).

————. *The Emphatic Civilization: The Race to Global Consciousness in a World in Crisis* (Penguin Group, 2009).

Ross, Andrew. *Nice Work if You Can Get It: Life and Labor in Precarious Times* (New York University Press, 2009).

Royte, Elizabeth. *Garbage Land: On the Secret Trail of Trash* (Back Bay Books, 2005).

Rushkoff, Douglas. *Life Inc.: How the World Became a Corporation and How to Take It Back* (Random House, 2009).

Sachs, Jeffrey. *Common Wealth: Economics for a Crowded Planet* (Penguin, 2008).

Schelling, Thomas C. *Choice and Consequence* (Harvard University Press, 1984).

Schor, Juliet B. *Born to Buy: The Commercialized Child and the New Consumer Culture* (Scribner, 2004).

————. *The Overspent American: Why We Want What We Don't Need* (Basic Books, 1998).

Schwartz, Barry. *The Paradox of Choice: Why More Is Less* (HarperPerennial, 2004).

Senge, Peter. *The Necessary Revolution: Working Together to Create a Sustainable World* (Doubleday, 2008).

Sennett, Richard. *The Culture of the New Capitalism* (Yale University Press, 2006).

Shirky, Clay. *Here Comes Everybody: The Power of Organizing Without Organizations* (Penguin, 2008).

Slade, Giles. *Made to Break: Technology and Obsolescence in America* (Harvard University Press, 2006).

Stiglitz, Joseph. *Making Globalization Work* (W. W. Norton & Company., 2007).

Strasser, Susan. *Waste and Want: A Social History of Trash* (Henry Holt, 1999).

Surowiecki, James. *The Wisdom of Crowds* (Anchor Books, 2005).

Tapscott, Don, and Anthony D. Williams. *Wikinomics: How Mass Collaboration Changes Everything* (Portfolio, 2008).

Thackara, John. *In the Bubble: Designing in a Complex World* (MIT Press, 2006).

Thaler, Richard, and Cass R. Sunstein. *Nudge: Improving Decisions About Health, Wealth, and Happiness* (Penguin, 2009).

Tomasello, Michael. *Why We Cooperate* (MIT Press, 2009).

Turner, Fred. *From Counterculture to Cyberculture: Stewart Brand, the Whole Earth Network, and the Rise of Digital Utopianism* (University of Chicago Press, 2006).

Wilkinson, Richard, and Kate Pickett. *The Spirit Level: Why Greater Equality Makes Societies Stronger* (Bloomsbury Press, 2009).

NOTES

INTRODUCTION: What's Mine Is Yours

1. Statistics on online networks taken from 'A Day on the Internet', www.onlineeducation.net/internet.

2. Abha Bhattarai, 'Bike-Sharing: Cycling to a City Near You', *Fast Company* (26 June 2009), www.fastcompany.com/blog/abha-bhattarai/abha-bhattarai/bike-sharing-cycling-city-near-you.

3. Statistics on Zilok taken from Reuters release, 'Rent Your Way Out of the Credit Crunch Online' (5 December 2008), http://www.reuters.com/article/idUSTRE4B44DE20081205.

4. Statistics on bartering taken from William Lee Adams, 'Bartering: Have Hotel, Need Haircut', *Time* (2 November 2009), http://www.time.com/time/magazine/article/0,9171,1931665,00.html.

5. Statistics on Freecyle taken from Freecycle press release, 'Largest Environmental Web Community in the World' (9 September 2008), www.freecycle.org/pressreleases/08-09-09_Freecycle_press_release.pdf?.

6. Statistics on CouchSurfing: http://traffic.alexa.com/graph?w=900&h=500&r=3m&y=p&u=CouchSurfing.org/&u=hospitalityclub.org&u=globalfreeloaders.com&u=place2stay.net&u=servas.org and www.CouchSurfing.org/statistics.html.

7. Statistics on allotment waiting lists were widely reported in the British media in August 2009, such as 'Forty-Year Wait for Allotments', BBC coverage: http://news.bbc.co.uk/2/hi/uk_news/england/london/8193100.stm.

8. Joseph Pisani, 'Car Sharing Takes Off', CNBC (4 December 2009), http://76.12.4.249/artman2/uploads/1/Car_Sharing_Takes_Off_-_CNBC.pdf.

9. David Zhao, 'Carsharing: A Sustainable and Innovative Personal Transport Solution', Frost & Sullivan Automotive Practice (28 January 2010), www.frost.com/prod/servlet/market-insight-top.pag?Src=RSS&docid=190795176.

10. Statistics from Gartner Research (5 January 2010). Retrieved January 2010, www.gartner.com/it/page.jsp?id=1272313.

11. Value of the market sector of used children's clothing provided by James Reinhart, founder of thredUP.

12. L.S., 'Collaborative Consumption', posted on the Economist blog (22 April 2010), http://www5.economist.com/blogs/babbage/2010/04/peer_to_peer_car_rentals.

13. Charles Leadbeater, We-Think: Mass Innovation Not Mass Production (Profile Books, 2008), 26.

14. Mark Levine, 'Share My Ride', The New York Times (5 March 2009), http://www.nytimes.com/2009/03/08/magazine/08Zipcar-t.html.

15. Lewis Carroll, Through the Looking-Glass (Macmillan, 1871), 205.

16. This idea was raised in the blog post 'Socialism or Not: Lessig Responds to Kelly', Adrian J. Ivakhiv (31 May 2009), http://aivakhiv.blog.uvm.edu/2009/05/socialism_or_not_lessig_responds_to_kelly.html.

17. Michael Spence, 'Markets Aren't Everything', Forbes.com (12 October 2009), www.forbes.com/2009/10/12/economics-nobel-elinor-ostrom-oliver-williamson-opinions-contributors-michael-spence.html.

18. Juliet B. Schor, The Overspent American: Why We Want What We Don't Need (Basic Books, 1998).

CHAPTER ONE: Enough Is Enough

1. Susan Casey, 'Our Oceans Are Turning into Plastic . . . Are We?' Best Life Magazine (20 February 2007).

2. Ibid.

3. Ibid.

4. This section was heavily influenced by Richard Grant's, 'Drowning in Plastic: The Great Pacific Garbage Patch Is Twice the Size of France', Daily Telegraph (24 April 2009), www.telegraph.co.uk/earth/

environment/5208645/Drowning-in-plastic-The-Great-Pacific-Garbage-Patch-is-twice-the-size-of-France.html.

5. Statistics on annual consumption of plastic materials come from 'Plastics Recycling Information'. Retrieved August 2009, www.wasteonline.org.uk/resources/InformationSheets/Plastics.htm.

6. Thomas M. Kostigen, 'The World's Largest Dump: The Great Pacific Garbage Patch', *Discover Magazine* (10 July 10 2008), http://discovermagazine.com/2008/jul/10-the-worlds-largest-dump.

7. Paul Hawken, Amory Lovins and L. Hunter Lovins, *Natural Capitalism* (Rocky Mountain Institute, 1999), 4, www.natcap.org/sitepages/pid5.php.

8. Tim Radford, 'Two-Thirds of World's Resources "Used Up"', *Guardian* (30 March 30 2005), www.guardian.co.uk/science/2005/mar/30/environment.research.

9. Ervin Laszlo, *The Chaos Point: The World at the Crossroads* (Hampton Roads Publishing Company, 2006), 17.

10. Global Footprint Network and WWF's Living Planet Report (September 2009), www.footprintnetwork.org/images/uploads/EO_Day_Media_Backgrounder.pdf.

11. Victor Lebow, 'Price Competition in 1955', *Journal of Retailing* (Spring 1955), www.scribd.com/doc/965920/LebowArticle.

12. Tim Jackson, 'Motivating Sustainable Consumption: A Review of Evidence on Consumer Behaviour and Behavioural Change', published in a paper by the Centre for Environmental Strategy, University of Surrey (2005), www.epa.gov/sustainability/Workshop0505/5d_Jackson_Tim.pdf.

13. Statistics on PC energy usage are from the 2009 P.C. US Energy Report, www.1e.com/EnergyCampaign/downloads/PC_EnergyReport 2009-US.pdf.

14. The artist Chris Jordan talked about this idea during his talk at the TED conference (June 2008). The video can be viewed at www.ted.com/talks/chris_jordan_pictures_some_shocking_stats.html.

15. 'Dixie Cup Company History', Lafayette College Libraries (August 1995), www.lafayette.edu/~library/special/dixie/company.html.

16. Jordan, TED talk.

17. Giles Slade, *Made to Break: Technology and Obsolescence in America* (Harvard University Press, 2006), 25.

18. Susan Strasser, *Waste and Want: A Social History of Trash* (Henry Holt and Company, 1999). Strasser talks at length about the connections between disposability and woman's liberation.

19. Kay Bushnell, 'Plastic Bags: Smothered by Plastic', a paper produced by the Sierra Club, www.sierraclub.org/sustainable_consumption/articles/bags1.asp.

20. Hawken et al., *Natural Capitalism*.

21. Sarah Graham, 'Making Microchips Takes Mountains of Materials', *Scientific American* (6 November 2002).

22. Slade, *Made to Break*, 5.

23. 'The E Waste Problem', posted on the Greenpeace website, www.greenpeace.org/international/campaigns/toxics/electronics/the-e-waste-problem.

24. John Thackara, *Inside the Bubble* (MIT Press, 2006), 22.

25. Neal Lawson, *All Consuming* (Penguin, 2009), 41.

26. Brian Walsh, 'Meet Dave, the Man Who Never Takes Out the Trash', *Time* (22 September 2008), www.time.com/time/health/article/0,8599,1843163,00.html.

27. Ibid.

28. Annie Leonard, *The Story of Stuff* (Free Press, 2010). The transcript of the video can be found at www.storyofstuff.com/pdfs/annie_leonard_footnoted_sript.pdf.

29. Ibid.

30. Clive Hamilton, 'Why Consumer Capitalism Loves Waste', quoted in his speech to the 6th Asia Pacific Roundtable for Sustainable Consumption and Production (October 2005), www.clivehamilton.net.au/cms/media/documents/articles/Consumer_Capitalism_Loves_Waste.pdf.

31. Ibid.

32. Jon Mooallem, 'The Self-Storage Self', *The New York Times* (2 September 2009), www.nytimes.com/2009/09/06/magazine/06self-storage-t.html?pagewanted=1&_r=1.

33. Statistics on growth and size of the self-storage industry come from the Self Storage Association. Last checked on February 2010, www. selfstorageassociation.org.

34. Chris Arnold, 'Americans Keeping More Possessions "Off-Site"', for a segment on National Public Radio (20 May 20 2005), www.npr.org/templates/story/story.php?storyId=4660790.

35. Martin John Brown, 'Too Much Stuff! America's New Love Affair with Self-Storage', AlterNet (June 4, 2008), www.alternet.org/work place/86998.

36. Ibid.

37. Story of Rich Ellmer comes from Rob D'Amico, 'What's in Store? Has Mini-Storage Become Mega-Storage', Austin Chronicle (1 September 2000), http://www.austinchronicle.com/gyrobase/Issue/story?oid=oid%3A78464.

38. Statistics on the changing size of American homes taken from surveys and research conducted by the National Association of Home Builders, www.nahb.org. Statistics last checked February 2010.

39. George Carlin's classic stand-up routine about the importance of 'stuff' in our lives from his appearance at Comic Relief (1986). It can be viewed at www.youtube.com/watch?v=MvgN5gCuLac.

40. Eric Fromm, To Have or to Be? (1976). His thesis states that people exist in one of two states – the 'having mode' or the 'being mode'. In the having mode, one concentrates on material possessions, acquisitiveness, power and aggression. The having mode is the basis of such 'universal evils' as greed, envy (jealousy) and violence. In the being mode, which is based in/on love, one concentrates on sharing and engages in meaningful, creative and productive activity. See www.physicsforums.com/archive/index.php/t-78564.html.

41. Richard Layard, 'Has Social Science Got a Clue?' Part of the Lionel Robbins Memorial Lectures delivered at the London School of Economics, 2–5 March 2003, http://cep.lse.ac.uk/events/lectures/layard/RL030303.pdf.

42. David Myers, The American Paradox: Spiritual Hunger in the Age of Plenty, as referenced in Barry Schwartz, The Paradox of Choice: Why More Is Less (HarperPerennial, 2004), 108.

43. Robert Lane, *The Loss of Happiness in Market Democracies* (Yale University Press, 2000). Quoted on p. 13 in a report produced by WWF, Anthony Kleanthous and Jules Peck, 'Let Them Eat Cake', www.wwf.org.uk/filelibrary/pdf/let_them_eat_cake_abridged.pdf.

44. 'Margin of discontent' was a term coined in E. J. Mishan, *The Costs of Economic Growth* (Staples Press, 1967), 112.

45. The notion of 'having driving up the wanting' is discussed in Clive Hamilton, *Growth Fetish* (Allen & Unwin, 2003).

46. Susan Fournier and Michael Guiry, 'An Emerald Green Jaguar, a House on Nantucket and an African Safari: Wish Lists and Consumption Dreams in Materialist Society', *Advances in Consumer Research* 20 (1993), 352–358.

CHAPTER TWO: All-Consuming

1. Thorstein Veblen, *The Theory of the Leisure Class* (The Macmillan Company, 1899).

2. Robert Lane, *The Loss of Happiness in Market Democracies* (Yale University Press, 2000), 176.

3. Clive Hamilton, 'The Social Roots of the Environmental Crisis', www.uri.edu/artsci/ecn/starkey/ECN398%20-Ecology,%20Economy,%20Society/Starkey_Micro_2e_c10.pdf.

4. Margaret Atwood, *Payback: Debt and the Shadow Side of Wealth* (Bloomsbury, 2008), 11.

5. Edward Bernays, *Propaganda* (Ig, first published 1928, quote taken from 2005 ed.), 71.

6. The story of Bernays and the 'Freedom of the Torches' is a featured article on 'Culture Wars', www.culturewars.com/CultureWars/1999/torches.html.

7. Allan M Brandt, 'Recruiting Women Smokers: The Engineering of Consent', *Journal of the American Medical Women's Association* 51, no. 1–2 (1996): 63–66, http://dash.harvard.edu/bitstream/handle/1/3372908/Brandt_Recruiting.pdf?sequence=1.

8. Douglas Rushkoff, *Life Inc.: How the World Became a Corporation and How to Take It Back* (Random House, 2009), 113.

9. Neal Lawson, *All Consuming* (Penguin, 2009), 41.

10. Grant Grand McCracken, *Diderot Unities and the Diderot Effect in Culture and Consumption* (Indiana University Press, 1988).

11. John Jervis, *Patterns of Western Culture and Civilization* (Wiley-Blackwell, 1999), 108.

12. Rushkoff, *Life Inc.*, 50.

13. Richard A. Feinberg, 'Credit Cards as Spending Facilitating Stimuli: A Conditioning Interpretation', *Journal of Consumer Research* 13, no. 3 (1986): 348–56.

14. Drazen Prelec and Duncan Simester, 'Always Leave Home Without It: A Further Investigation of the Credit Card Effect on Willingness to Pay', *Springer Netherlands* 12, no. 1 (February 2001).

15. This experiment is well described in Stuart Vyse, *Going Broke* (Oxford University Press, 2008), 40.

16. Dilip Soman, 'Effects of Payment Mechanism on Spending Behaviour: The Role of Rehearsal and Immediacy of Payments', *Journal of Consumer Research* 27 (March 2001).

17. In *The Decisive Moment*, Jonah Lehrer made a similar observation: 'When we pay for something with cash, the purchase involves an actual loss – our wallet is literally lighter' (Canongate, 2009), 89.

18. Mickey Butts talks about this idea in 'Why We Charge: What Behavioural Economics Can Tell Us' (19 August 2003). This is a working article written by Butts while on the Knight-Bagehot fellowship for business journalists at Columbia Journalism School and Columbia Business School, http://www.mickeybutts.com/wj_business.html.

19. Ibid.

20. Joe Nocera, *A Piece of the Action: How the Middle Class Joined the Money Class*, as quoted in *Vanity Fair*, 'Rethinking the American Dream', www.vanityfair.com/culture/features/2009/04/american-dream200904.

21. George A. Akerlof and Robert J. Shiller, *Animal Spirits: How Human Psychology Drives the Economy and Why It Matters for Global Capitalism* (Princeton University Press, 2009), 128.

22. Steve Rhode, founder of myvesta.org, found that 26 per cent of his company's clients say they never look at the statement. Quoted in Mickey Butts, 'Why We Charge: What Behavioural Economics Can Tell Us'.

23. Juliet B. Schor, *The Overspent American: Why We Want What We Don't Need* (HarperCollins, 1998), 72.

24. Demos, www.demos.org, April 2008.

25. While we were writing this book, President Obama signed the Credit Card Accountability, Responsibility and Disclosure (CARD) act. By July 2010, credit card companies had to meet an array of new requirements for disclosing fees, rates and terms on monthly statements. For decades, these numbers have been 'conveniently' and intentionally left out because the credit card companies wanted debt to feel 'free' and guiltless.

26. Interview with Elizabeth Warren from 'The Secret History of the Credit Card', produced by *Frontline* and *The New York Times*, www.pbs.org/wgbh/pages/frontline/shows/credit/interviews/warren.html.

27. Lehrer, *The Decisive Moment*, 91.

28. Tim Harford, 'Your Brain on Credit', Forbes.com (March 2009), www.forbes.com/2009/03/19/credit-poor-judgement-markets-tim-harford.html.

29. This first shopping centre, called Southdale, was in the town of Edina, just outside Minneapolis. Malcolm Gladwell talks about the Gruen Effect in 'The Terrazzo Jungle' in *The New Yorker* (March 2004), www.newyorker.com/archive/2004/03/15/040315fa_fact1.

30. Ibid.

31. Vance Packard, *The Waste Makers* (David McKay, 1960), 35.

32. Aldous Huxley, *Brave New World* (Penguin, 1959), 49.

33. Giles Slade, *Made to Break: Technology and Obsolescence in America* (Harvard University Press, 2006), 263–264.

34. Ibid.

35. Liveblog: 'Rock and Roll' Apple iPod Event. *Ars Technica*, 9 September 2009, http://arstechnica.com/apple/news/2009/09/liveblog-rock-and-roll-apple-ipod-event.ars. Retrieved 9 August 2009.

36. Heidi Dawley, 'The Disorder of These Times: Neophilia', blog post for *Media Life* (June 2006), www.medialifemagazine.com/artman/publish/article_5439.asp.

37. Charles Kettering, 'Keep the Consumer Dissatisfied,' *Nation's Business* 17, no. 1 (January 1929): 30–31, 79.

38. Susan Strasser, *Waste and Want: A Social History of Trash* (Henry Holt, 1999), 193.

39. Packard, *The Waste Makers*, 20.

40. 'Ten Great Public Health Achievements – United States, 1900–1999', CDC (1999), *Morbidity Mortality Weekly Report* 48, no. 12: 241–243. PMID 10220250, http://www.ncbi.nlm.nih.gov/pubmed/10220250.

41. Packard, *The Waste Makers*, 25.

42. Television Audience Report by Nielsen. Retrieved August 2009, http://blog.nielsen.com/nielsenwire/media_entertainment/ more-than-half-the-homes-in-us-have-three-or-more-tvs/.

43. Packard, *The Waste Makers*, 25.

44. *Progress Paradox*, cited in David Camp, 'Rethinking the American Dream', *Vanity Fair* (April 2009), www.vanityfair.com/culture/ features/2009/04/american-dream200904.

45. Jonathan Haidt, *The Happiness Hypothesis: Finding Modern Truth in Ancient Wisdom* (Basic Books, 2006), 101.

46. Jon Mooallem, 'The Self-Storage Self', *The New York Times* (2 September 2009), http://www.nytimes.com/2009/09/06/magazine/06self-storage-t.html?pagewanted=1.

47. Lawson, *All Consuming*, 11.

CHAPTER THREE: From Generation Me to Generation We

1. Adam Smith, *The Wealth of Nations* (W. Strahan and T. Cadell, 1776).

2. '18th Century London – Its Daily Life and Hazards', http://forums. canadiancontent.net/history/48176-18th-century-london-its-daily. html.

3. David Korten, *When Corporations Rule the World* (Berrett-Koehler Publishers, 1995), http://deoxy.org/korten_betrayal.htm.

4. Douglas Rushkoff, *Life Inc.: How the World Became a Corporation and How to Take It Back* (Random House, 2009), 51.

5. Bill McKibben, *Deep Economy: The Wealth of Communities and the Durable Future* (Times Books, 2007), 117.

6. 'Who Needs Neighbours?' BBC report (July 2006), http://news.bbc. co.uk/2/hi/programmes/breakfast/5163976.stm.

7. The notion of social capital including Putnam's definition is
    discussed in Gene A. Brewer, 'Building Social Capital: Civic Attitudes
    and Behaviour of Public Servants', *Journal of Public Administration Research
    and Theory* 3 (2003).

8. Robert Putnam, 'Bowling Alone: America's Declining Capitalism'.
    The article was published in *Journal of Democracy* in 1995 and later
    turned into a book published by Simon and Schuster in 2000. See
    http://xroads.virginia.edu/~HYPER/DETOC/assoc/bowling.html.

9. Statistics taken from the US Department of Commerce, Bureau of
    Economic Analysis, www.bea.gov/national/nipaweb/TablePrint.asp?
    FirstYear=1939&LastYear=2000&Freq=Year&SelectedTable=5&View
    Series=NO&Java=no&MaxValue=14546.7&MaxChars=8&Request3
    Place=N&3Place=N&FromView=YES&Legal=&Land=.

10. 'NAFTA: Embracing Change – North American Free Trade
    Agreement', a speech given by President Bill Clinton on 13
    September 1993. Transcript, US Department of State Dispatch, http://
    findarticles.com/p/articles/mi_m1584/is_n37_v4/ai_14276333/.

11. E. G. West, *Adam Smith: The Man and His Works* (Liberty Fund Inc., 1969).

12. Benjamin Kline Hunnicutt, *Kellogg's Six-Hour Day* (Temple University
    Press, 1996), www.temple.edu/tempress/titles/1155_reg.html.

13. Ibid.

14. Ibid.

15. Juliet B. Schor, *The Overworked American: The Unexpected Decline of Leisure*
    (Basic Books, 1993).

16. Don Fitz, 'What's Wrong with a 30-Hour Work Week?' posted on his
    blog 'Climate and Capitalism' (May 2009), http://
    climateandcapitalism.com/?p=691.

17. As quoted in Jeff Kaplan, 'The Gospel of Consumption', *Orion* (6 May
    2008), www.orionmagazine.org/index.php/articles/article/2962/.

18. Donna Fenn, 'Cool, Determined & Under 30', *Inc.* (1 October 2008),
    www.inc.com/magazine/20081001/cool-determined-amp-
    under-30_pagen_3.html?.

19. 'Etsy Lets Artists Create a Living', article posted 1 July 2008, on
    www.rarebirdinc.com/news/articles/etsy.html.

20. Jeff Jarvis, *What Would Google Do?* (HarperBusiness, 2009), 57.

21. Rob Walker, 'Handmade 2.0', *The New York Times* (12 December 2007), http://www.nytimes.com/2007/12/16/magazine/16Crafts-t.html.

22. 'Farmers Markets and Local Food Marketing: Farmers Market Growth: 1994–2009', USDA Agricultural Marketing Service, www.ams.usda.gov/AMSv1.0/FarmersMarkets.

23. Quoted in Bill McKibben, *Deep Economy: The Wealth of Communities and the Durable Future* (Times Books, 2007), 105. The research is from Brian Halweil, *Eat Here: Homegrown Pleasures in a Global Supermarket*, Worldwatch Institute (W. W. Norton, 2004), 11–12.

24. Pablo Paster, 'Sowing the Seeds of Sustainability: Victory Gardens Are Back!' Treehugger.com (August 2009), www.treehugger.com/files/2009/06/victory-gardens-are-back.php.

25. Bruce Horowitz, 'Recession Grows Interest in Seeds, Vegetable Gardening', *USA Today* (20 February 2009), www.usatoday.com/money/industries/food/2009-02-19-recession-vegetable-seeds_N.htm.

26. Michael Pollan, *The Omnivore's Dilemma: A Natural History of Four Meals* (Penguin Press, 2006), 258.

27. Ellen McGirt, 'How Chris Hughes Helped Launch Facebook and the Barack Obama Campaign', *Fast Company* (April 2009), www.fastcompany.com/magazine/134/boy-wonder.html.

28. Rahaf Harfoush, *Yes We Did! An Inside Look at How Social Media Built the Obama Brand* (New Riders Press, 2009). Sample chapter can be seen at http://ptgmedia.pearsoncmg.com/images/9780321631534/samplechapter/0321631536_ch6_yeswedid.pdf.

29. McGirt, 'How Chris Hughes Helped Launch Facebook and the Barack Obama Campaign'.

30. Anjana Ahuja, 'Estonia's Bank of Happiness: Trading Goods and Deeds', *The Times* online (April 2008), http://women.timesonline.co.uk/tol/life_and_style/women/the_way_we_live/article6053885.ece.

31. Sharon Jayson, 'Generation Y Gets Involved', *USA Today* (24 October 2006), www.usatoday.com/news/nation/2006-10-23-gen-next-cover_x.htm.

32. McKibben, *Deep Economy*, 1.

33. Daniel Kimmage, 'Fight Terror with YouTube', *The New York Times* (26 June 2008), www.nytimes.com/2008/06/26/opinion/26kimmage. html.

34. Don Tapscott and Anthony D. Williams, *Wikinomics: How Mass Collaboration Changes Everything* (Portfolio, 2008).

35. The story of Linux is well documented in Sam Williams, *Free as in Freedom* (O'Reilly Books, 2002).

36. Clay Shirky, *Here Comes Everybody: The Power of Organizing Without Organizations* (Penguin, 2008), 241.

37. Gary Rivlin, 'Leader of the Free World', *Wired* (November 2007), www.wired.com/wired/archive/11.11/linus_pr.html.

38. Statistics taken from the 'Linux Counter Summary Report'. Retrieved 22 February 2010, http://counter.li.org/reports/short. php?orderby=users#table.

39. Statistics taken from Clickworkers website. Retrieved October 2009, http://clickworkers.arc.nasa.gov/documents/crater-marking.pdf.

40. 'Clickworkers Results: Crater Marketing Activity' (3 July 2001), http://clickworkers.arc.nasa.gov/documents/crater-marking.pdf. As quoted in Yochai Benkler, 'The Wealth of Networks: How Social Production Transforms Markets and Freedom'. Published under a Creative Commons Licence,.http://yupnet.org/benkler/.

41. Statistics taken from Facebook's FarmVille application page. Retrieved 22 April 2010, http://www.facebook.com/home.php#!/FarmVille.

42. Statistics taken from Meetup website. Retrieved 22 February 2010, www.meetup.com/about/.

43. Scott Heiferman and Jeremy Heimans, 'We Are the Stimulus', *Huffington Post* (12 March 2009), www.huffingtonpost.com/scott-heiferman-and-jeremy-heimans/we-are-the-stimulus_b_174511. html.

44. Eliot Van Buskirk, 'Yes, We Plan: How Altruism and Advertising Could Change the World', Wired.com (3 March 2010), www.wired. com/epicenter/2009/03/yes-we-plan-how/.

45. Charles Leadbeater spoke about this idea in an informal Q&A after a conference at Reboot Britain.

46. Q&A with Cindy Gallop: 'Tackling Porn, Feminism and Big Dreams', TED blog (2 December 2009), http://blog.ted.com/2009/12/qa_ with_cindy_g.php.

47. Thomas Friedman, 'The Inflection Is Near?' *The New York Times* (7 March 2009), www.nytimes.com/2009/03/08/opinion/08friedman. html?_r=1.

CHAPTER FOUR: The Rise of Collaborative Consumption

1. The concept of 'weak ties' was developed in Mark Granovetter, 'The Strength of Weak Ties', *American Journal of Sociology* 78, no. 6 (May 1973): 1360–1380.

2. Michael Tomasello's research and new book *Why We Cooperate* were covered in Nicholas Wade, 'Why We May Be Born with an Urge to Help', *The New York Times* (30 November 2009), www.nytimes. com/2009/12/01/science/01human.html?pagewanted=1.

3. Michael Tomasello, *Why We Cooperate* (MIT Press, 2009), 5.

4. Statistics retrieved from 'The Rise and Rise of eBay', Nielsen// NetRatings. Retrieved October 2009, www.nielsen-online.com/pr/ pr_050823_uk.pdf.

5. Fred Turner, *From Counterculture to Cyberculture: Stewart Brand, the Whole Earth Network, and the Rise of Digital Utopianism* (Chicago University Press, 2006).

6. 'Zipcar Rolls Out National Low-Car Diet'. Zipcar press release (21 July 2009), http://green.autoblog.com/2009/08/25/zipcars-low-car- diet-results-save-money-lose-weight.

7. Ibid.

8. Philip Ball, *Critical Mass: How One Thing Leads to Another* (Farrar, Straus and Giroux, 2006). As cited on Wikipedia, http://en.wikipedia.org/ wiki/Critical_mass_(sociodynamics).

9. 'Bixi by the Numbers', www.bixi.com. Retrieved August 2009.

10. Noah J. Goldstein., Robert B. Cialdini and Vladas Griskevicius, 'A Room with a Viewpoint: Using Normative Appeals to Motivate Environmental Conservation in a Hotel Setting', *Journal of Consumer Research* 35 (August 2008), www.csom.umn.edu/assets/118359.pdf.

11. Cialdini quoted in Bonnie Tsui, 'Greening with Envy: How Knowing Your Neighbour's Electric Bill Can Help You to Cut Yours', *Atlantic* (July/August 2009), www.theatlantic.com/doc/200907/green-envy.

12. Alex C. Michalos, *Essays on the Quality of Life* (Kluwer Academic Publishers, 2003), 137.

13. Alex Steffen, 'Use Community: Smaller Footprints, Cooler Stuff and More Cash', *Worldchanging* (15 February 2007), www.worldchanging. com/archives//006082.html.

14. Robin Chase referred to this idea in a *GOOD* interview with Eric Steuer, 'Robin Chase on the (Financial) Value of Sharing' (9 July 2009), www. good.is/post/robin-chase-on-the-financial-value-of-sharing/.

15. Statistics taken from Morgan Stanley, 'The Mobile Internet Report' (15 December 2009). Key excerpts can be found at www.emarketer. com/Reports/All/Emarketer_2000639.aspx.

16. Mark Diacono, 'Mr Green, Meet Mrs Brown: Landshare Explained', *Guardian* (June 2009), www.guardian.co.uk/lifeandstyle/ gardeningblog/2009/jun/05/landshare-hugh-fearnley-whittingstall.

17. 'Commons Sense', *Economist* (31 July 2008), www.cs.ucl.ac.uk/staff/d. quercia/others/commons.pdf.

18. 'The Tragedy of the Commons' is an influential article written by Garrett Hardin. First published in *Science* 162, no. 3859 (13 December 1968): 1243–1248.

19. The idea of traffic congestion and 'The Tragedy of the Commons' is documented in Garrett Hardin, *Living Within Means* (Oxford University Press, 1993). It is also well described in a blog post on *Seed*, www. seed.slb.com/subcontent.aspx?id=4110.

20. David Bollier, 'Elinor Ostrom and the Digital Commons', *Forbes* (13 October 2009), www.forbes.com/2009/10/13/open-source-net- neutrality-elinor-ostrom-nobel-opinions-contributors-david-bollier. html.

21. David Bollier, *Viral Spiral: How the Commoners Built a Digital Republic of Their Own*, 4. Published under a Creative Commons licence and available for download at www.viralspiral.cc/download-book.

22. 'Reviews and reputation' was an idea discussed at an informal Q&A Botsman and Rogers conducted at *Meet Up* in January 2010. The articulation of this idea appeared in a follow-up blog piece by Jesse

Richards, www.secretpeace.com/2010/01/collaborative-consumption.html.

23. Charles Leadbeater, *We-Think: Mass Innovation Not Mass Production* (Profile Books, 2008), 4.

CHAPTER FIVE: Better Than Ownership

1. Kevin Kelly, 'Better Than Owning', posted on his blog Technium (21 January 2009), www.kk.org/thetechnium/archives/2009/01/better_than_own.php.

2. We discussed the ideas of 'use by association' in an interview with Robin Chase, founder of Zipcar, in May 2009.

3. Chris Arkenberg, 'Dematerialize: Change the Ways We Relate to Product & Ownership', posted on his blog urbeingrecorded (27 March 2009), www.urbeingrecorded.com/news/2009/03/27/dematerialize-changing-the-ways-we-relate-to-product-ownership/.

4. Christopher L. Weber, Jonathan G. Koomey and H. Scott Matthews, 'The Energy and Climate Impacts of Different Music Delivery Methods', Carnegie Mellon University, Department of Civil and Environmental Engineering and Lawrence Berkeley National Laboratory and Stanford University (17 August 2009), http://download.intel.com/pressroom/pdf/CDsvsdownloadsrelease.pdf.

5. Jeremy Rifkin, *The Age of Access: The New Culture of Hypercapitalism, Where All of Life Is a Paid-For Experience* (Tarcher/Putnam, 2001), 6.

6. Peter K. Nevitt, Frank J. Fabozzi and Jojy Vaniss Mathew, *Equipment Leasing* (Wiley, 2000), 21.

7. Jeffrey Taylor, 'The History of Leasing', http://fbibusiness.com/history_of_leasing.htm.

8. Statistics taken from the American Rental Association. Retrieved August 2009, www.ararental.org.

9. R. Meijkamp, *Changing Consumer Behaviour Through Eco-Efficient Services: An Empirical Study of Car Sharing in the Netherlands*, Design for Sustainability Research Programme, Delft University of Technology (2000), 296.

10. Reed Hastings quoted in Amy Zipkin, 'Out of Africa, onto the Web', *The New York Times* (17 December 2006), www.nytimes.com/2006/12/17/jobs/17boss.html?_r=2.

11. Joan O'C. Hamilton, 'Home Movies', *Stanford Magazine*, www.
     stanfordalumni.org/news/magazine/2006/janfeb/features/netflix.
     html.

12. Statistics retrieved from Netflix.com, September 2009, www.netflix.
     com/MediaCenter?id=5379&hnjr=8#facts.

13. Ibid.

14. Quote taken from interview with Zilok CEO on NBC (3 June 2008).
     Segment can be viewed at www.youtube.com/watch?v=aLko8EPEzs
     &feature=related.

15. 'Life for Rent', *Scotland on Sunday* (8 November 2009), http://
     scotlandonsunday.scotsman.com/comment/Life-for-rent.5805095.jp.

16. Report published by Waste Resources Action Program (November
     2009). The report is referenced in Ben Webster, 'Rent Clothes to Cut
     Carbon Emissions', *The Times* (4 November 2009), www.timesonline.
     co.uk/tol/news/environment/article6901829.ece.

17. Andrew Carnegie, *The Autobiography of Andrew Carnegie* (Constable & Co.
     Ltd, 1920), 6.

18. Quote is from an interview we conducted with LiveWork.

19. Alex Steffen, 'Service Envy: Branding Experience Instead of Stuff' (28
     June 2006). World Changing, www.worldchanging.com/
     archives/004609.html.

20. Lydia Boyd, 'Brief History of Buses and Rental Cars in the US', Duke
     University Libraries, http://library.duke.edu/digitalcollections/
     adaccess/carandbus.html.

21. Database of car-sharing companies can be found at http://ecoplan.
     org/carshare/general/cities.htm#latest.

22. Joel Makower, 'Reinventing Mobility: It's Not Just the Cars, Stupid',
     GreenBiz.com (7 August 2009), www.greenbiz.com/
     blog/2009/04/07/reinventing-mobility-its-not-just-cars-stupid.

23. Driving costs retrieved from AAA, www.aaanewsroom.net/Assets/
     Files/200844921220.DrivingCosts2008.pdf.

24. Paul Keegan, 'Zipcar: The Best New Idea in Business', CNNMoney.
     com (27 August 2009), http://money.cnn.com/2009/08/26/news/
     companies/zipcar_car_rentals.fortune/.

25. Reid J. Lifset, 'Moving from Products to Services', *Journal of Industrial Ecology* 4, no. 1 (13 February 2002), www.greenbiz.com/research/report/2002/02/14/moving-products-services.

26. Keegan, 'Zipcar: The Best New Idea in Business'.

27. Mark Levine discussed a similar idea in 'Share My Ride', *The New York Times* (5 March 2009), http://www.nytimes.com/2009/03/08/magazine /08Zipcar-t.html.

28. Makower, 'Reinventing Mobility: It's Not Just the Cars, Stupid'.

29. Ray Anderson, *Mid-Course Correction: Toward a Sustainable Enterprise* (Chelsea Green Publishing Company, 1999).

30. 'Ray Anderson, Visionary Leader', World Business Academy (2005), www.visionarylead.org/vl/ray_anderson.htm.

31. Charles Fishman, 'Sustainable Growth – Interface Inc.', *Fast Company* (31 March 1998), www.fastcompany.com/magazine/14/sustaing.html.

32. Walter R. Stahel, *The Industrial Green Game* (National Academy Press, 1997), 91.

33. John Thackara, *Inside the Bubble* (MIT Press, 2006), 224.

34. Rifkin, *The Age of Access*, 93.

35. Fishman, 'Sustainable Growth'.

36. Ray Anderson, 'The Business Logic of Sustainability', a TED talk (February 2009), www.ted.com/talks/ray_anderson_on_the_business_logic_of_sustainability.html.

CHAPTER SIX: What Goes Around Comes Around

1. 'Largest Environmental Web Community in the World', Freecycle press release (9 September 2008), www.freecycle.org/pressreleases/08-09-09_Freecycle_press_release.pdf.

2. Statistics on membership numbers and group numbers retrieved from www.freecycle.org. Last checked February 2010.

3. R. H. Coase, 'The Nature of the Firm', *Economica*, New Series, 4, no. 16 (November 1937).

4. Heath Row, 'Ridiculously Easy Group Forming', *Fast Company* (15 March 2004), www.fastcompany.com/blog/heath-row/ridiculously-easy-group-forming.

5. Paul Hawken, Amory B. Lovins and Hunter L. Lovins, *Natural Capitalism* (Rocky Mountain Institute, 1999).

6. Rosanne Bersten, 'The Gift Economy', published on the blog NETT (13 October 2009), http://nett.com.au/marketing/quick-fix/the-gift-economy/11544.html.

7. Rob Walker, 'Unconsumption', *The New York Times* (7 January 2007), www.nytimes.com/2007/01/07/magazine/07wwln_consumed.t.html.

8. Jorge Moll et al., 'Human Fronto-Mesolimbic Networks Guides Decisions About Charitable Donation', *Proceedings of the National Academy of Sciences* 103 (2006), www.pnas.org/content/103/42/15623.full. This experiment was mentioned in Raj Patel, *The Value of Nothing: How to Reshape Market Economy and Redefine Democracy* (Picador, 2009), 32.

9. Lewis Hyde, *The Gift: How the Creative Spirit Transforms the World* (Canongate, 2006), 16.

10. Robert B. Cialdini, *Influence, Science and Practice* (Scott, Foresman and Company, 1985). Summary notes can be found at www.icsahome.com/infoserv_articles/cialdini_robert_influence.htm.

11. Richard Alexander, *The Biology of Moral Systems* (Walter de Gruyter & Co, 1987).

12. David J. Cheal, *The Gift Economy* (Routledge, 1998), 1–19.

13. Gary Wolf, 'Why Craigslist Is Such a Mess', *Wired* (24 August 2009), www.wired.com/entertainment/theweb/magazine/17-09/ff_craigslist.

14. Statistics taken from craigslist.org. Retrieved October 2009, http://siteanalytics.compete.com/craigslist.org/.

15. Jeff Jarvis, *What Would Google Do?* (HarperBusiness, 2009), 117.

16. Wolf, 'Why Craigslist Is Such a Mess'.

17. Gary Wolf, 'Craigslist Credo: More Minimal', *Wired* (September 2009), www.wired.com/epicenter/2009/09/the-craigslist-credo-more-minimal/.

18. 'eBay Champions Smart Ways to Shop Green', eBay press release (4 March 2009), www.businesswire.com/portal/site/home/permalink/?ndmViewId=news_view&newsId=20090304005278&newsLang=en.

19. Christoph Uhlhaas, 'Is Greed Good?' *Scientific American Mind* (August/September 2007), www.sciamdigital.com/index.cfm?fa=Products.ViewIssuePreview&ARTICLEID_CHAR=0950A3EC-3048-8A5E-10BB9808E7E70922.

20. P. Resnick et al., 'The Value of Reputation on eBay: A Controlled Experiment', *Experimental Economics* 9, no. 2 (2006): 79–101.

21. Bart Wilson, 'Fair's Fair', *Atlantic* (25 January 2009), http://business.theatlantic.com/2009/01/fairs_fair.php.

22. Jonah Lehrer, *The Decisive Moment* (Text Publishing Company, 2009), 176.

23. Uhlhaas, 'Is Greed Good?'

24. Christian Mayer, 'Playing Games', Max Planck Research (January 2003), www.mpg.de/english/illustrationsDocumentation/multimedia/mpResearch/2003/heft01/1_03MPR_64_69.pdf.

25. Robert D. Hof, 'Pierre Omidyar on Connecting People', in an interview, *BusinessWeek* (20 June 2005).

26. From the founder's note on ebay.com, http://pages.ebay.com.au/services/forum/feedback-foundersnote.html.

27. Mayer, 'Playing Games'.

28. Resnick et al., 'The Value of Reputation on eBay: A Controlled Experiment'.

29. Ori Brafman and Rod A. Beckstrom, *The Starfish and the Spider: The Unstoppable Power of Leaderless Organizations* (Penguin, 2006), 164.

30. 'eBay Boomers', *Guardian* (26 September 2009), www.guardian.co.uk/lifeandstyle/2004/sep/26/shopping.technology.

31. Robert Axelrod, *The Evolution of Cooperation* (Basic Books, 1984).

32. Andy Hobsbawn, 'Small Is the Next Big Thing', http://smallbig.typepad.com/files/pdf/small-is-the-next-big-thing.pdf.

33. eBay 2009 Analyst Day slide presentation. Retrieved October 2009, www.slideshare.net/evanwolf/ebay-2009-analyst-day.

34. Magaret Atwood, *Payback: Debt and the Shadow Side of Wealth* (Bloomsbury, 2009), 162.

35. Chris Anderson, *The Long Tail: Why the Future of Business Is Selling Less of More* (Hyperion, 2006).

36. 'SwapTree Launches Free Swapping Service', press release (28 June 2007), www.redorbit.com/news/technology/983395/swaptree_launches_free_swapping_service__trade_books_cds_dvds/index.html.

37. Daniel Nissanoff, *FutureShop: How the New Auction Culture Will Revolutionize the Way We Buy, Sell, and Get Things We Really Want* (Penguin, 2006).

CHAPTER SEVEN: We Are All in This Together

1.   The phrase 'double coincidence of wants' was first used by William Stanley Jevons in *Money and the Mechanism of Exchange* (New York: D. Appleton and Co, 1875): '[T]he first difficulty in barter is to find two persons whose disposable possessions mutually suit each other's wants. There may be many people wanting, and many possessing those things wanted; but to allow of an act of barter there must be a double coincidence, which will rarely happen.'

2.   William Lee Adams, 'Bartering: Have Hotel, Need Haircut,' *Time* (2 November 2009), http://www.time.com/time/magazine/article/0,9171,1931665,00.html?xid=rss-topstories#ixzz0bSh9E5RS.

3.   The anecdote about Yvonne Hill is from Tom Rawstorne, 'Swap Shop Britain: How You Can Afford the Lifestyle of Your Dreams by Bartering', *Daily Mail* (19 November 2009), www.dailymail.co.uk/news/article-1229101/Swap-shop-Britain-How-afford-lifestyle-dreams-bartering.html#ixzz0XGSY0jPH.

4.   Statistics taken from www.timebanks.org. Retrieved October 2009.

5.   Edgar S. Cahn, 'Priceless Money: Banking Time for Changing Times', (2006), www.timebanking.org/documents/Publications/Priceless-money-edgar-cahn-book.doc.

6.   Anjana Ahuja, 'Estonia's Bank of Happiness: Trading Good Deeds', *The Times* (8 April 2009), http://women.timesonline.co.uk/tol/life_and_style/women/the_way_we_live/article6053885.ece.

7.   Umair Haque, 'The Great to Good Manifesto', *Harvard Business Review* (3 February 2010), http://blogs.hbr.org/haque/2010/02/great_to_good.html.

8.   Rushkoff was featured in Andy Jordan, 'The Coming Currency Revolution', *Wall Street Journal* (September 2009), http://online.wsj.

com/video/the-coming-currency-revolution/25225F5A-B979-4609-A55D-1BAE9A1BA158.html.

9. Description of VEN can be found at www.crunchbase.com/company/hub-culture.

10. 'Brits Put Their Faith in Traditional Banking Values', research report published by Mintel (2008), www.marketresearchworld.net/index.php?option=com_content&task=view&id=2294&Itemid=77.

11. Carlota Perez, *Technological Revolutions and Financial Capital: The Dynamics of Bubbles and Golden Ages* (Edward Elgar Publishing, 2002).

12. Pierre Omidyar, 'From Self to Society: Citizenship to Community for a World of Change', keynote address at Tufts University (May 2002), http://enews.tufts.edu/stories/052002Omidyar_Pierre_keynote.htm.

13. Michael K. Hulme and Collette Wright, 'Internet Based Social Lending: Past, Present and Future', *Social Futures Observatory* (October 2006): 11, www.socialfuturesobservatory.co.uk/pdf_download/internetbasedsociallending.pdf.

14. 'Credit Card Default Rate Hits Record High', Reuters (15 June 2009).

15. Kiera Butler, 'Practical Values: Work Well with Others', *Mother Jones* (18 January 2008), http://motherjones.com/politics/2008/01/practical-values-works-well-others.

16. Ibid.

17. 'A Conversation with Daniel Pink', *Information Outlook* (November 2001), www.conversationagent.com/2008/04/conversation-wi.html.

18. Christophe Aguiton and Dominique Cardon, 'The Strength of Weak Cooperation: An Attempt to Understand the Meaning of Web 2.0', *International Journal of Digital Economics* 65 (2007): 51–65.

19. Stephanie Smith, 'Good Guide: R. Buckminster Fuller', *GOOD* (14 August 2007), www.good.is/post/good-guide-r-buckminster-fuller/.

20. Jennifer Sharpe, 'A Social Experiment: Communes in Cul-De-Sacs', NPR radio interview (2 April 2009), www.npr.org/templates/story/story.php?storyId=102651496.

21. Wikipedia definition of a commune posted at http://en.wikipedia.org/wiki/Commune_(intentional_community).

22. Ariel Schwartz, 'WeCommune: Social Networking Communes', *Fast Company* (June 2009), http://origin-www.fastcompany.com/blog/ariel-schwartz/sustainability/wecommune-social-networking-communes?.

23. James Surowiecki, *The Wisdom of Crowds* (Anchor Books, 2005), 86.

24. Allison Arieff, 'Q&A: Sharing the Plenty in the Third Economy', GOOD (24 March 2010), http://www.refresheverything.com/blog/2010/03/24/qa-sharing-the-plenty-in-the-third-economy/.

25. Dave LeBlanc, 'Welcome to the Commune on the Cul-de-Sac', CTVglobemedia Publishing Inc. (17 October 2009), http://www.theglobeandmail.com/real-estate/welcome-to-the-commune-on-the-cul-de-sac/article1325290/.

26. Allison Arieff, 'Saving the Suburbs', *The New York Times* (3 February 2009), http://arieff.blogs.nytimes.com/2009/02/03/saving-the-suburbs-part-2/.

27. Stories from DaveZillion website. Retrieved November 2009, http://davezillion.com/success_stories.php.

28. Tim O'Reilly, 'The Architecture of Participation', published on his blog O'Reilly (June 2004), www.oreillynet.com/pub/a/oreilly/tim/articles/architecture_of_participation.html.

29. CouchSurfing's Mission Statement, from CouchSurfing website. Retrieved November 2009, www.CouchSurfing.org/about.html/mission.

30. Statistics retrieved February 2010 from www.CouchSurfing.org/index.html.

31. Jeff Miranda, 'Take the Couch', *Boston Globe* (22 August 2007), www.boston.com/yourlife/articles/2007/08/22/take_the_couch/.

32. Mark Granovetter, 'The Strength of Weak Ties', *American Journal of Sociology* 78, no. 6 (May 1973): 1360–1380.

33. Debra Lauterbach, Hung Truong, Tanuj Shah and Lada Adamic, 'Surfing a Web of Trust: Reputation and Reciprocity on CouchSurfing. com', *IEEE International Conference* 4 (2009): 348.

34. Traveller CouchSurfing story from Lisa Lubin, 'You Meet the Darndest People While CouchSurfing', *Chicago Tribune* (9 August

2009), www.chicagotribune.com/travel/chi-0809-couch-surfingaug09,0,208222.story.

35. Paul J. Zak, 'CouchSurfing 101', *Psychology Today*, The Moral Molecule blog (October 2008), www.psychologytoday.com/blog/the-moral-molecule/200810/CouchSurfing-101.

36. Bill McKibben, *Deep Economy: The Wealth of Communities and the Durable Future* (Times Books, 2007), 105.

CHAPTER EIGHT: Collaborative Design

1. Kevin Kelly, 'Was Moore's Law Inevitable?' posted by the author on his blog Technium (17 July 2009), www.kk.org/thetechnium/archives/2009/07/was_moores_law.php.

2. Damien Broderick, *The Spike: How Our Lives Are Being Transformed by Rapidly Advancing Technologies* (Tom Doherty Associates, 2001).

3. Information on the Slice Precision Cutter: www.laprimashops.com. Retrieved January 2010.

4. Karim Rashid's manifesto is taken from his website, www.karimrashid.com/manifesto_fr.html. Retrieved January 2010.

5. Paul Hawken, Amory Lovins and Hunter L. Lovins, *Natural Capitalism: Creating the Next Industrial Revolution* (Back Bay Books, 2008).

6. William McDonough and Michael Braungart, 'Redefining Green: A New Definition of Quality Empowers the Next Wave of Design', published by William A. McDonough on his website McDonough. com (2005). Adapted from an article published in *Perspective* (Spring 2003), www.mcdonough.com/writings/redefining_green.htm.

7. John Thackara, *In the Bubble: Designing in a Complex World* (MIT Press, 2006), 7.

8. 'Eco-Patent Commons', from World Business Council for Sustainable Development (updated March 2009), www.wbcsd.org/templates/TemplateWBCSD5/layout.asp?type=p&MenuId=MTQ3NQ&doOpen=1&ClickMenu=LeftMenu.

9. Thomas Goetz, 'Open Source Everywhere', *Wired* (November 2003), www.wired.com/wired/archive/11.11/opensource_pr.html.

10. Ezio Manzini and Jegou François, *Collaborative Services: Social Innovation and Design for Sustainability* (Poli Design, 2008), 111.

11. Terms for this section come from Manzini's work on *Collaborative Services*; quotes come from an interview with him on 7 December 2009.

12. Oksana Mont, 'Innovative Approaches to Optimising Design and Use of Durable Consumer Goods', *International Journal of Product Development* (2008): 228.

13. Thackara, *In the Bubble: Designing for a Complex World*, 100.

CHAPTER NINE: Community Is the Brand

1. Abraham Maslow, 'A Theory of Human Motivation', originally published in *Psychological Review* 50 (1943): 370–396.

2. Louise Story, 'The New Advertising Outlet: Your Life,' *The New York Times* (14 October 2007), www.nytimes.com/2007/10/14/business/media/14ad.html?_r=1.

3. Mark McClusky, 'The Nike Experiment: How the Shoe Giant Unleashed the Power of Personal Metrics', *Wired* (22 June 2009), www.wired.com/medtech/health/magazine/17-07/lbnp_nike.

4. 'The Consumer Decides: Nike Focuses Competitive Strategy on Customization and Creating Personal Consumer Experiences' (26 February 2007), http://mass-customization.blogs.com/mass_customization_open_i/2007/02/the_consumer_de.html.

5. 'Nike + Community = Leadership', blog post on Go Big Always (30 April, 2008), http://gobigalways.com/nike.

6. 'Skype Fast Facts', press release (Q4 2008), http://ebayinkblog.com/wp-content/uploads/2009/01/skype-fast-facts-q4-08.pdf.

7. Geoffrey Heal and Howard Kunreuther, 'Social Reinforcement: Cascades, Entrapment and Tipping', Wharton School, University of Pennsylvania (December 2008), http://opim.wharton.upenn.edu/risk/library/WP2009-03-09_GH,HK_SocReinf.pdf.

8. The video of Dyfedpotter can be seen on YouTube. Retrieved November 2009, www.youtube.com/user/dyfedpotter.

9. Erik Qualman, *Socialnomics: How Social Media Transforms the Way We Live and Do Business* (John Wiley, 2009).

10. 'It Takes a Community to Build a Brand'. Presentation, Slideshare. com, www.slideshare.net/agentwildfire/it-takes-a-community-to-raise-a-brand-not-a-campaign-presentation.

11. Stewart Butterfield and Caterina Fake, 'How We Did It: Stewart Butterfield and Caterina Fake, Co-Founders, Flickr', *Inc.* (1 December 2006), www.inc.com/magazine/20061201/hidi-butterfield-fake. html.

12. Raymund Flandez, 'Building an Online Community of Loyal and Vocal Users', *Wall Street Journal* (6 March 2008), http://online.wsj. com/article/SB120467374049811663.html.

13. Example is taken from Giles Andrews's transcript from the 2009 'US Now' film project about the power of mass collaboration, government and the Internet, http://www.usnowfilm.com/logs/6.

14. Clare Murphy, 'Recession? What Recession?' *Guardian*, www.guardian. co.uk/inspire-innovate/recessions.

15. Abran Sauer, 'Craigslist', *Brandchannel* (12 March 2007), www. brandchannel.com/features_profile.asp?pr_id=326.

CHAPTER TEN: The Evolution of Collaborative Consumption

1. Carol Kaesuk Yoon, 'Bacteria Seen to Evolve in Spurts', *The New York Times* (June 1996), www.nytimes.com/1996/06/25/science/ bacteria-seen-to-evolve-in-spurts.html.

2. Arnold Toynbee, *Lectures on the Industrial Revolution in England: Popular Addresses, Notes and Other Fragments* (London, 1884).

3. Kevin Kelly, 'Kevin Kelly on the Next 5,000 Days of the Web', video on Ted.com (July 2008), www.ted.com/index.php/talks/kevin_ kelly_on_the_next_5_000_days_of_the_web.html.

4. Clifford Stoll, 'Why the Web Won't be Nirvana', *Newsweek* (February 1995), www.newsweek.com/id/106554/page/1.

5. Tim Cooper and Sian Evans, 'Products to Services', a report for Friends of the Earth, Centre for Sustainable Consumption, Sheffield Hallam University, www.foe.co.uk/resource/reports/products_ services.pdf.

6. 'The Water Saver Home', developed by the California Urban Water Conservation Council in cooperation with EPA (June 2002), www. epa.gov/watersense/docs/waterconservation_final_508.pdf.

7. Jo M. F. Box, 'Extending Product Lifetime: Prospects and Opportunities', *European Journal of Marketing* 17, no. 4, 1993.

8. 'Future Travel', an interview with Casey Fenton by Rachel Botsman. Shareable.net (10 February 2010), http://shareable.net/blog/future-travel.

9. Nikhil Swaminathan, 'For the Brain, Cash Is Good, Status Is Better', *Scientific American* (24 April 2008), www.scientificamerican.com/article.cfm?id=for-the-brain-status-is-better.

10. Craig Newmark, 'Trust and Reputation Systems: Redistributing Power and Influence' (April 2010), http://www.cnewmark.com/2010/04/trust-and-reputation-systems-redistributing-power-and-influence.html.

11. Saamah Abdallah, 'Sarkozy and Stiglitz Challenge GDP "Fetish",' *New Economics Forum* (September 2009), http://neftriplecrunch.wordpress.com/2009/09/14/sarkozy-and-stiglitz-challenge-gdp-fetish/.

12. 'Sarkozy Adds to Call for GDP Alternative', *Wall Street Journal* (September 2009), http://blogs.wsj.com/economics/2009/09/14/sarkozy-adds-to-calls-for-gdp-alternative/tab/article/.

13. 'Economists Search for New Definition of Well-Being', *Spiegel* online (September 2009), www.spiegel.de/international/business/0,1518,650532,00.html.

14. Philip Aldrick, 'Nicolas Sarkozy Wants "Well-Being" Measure to Replace GDP', *Daily Telegraph* (September 2009), www.telegraph.co.uk/finance/economics/6189582/Nicolas-Sarkozy-wants-well-being-measure-to-replace-GDP.html.

15. Thomas Friedman, 'The Inflection Is Near?' *The New York Times* (March 2009), www.nytimes.com/2009/03/08/opinion/08friedman.html.

COLLABORATIVE CONSUMPTION HUB
www.collaborativeconsumption.com

We have created the hub www.collaborativeconsumption.com to become a collaborative repository of ideas and resources built by the readers of this book. As the Collaborative Consumption movement evolves, so will the online hub – providing tools, resources and stories that discuss, inform and inspire its growth. We invite you to edit and add to the ideas we have started.

On the hub you will also find a whole range of Spreadables that is under a Creative Commons licence for you to freely share. We also encourage you to swap, barter or pass on this book. If you go to collaborativeconsumption.com and create a nickname for your copy, you will be able to track where your book travels.

Many of the founders we spoke to during the course of writing this book expressed a desire for us to help people see the similarities between different examples of Collaborative Consumption: in other words, to show how Netflix, Zipcar, eBay and Zopa are all connected. We hope we have risen to the challenge! More and more examples of Collaborative Consumption are popping up every day, everywhere. We have created a Collaborative Consumption icon for all to use to show they are part of this exciting groundswell.

With thanks,
Rachel and Roo

UK EXAMPLES OF SYSTEMS OF COLLABORATIVE CONSUMPTION

There are three systems of Collaborative Consumption.

Product Service Systems

Paying for the benefit of using a product without needing to own the product outright. Disrupting traditional industries based on models of individual private ownership.

CAR SHARING

City Car Club www.citycarclub.co.uk
Streetcar www.streetcar.co.uk
Car Clubs www.carplus.org.uk
CARvenience by Avis hourly car rental www.avis.co.uk
hOURCARS Salisbury http://homepages.phonecoop.coop/
     pcc1201/hourcars/

PEER-TO-PEER CAR SHARING

Whipcar www.whipcar.com

RIDE SHARING

LiftShare www.liftshare.com
National CarShare www.nationalcarshare.co.uk
Carbon Heroes www.carbonheroes.com
ShareACar www.shareacar.com

ShareAJourney www.shareajourney.com
CatchALift www.uk.catchalift.com
goCarShare www.gocarshare.com
RideKicks www.ridekicks.com

BIKE SHARING
Barclays Cycle Hire www.tfl.gov.uk
Byke www.byke.mobi
Citybyke www.citybyke.co.uk

TAXI SHARING
BioTravel www.biotravel.co.uk
Taxi2 www.taxi.to

PEER-TO-PEER RENTAL
The Hire Hub www.thehirehub.co.uk
Ecomodo www.ecomodo.com
Zilok http://uk.zilok.com
Erento www.erento.co.uk
Thingloop www.thingloop.com
GetItWithMe www.getitwithme.com

TOY AND BABY GOODS RENTAL
MiniLodgers www.minilodgers.co.uk
Busy Bee Babies Scotland www.busybeebabies.co.uk
Daisy's Party Toys www.daisyspartytoys.co.uk
Baby Equipment Hire UK Scotland www.babyequipmenthireuk.
  com

FASHION AND ACCESSORIES RENTAL
Fashion Hire www.fashionhire.co.uk
Girl Meets Dress www.girlmeetsdress.com

GetAhead Hats www.getaheadhats.co.uk
Kennedy Purple www.kennedypurple.com
Erento www.erento.co.uk
One Night Stand www.onenightstand.co.uk

FILM RENTAL
LoveFilm www.lovefilm.com
Blockbuster www.blockbuster.co.uk
FutureMovies www.futuremovies.co.uk
Virgin Online Movies http://onlinemovies.virginmedia.com

Redistribution Markets

Redistributing used or pre-owned goods from where they are not needed to somewhere where they are.

BIG MARKETPLACES
craigslist http://london.craigslist.co.uk
Gumtree www.gumtree.com
Freecycle www.uk.freecycle.org
eBay www.ebay.co.uk

SWAP SITES FOR LIKE GOODS/GOODS OF SIMILAR VALUE
Barter Swap www.u-exchange.com
Swapshop www.swapshop.co.uk
ReadItSwapIt www.readitswapit.co.uk
iSwap www.iswap.co.uk
Swapz www.swapz.co.uk
BookHopper www.bookhopper.co.uk

CLOTHING SWAPS
Swishing www.swishing.org
Big Wardrobe www.bigwardrobe.com
Covert Candy www.covertcandy.co.uk
SwapStyle www.swapstyle.com

FOOD
Incredible Edibles www.incredible-edible-todmorden.co.uk
Lourish http://lourish.com
HouseBites www.housebites.com

Collaborative Lifestyles

It's not just physical goods that can be shared, swapped, and bartered. People with similar interests are banding together to share and exchange less tangible assets such as time, space, skills and money.

CO-WORKING SPACES
Hub Culture www.hubculture.com
Le Bureau www.lebu.co.uk
Lemon Studios www.lemonstudioslondon.com
The Cube London www.thecubelondon.com
The Tuttle Club www.tuttleclub.wordpress.com
The Hub www.the-hub.net
The Trampery www.thetrampery.com
TechHub www.techhub.com

PEER-TO-PEER SOCIAL LENDING
Zopa http://uk.zopa.com
YES-Secure www.yes-secure.com
Quakle www.quakle.co.uk
Funding Circle www.fundingcircle.com

SOCIAL CURRENCIES

LETS www.letslinkuk.net

CamdenShares www.camdenshares.org.uk

Streetbank www.streetbank.com

SPICE Timebank Wales www.justaddspice.org

Freeconomy www.justfortheloveofit.org

Brixton Skillshare http://brixtonblog.wordpress.com

Haringey Skillshare www.haringeyskillshare.wikispaces.com

CROWDFUNDING

CrowdCube www.crowdcube.com

Fundbreak UK www.fundbreak.co.uk

TRAVEL

Crashpadder www.crashpadder.com

One Fine Stay www.onefinestay.com

Single Spot Camping www.singlespotcamping.com

BARTERING

Bartercard http://uk.bartercard.com

U-exchange www.u-exchange.com

Miroma Media trading www.miroma.com

PEER-TO-PEER SHARING OF GARDENS, PARKING SPACES, STORAGE

Landshare www.landshare.net

Yours2Share www.yours2share.com

Parkatmyhouse www.parkatmyhouse.com

Grow Your Neighbour's Own www.growyourneighboursown.
    org.uk

Edinburgh Garden Share Scheme http://edinburghgardenshare.
    org.uk

Park-UK www.park-uk.com

Garden Swap Shop www.gardenswapshop.co.uk
Somewhereto... www.somewhereto.org
SpareGround www.spareground.co.uk

INDEX